THE ITALIAN RENAISSANCE

For Maria Lúcia

PETER BURKE

THE ITALIAN RENAISSANCE

Culture and Society in Italy

POLITY PRESS

Copyright © Peter Burke, 1986

First edition 1972 by Batsford, UK. Scribner, US.
Paperback edition published by Collins Fontana 1974.
This revised edition first published 1987 by Polity Press
in association with Basil Blackwell

Editorial Office:
Polity Press, Dales Brewery, Gwydir Street,
Cambridge CB1 2LJ, UK

Basil Blackwell Ltd
108 Cowley Road, Oxford OX4 1JF, UK

British Library Cataloguing in Publication Data

Burke, Peter
    The Italian renaissance: culture and society in Italy.
    1. Renaissance — Italy
    I. Title II. Burke, Peter. Culture and Society in Renaissance Italy, 1420–1540
    945′.05

    ISBN 0-7456-0380-7
    ISBN 0-7456-0381-5 Pbk

Typeset in 10½ on 12 pt Sabon by Gecko Limited, Bicester, Oxon
Printed in Great Britain by Butler & Tanner, Ltd, Frome

Contents

————————◆◆◆◆————————

PART III THE WIDER SOCIETY

INTRODUCTION

A T the beginning of the fifteenth century, Italy was neither a social nor a cultural unit, although the concept *Italia* existed, and some educated men in other regions could understand Tuscan. It was simply a geographical expression; but geography influences both society and culture. Their geography encouraged Italians to devote more attention than their neighbours did to commerce and industry. Italy's central location in Europe, and easy access to the sea, gave its merchants the opportunity to become middlemen between East and West, while its terrain, one-fifth mountainous and three-fifths hilly, discouraged agriculture. It is hardly surprising then that Italian cities – Genoa, Venice, Florence – played a leading part in the commercial revolution of the thirteenth century, or that in 1300 some 23 cities in north and central Italy had a population of 20,000 or more apiece. City-republics were the dominant form of political organization in the twelfth and early thirteenth centuries. A relatively numerous urban population and a high degree of urban autonomy underpinned the unusual importance of the educated layman. It would be hard to understand the cultural and social developments of the fifteenth and sixteenth centuries without reference to these preconditions and traditions (Waley, 1969; Martines, 1979, chs 1–4; Larner, 1980).

In the late thirteenth and early fourteenth centuries, a number of citystates lost their independence, and in the 1340s Italians, like other Europeans, were hit by slump and plague. However, the tradition of the urban way of life and the educated laity survived, and it is central to this study. The majority of the Italian population (about nine or ten million people altogether) were peasants, living for the most part in extreme poverty and probably untouched by the Renaissance. They had a culture and it is well worth study, but it is not the subject of this book, which is concerned with the social context of new developments in the arts.

Writing in 1860, the great Swiss historian Jacob Burckhardt saw the Renaissance as a modern culture created by a modern society. Today, it looks rather more archaic. The shift in attitude is due in part to scholarly research on continuities between the Middle Ages and the Renaissance, but much more to changes in conceptions of the 'modern'. Since 1860 the classical tradition has withered away, the

1

tradition of representational art has been broken and rural societies have turned into urban – industrial ones on a scale which dwarfs fifteenth- or sixteenth-century cities and their crafts. Renaissance Italy now looks 'underdeveloped', in the sense that the majority of the population worked on the land, many were illiterate and all were dependent on animate sources of power. This perspective makes the cultural innovations of the period all the more remarkable.

To understand and explain these innovations – which came in the course of time to constitute a new tradition – is the aim of this book, as it has been the aim of many earlier studies of the Renaissance. What makes this book somewhat more distinctive is the aspiration to write not only a cultural history but also a social history of the movement, and to deal in particular with the relation between culture and society. Neither term is easy to define. By 'culture' I mean essentially attitudes and values and their expressions or embodiments in texts, artefacts and performances. Culture is the realm of the imaginary and the symbolic. As for 'society', the term is shorthand for the economic, social and political structure, an invisible structure which reveals itself in the pattern of social relationships characteristic of a particular place and time.

The essential argument, which I shall try to make as explicit as possible in the chapters that follow, is that we cannot understand the culture of Renaissance Italy if we look only at the conscious intentions of the artists, writers and performers who produced the paintings, poems, treatises, plays, songs, buildings and so on. Understanding these individual intentions – so far as we now can, hampered as we are by gaps in the evidence and by the differences between our categories, assumptions and values and theirs – is certainly necessary but it is not sufficient for the understanding of the Renaissance.

There are several different reasons why this approach is not sufficient in itself. Although Botticelli, for example, expressed his individuality on panel or canvas so clearly that is is not difficult, 500 years later, to recognize certain works as his, he was not an entirely free agent. Whatever contemporary artists do – and their liberty is often exaggerated – Renaissance artists generally did more or less what they were told. The constraints on them are part of their history.

Yet it would be as much a caricature to portray a Botticelli forced to produce the *Primavera* against his will as it would be to show the idea of it coming one morning quite spontaneously into his head. Romantic notions of the spontaneous expression of individuality were not available to him. The role of painter which he played was the one defined by (or at any rate in) his own culture. In a sense this social definition of a role is a kind of constraint; we are all, as the

French historian Fernand Braudel liked to put it, 'imprisoned' by our assumptions, our mentalities. It is not possible to think all kinds of thought at all times, as another French historian, Lucien Febvre, used to say. At the same time, there are societies, and Renaissance Italy was one of them, where alternative definitions of the artist's role – and of much else – were available. This pluralism may well have been a precondition of the other achievements of the period. In any case, Braudel's metaphor is in some ways misleading. Without social experiences and without cultural traditions to help us make sense of those experiences, it would be impossible to think or imagine anything at all. The problem for posterity is that the Renaissance has become, almost as much as the Middle Ages, an alien, or at the least a 'half-alien', culture.[1] What one takes for granted, the other finds questionable, so that misunderstandings are frequent. The artists and writers of the period are becoming increasingly remote from us – or we from them.

It is for this reason that the focus of this book will not be on individuals – though some of them, Michelangelo for example, never let us forget their individuality – so much as on traditions. Its concern will not only be with what linguists call the 'message', the particular act of communication, but also with the 'code', the language or more generally the cultural tradition which both limits what can be said and makes a message possible.

The main theme is that of the break with one code or tradition, that of the medieval ('German', 'Gothic', 'barbaric') past, and the development of another, modelled more closely on classical antiquity. These changing traditions have some relationship not only to the past but to the general history of the time: economic booms and slumps, political crises and the less dramatic and more gradual transformations of the social structure.

My aim here is to avoid the weaknesses of two earlier approaches to the Renaissance, discussed in more detail in chapter 2. The first is *Geistesgeschichte* and the second is historical materialism, otherwise known as Marxism.

Geistesgeschichte, literally 'the history of spirit', was an approach to history stressing the 'spirit of the age' which expressed itself in every form of activity, including the arts and above all philosophy. Historians of this persuasion, including Jacob Burckhardt, still the greatest historian of the Renaissance, begin with ideas rather than with everyday life, stress consensus at the expense of cultural and social conflict and assume somewhat vague connections between

---

[1] I take this useful concept from Medcalf (1981).

different activities. Historical materialists, on the other hand, start with their feet on the earth of everyday life and move upwards to ideas, stress conflict at the expense of consensus and tend to assume that culture, which is an expression of 'ideology', is determined – directly or indirectly – by the economic and social 'base'. The middle position which I occupy here is not unlike that held by members of the French 'Annales School' (notably Marc Bloch, Lucien Febvre and Fernand Braudel). My concern with comparative history and the history of mentalities owes a good deal to their example. The aim of this study is an open social history which explores connections between culture and society without assuming that the imaginary is determined by economic or social forces. This open social history makes use of the concepts of a number of social theorists – Karl Mannheim, for example, Emile Durkheim and Max Weber – without accepting any one theoretical package. Mannheim's discussion of worldviews and generations, Durkheim's social explanations of self-consciousness and competitive behaviour and Weber's concepts of bureaucracy and secularization all have their relevance to Renaissance Italy and it is possible to draw them together into a synthesis.

Also relevant to a historian of the Renaissance is the work of some social or cultural anthropologists: the many anthropological studies of religion, magic and witchcraft, for example, or Edward Evans-Pritchard's (1940) analysis of the perception of space and time among the Nuer of the Sudan, or Paul Bohannan's (1961) discussion of the communal aspect of the 'art' of the Tiv of central Nigeria. It is worth bearing in mind throughout this study that some of its central concepts (notably 'art', 'artist' and 'literature') are Western ones, which were still in the process of formation in the fifteenth and sixteenth centuries. We need to be able to stand back from our own concepts, to defamiliarize ourselves with them, to place them mentally (if not always typographically) in inverted commas. To achieve this end it may be useful to compare and contrast Western culture with others, such as the African examples just mentioned or that of early modern Japan, which is discussed in the final chapter.

The plan adopted in this study is that of working outwards from a centre. This centre is what we call the art, humanism, literature and music of Renaissance Italy, and it is described in Chapter 1. It is in a sense the problem that the rest of the book tries to solve. Why did the arts take these particular forms in these cities and centuries? Chapter 2 gives a brief account of the various solutions propounded from that day to this. (Giorgio Vasari, writing at the end of the period, was already aware of the need to offer an explanation for the recent artistic achievements of the Tuscans.)

The second part of the book is concerned with the immediate social environment of the arts. First, what sort of people produced the paintings, buildings, poems we so much admire? Six hundred of the best-known artists and writers are studied in particular detail. Secondly, for whom did this 'creative elite' produce their texts, artefacts and performances? What did the patrons expect for their money? Widening out from these two groups, I look at the uses in Renaissance society of what we call 'works of art' and at the responses of contemporary viewers and listeners, at the taste of the time. These chapters may be regarded as contributions to a 'micro-social' history.

Some people think that the social history of the arts should stop at this point, but I believe that this leaves the job half done, and so the third and last part of the book widens out still further. A description of contemporary standards of taste does not make full sense if we do not know something about the dominant worldview of the time. The artists and their patrons, two different social groups, need to be re-placed in the general social framework if we are to understand their ideals, intentions or demands. Finally, there is the problem of change, more exactly the problem of the relation between cultural and social change. Every chapter discusses specific changes during the period, but the last two chapters attempt to draw these different threads together, and also to illuminate Italian developments by means of comparisons and contrasts with a neighbouring culture, that of The Netherlands in the same period, and a culture more remote in both space and time, Japan in its famous 'Genroku era'.

This book was originally devised and written in the 1960s, at a time when – despite the work of Raymond Williams (1958) on *Culture and Society*, which inspired the original title – it still seemed somewhat daring to approach Leonardo, Michelangelo or Ariosto in this way. Art historians, literary critics and 'plain' historians did not have too much to say to one another. In the past 20 years or so, a common interest in the social history of art and literature has drawn them together, so closely that it is not always possible to tell them apart. There has probably been more research on the social history of the arts in the past 20 years than in the previous 60, and a good deal of it has been concerned with Renaissance Italy. It includes not only important individual contributions but also grand collective enter-prises organized in Turin, Paris and elsewhere.[2]

At the same time (or rather, as a result of this research) we have become aware that modern notions of 'art', like modern notions of

---

[2] Notably the *Storia dell'arte italiana* (12 vols in 14, Turin, 1979–83); *Letteratura italiana*, ed. A. Asor Rosa (in progress, Turin 1982–); and the 13 occasional volumes produced so far by the French *Centre interuniversitaire de recherche sur la Renaissance italienne* directed by André Rochon, the last of which is entitled '*Culture et société*'. Specific essays in these collections are cited below as appropriate.

'literature', are not universal but bound to particular periods in particular cultures.[3] Poems and paintings have different uses (a point discussed at length in chapter 5). This awareness makes the socially constructed identity of 'art historian' or 'literary critic' difficult to sustain. We are all cultural historians now (Burke, 1983).

Cultural history, once (despite the precedents of Burckhardt and Huizinga) a small subject on the margin of 'proper' history, has both expanded and fragmented. There is no consensus about the methods of this kind of history or even about its aims. Traditional *Geistesgeschichte* has been discredited; the newer 'history of ideas; developed in reaction against it by the American philosopher – historian Arthur Lovejoy and his collaborators, no longer seems as attractive as it once did; the French 'history of mentalities' still appears glamorous but is thought by many to be meretricious (see Burke, 1986). The traditional Marxist view of culture as a reflection of society, which underlies the work of Raymond Williams as it did that of such social historians of the Renaissance as Frederick Antal and Arnold Hauser, has been challenged by other approaches.[4] New styles of cultural history have developed since the 1960s, distinguished by broader definitions of culture and more subtle and complex views of its relation to society.[5] It may be useful to distinguish four overlapping approaches which place their respective emphases on popular culture, social anthropology, politics and language.

The discovery of popular culture is part of a wider movement to write history from below, a movement which has been led by Marxists (Edward Thompson, for example), although it is not confined to them. In 1860, it was natural for Burckhardt to concern himself with the attitudes and values of a minority of the population of Italy. It is now equally natural to ask what everyone else was thinking, feeling or doing at the time, and to explore their culture.[6] Carlo Ginzburg's (1976) study of the worldview of Menocchio Scandella, a sixteenth-century miller from a village in Friuli whose attitudes were too unorthodox for his own good, is an outstanding example of the new wave of research on popular culture. Unfortunately, the two concepts basic to this approach, 'popular' and 'culture', are both extremely difficult to pin down. Who are the

---

[3] On art, see Alsop (1982); on literature, see Eagleton (1983), pp. 1–16.

[4] Antal (1947), Hauser (1951) and Williams (1958). Contrast the more subtle approaches discussed in Jameson (1971) and Williams (1977), and exemplified in Clark (1973) and Barrell (1980).

[5] These views are made usefully explicit in Baxandall (1985) and other essays in the same issue of the Journal, under the rubric 'Art or Society: must we choose?'

[6] This was my own reaction after finishing this book in 1970. The attempt to answer the question led to Burke (1978).

people? Everyone, or the non-elite? And, if the latter, are they to be defined in social, political or cultural terms, as those who lack status, power or education? Do they in fact lack 'education' or only what an elite defines as education? In other words, what is culture? The recent trend – in the wake of such social theorists as Pierre Bourdieu – is to study the attitudes encoded in daily life or 'cultural practice', the local conventions for eating, drinking walking, talking, falling ill (or being perceived as ill) and so on (Bourdieu, 1972, 1979).

To study cultural practice and the values which underlie it is what social anthropologists do, so that Emmanuel Le Roy Ladurie's (1975) study of the village of Montaillou in the fourteenth century can be described with equal accuracy as a piece of history from below or as historical anthropology. It is at first sight rather odd that specialists in the study of the dead should be attracted by a discipline centred on fieldwork among the living, or that historians specializing for the most part on parts of the West should read ethnographies of Central Africa or Indonesia. However, this attraction is not a blind or irrational one. Historians of cultural practices need to defamiliarize themselves with their own culture in order not to take too much for granted, and exotic ethnography provides a means to this end. Social anthropologists have traditionally operated with a broad definition of culture. (Clifford Geertz, for example, distinguishes 'the general system of symbolic forms we call culture' from the particular system we call art.)[7] They are more concerned with theory than historians have traditionally been, and the so-called 'symbolic anthropologists' in particular have developed a useful vocabulary for analysing myths, rituals and symbols, and placing them in their social setting.

This setting includes politics. In the past decade or so, cultural historians have taken a more political turn. The 1960s formula 'culture and society' has been joined, or displaced, by 'cultural politics'. Political historians are discovering culture ('political culture', as they sometimes call it), while cultural historians have found it necessary to concern themselves with power. The concept 'cultural hegemony', developed by Antonio Gramsci in a fascist prison between the wars, has become common historical currency as a result of this trend; so has the concept of 'strategy'.[8] The concept of ideology has been refined and reformulated to analyse the various ways in which meaning or signification 'serves to sustain relations of domination' (Thompson, 1984, p. 131f). The history of political rituals has

---

[7] See Geertz (1983) which, incidentally, discusses Baxandall (1972) on Renaissance art.

[8] On hegemony, see Williams (1977), pp. 108–14; on strategy, see Bourdieu (1972), pp. 6f, 58f, discussed in the context of Renaissance art by Castelnuovo (1976), p. 48.

attracted particular attention as a means of studying the relation between culture and power.[9]

Rituals are often a means of persuasion, a kind of rhetoric, a form of language. Cultural historians have recently been taking a linguistic or rhetorical turn. Of course, the revival of interest in rhetoric on the part of literary critics is nothing new; but the subject is too important for historians to leave to the critics. Partly because it is impossible to use written sources critically without awareness of the conventions of literary genres (letters, wills, diaries and decrees no less than poems or plays); but also because speaking and writing are human activities which have their own relation to society (as ethnolinguists and sociolinguists remind us), and their own history. The social history of language is just beginning to be taken seriously. It involves a concern not only with the varieties of language spoken by different social groups in different periods, but also with the varieties employed by the same people in different social contexts, with the use of language to express or create social relationships (deference, intimacy, hostility and so on). The basic question is 'who speaks what language to whom and when?' [10]

Ritual, and visual arts and other cultural activities may usefully be regarded (in some respects at least) as languages, or better (because it does not impose a verbal model) as forms of communication. A group of social anthropologists who call themselves 'ethnographers of communication' concern themselves with who is 'saying' what to whom, in what situations and through what channels and codes, in a wide range of what they call 'communicative events', which between them make up a culture.[11]

This approach has very great potential for historians, who are no longer content with the classic style of cultural history (exemplified by Jacob Burckhardt and Johan Huizinga), but have not yet devised an acceptable alternative to it.[12] What would it be like to approach Renaissance Italy with this communication model of culture in mind? It would shift the focus of attention from great 'works of art' to a much wider range of messages or 'communicative events', such as popular songs, sermons, graffiti and rituals, official and unofficial,

---

[9] Two important examples, discussed below, are Trexler (1980) and Muir (1981).

[10] See Fishman (1965); and cf. formulation in Williams (1974), p. 120. For examples of historians' answers to this question, see the collection of essays on *The Social History of Language*, ed. P. Burke and R. Porter, forthcoming from Cambridge University Press.

[11] See Hymes (1964)) and, on the relation between culture and communication, Leach (1976).

[12] I try to put this approach into practice in my forthcoming *Historical Anthropology of Early Modern Italy*, which centres on the history of perception and communication.

from the Marriage of the Sea to Carnival. It would involve distinguishing between different kinds of sender and recipient of messages:
rulers and subjects, clergy and laity, the whole community and the
various families, factions, guilds, fraternities and individuals which
constituted it. It would involve distinguishing between learned and
popular culture, but also discussing the interaction between the two,
identifying the occasions on which the learned or the upper classes
participated in popular culture, the social situations in which they
spoke dialect rather than Latin or the literary Tuscan which was
beginning to become Italian. Such an approach would attempt to
distinguish the different purposes of communicative events: to obtain
obedience, to spread the truth, to make people laugh, to criticize the
established order, to make a good impression, to destroy rivals. Even
the limited range of messages which we now call the 'works of art' of
the Renaissance served this wide range of functions and more. The
family palace and the family portraits, for example, were forms of
conspicuous consumption and means of impression management
which no one who had or aspired to high status could afford to do
without.[13] Like the marriages of sons and daughters, the commissioning of what we call works of art formed an essential part of family
strategies for maintaining or advancing their social position.

The communication model also involves the study of how audiences, spectators or individual readers perceived and interpreted the
messages they received, since their minds were not like sheets of blank
paper but were on the contrary filled (as ours are, but differently from
ours), with stereotypes, assumptions and habits of thought. To avoid
anachronism, historians have to concern themselves with the responses of readers, listeners and beholders, with their 'horizon of
expectation'.[14] Finally, the study of Renaissance culture as communication would avoid the reductionism of some social approaches
to the arts, and oblige the historian to attend to form as well as
content, and to media (or 'codes') as well as messages.

In short, I would not and do not approach the culture and society
of Renaissance Italy in the same way now as I did in the 1960s. If I
were sitting down to write the book today, I would formulate some
questions and organize some chapters rather differently. The book
would actually be more difficult to write now, partly because the key
terms 'culture' and 'society' have so much less limited and less precise
meanings than they did 20 years ago. At any rate, no one else has

---

[13] On conspicuous consumption, see Elias (1969), especially ch. 3, and Burke (1982). On
impression management, see Goffman (1956).
[14] This concern is central to the controversial approaches to literature known as
'reception theory' and 'reader-response theory' (cf. Holub, 1984).

tried.[15] All the same, a good many of the same questions would have to be asked and – despite the wealth of recent research – a good many of the same answers would have to be given. A number of the new approaches which have just been discussed were at least adumbrated, if not always developed, in the first edition of this book. It already dealt, for instance, with popular culture, with ritual, with the expectations and responses of viewers or, to take a more precise example, with the use of images to bring rain, to ward off danger or to defame and humiliate criminals or enemies.[16]

I am grateful to the reviewers of earlier editions of this book for their constructive criticisms, and I have taken some of their suggestions to heart.[17] On one question, however, I remain unrepentant: that of quantitative methods. The discussion of the changing subject matter of paintings was founded on the analysis of a sample of some 2,000 paintings, while the chapter on artists and writers was based essentially on the analysis of 600 careers (facilitated by a computer, an ICT 1900, which has doubtless become an antique by now). The use of statistics struck one reviewer at least as 'pseudo-scientism'. On the other hand, this method of collective biography (or 'prosopography') has been followed in some subsequent studies of Renaissance Italy (Bec, 1983; De Caprio, 1983; King, 1986).[18] Quantitative history has become in turn fashionable and unfashionable. Both reactions are in my view unfortunate, but they suggest that a few words of clarification are needed in order to make at least two points. First, historians make implicitly quantitative statements whenever they use terms like 'more' or 'less', 'rise' or 'decline', without which they would find their task difficult indeed. If we are going to make quantitative statements, it is our duty to look for quantitative evidence. A common criticism of quantitative methods (in this study and elsewhere) has been that they generally tell us only what we know already. They do indeed sometimes confirm earlier conclusions but, like the discovery of new documents, they often put these conclusions on a firmer base. The second point concerns precision. The statistics are, as I remarked in the first edition of this book, speciously precise because the exact relation of the 'sample' analysed to the world outside it is uncertain. Hence it is useless, and misleading, in this field at least, to offer figures such as '7.25 per cent', and I have deliberately

---

[15] The study of the Italian Renaissance closest to mine is the work of a Soviet scholar, Batkin (1978). Cf. Martines (1979).

[16] See chapter 5. For developments, see Trexler (1972a), Ortalli (1979) and Edgerton (1985).

[17] I should like to record a particular debt to the comments of Hatfield (1973) and Kurczewski (1983).

[18] On the method more generally, see Stone (1971).

dealt in round numbers. However, in order to assess relative magnitudes and changes over time, which are the objects of the exercise, the calculation of rough absolute figures is probably the least unreliable means. In short, the justification for the method is purely pragmatic.

It remains to explain how exactly this edition differs from its two predecessors. In the first place, it includes a bibliography which contains not only the sources and secondary works used in the original version, but a considerable amount of more recent research, together with studies in other fields to which allusions are made in different parts of the book. References to this recent research have also been incorporated into the notes. In the second place, some information which seemed to clog the flow of the argument has been transferred to the notes and the text has been completely rewritten, mainly on stylistic grounds. The order of sentences, paragraphs and, on occasions, chapters has been changed to make the argument clearer. Some examples have been replaced with others which seem more appropriate, better documented or more fully discussed in the recent literature. The dates 1420–1540, which confine the Renaissance too narrowly and were chosen merely to demarcate the volume from another in the same series, have been taken still less seriously than before.[19] In essentials, however, I am the same author (despite grey hairs and increasing caution, if not wisdom), and this is the same book.

---

[19] The companion volume, on the period 1290–1420, was Larner (1971).

Part 1

The Problem

1

THE ARTS IN RENAISSANCE ITALY

THE aim of this book is to place, or re-place, the painting, sculpture, architecture, music, literature and learning of Renaissance Italy in their original environment, the society of the time, its 'culture' in the wider sense of that flexible term. In order to do this it is advisable to begin with a brief description of the main characteristics of the arts at this time. In this description the stress will fall on the viewpoint of posterity rather than that of contemporaries. (Their point of view is discussed in chapters 5–7.) Although they sometimes wrote of 'rebirth', they did not have a clear and distinct idea of the Renaissance as a period. They were interested in poetry and rhetoric but our idea of 'literature' would have been foreign to them, while a concept something like our 'work of art' was only just beginning to emerge at the end of the period.

This description will emphasize characteristics common to several arts more than those which seem to be restricted to one of them, and attempt to present the period as a whole (leaving the discussion of trends within it to chapter 10). The cultural unity of the age will not be assumed (as it was, for example, by Jacob Burckhardt), but it will be taken as a hypothesis to be tested.[1]

The conventional nineteenth-century view of the arts in Renaissance Italy (a view still widely shared today, despite the labours of art historians) might be summarized as follows. The arts flourished, and their new realism, secularism and individualism all show that the Middle Ages were over and that the modern world had begun. However, all these assumptions have been questioned by critics and historians alike. If they can be saved, it is at the price of radical reformulations.

To say that the arts 'flourished' in a particular society is to say, surely, that better work was produced there than in many other societies, which leads one straight out of the realm of the empirically verifiable. It no longer seems as obvious as it once did that medieval art is inferior to that of the Renaissance. Raphael has been judged a great artist and Ariosto a great writer from their own time to the

---

[1] The cases for and against the idea of the cultural unity of an age are concisely and elegantly presented in Huizinga (1929) and Gombrich (1969).

present, but there has been no such consensus about Michelangelo, Masaccio or Josquin des Près, however high their reputation now stands. All the same, few would quarrel with the suggestion that Renaissance Italy was a society where artistic achievements 'clustered'.[2] The clusters are most spectacular in painting, from Masaccio (or indeed from Giotto) to Titian; in sculpture, from Donatello (or from Nicola Pisano in the thirteenth century) to Michelangelo; and in architecture, from Brunelleschi to Palladio.

Literature is a more difficult case. After Dante and Petrarch, comes what has been called the 'century without poetry' (1375–1475), which is in turn followed by the achievements of Poliziano, Ariosto and many others. The fourteenth and the sixteenth centuries are great ages of Italian prose, but the fifteenth century is not (partly because scholars preferred to write in Latin). In the realm of ideas, there are many outstanding figures – Alberti, Leonardo, Machiavelli – and a major movement, that of the 'humanists', most exactly defined as the teachers of the 'humanities'.[3]

The most conspicuous gaps in this account of Italian achievements are to be found in music and mathematics. Although much fine music was composed in Renaissance Italy, most of it was the work of Netherlanders, and it is only in the sixteenth century that composers of the calibre of the Gabrielis and Costanzo Festa appear. In mathematics, the famous Bologna school belongs to the later sixteenth century.[4]

It is more useful to investigate innovation in the arts rather than 'flourishing' because the concept is more precise. In Italy, the fifteenth and sixteenth centuries were certainly a period of innovation in the arts, a time of new genres, new styles, new techniques. The period is full of 'firsts'. This was the age of the first oil-painting, the first woodcut, the first copperplate and the first printed book (though all these innovations came to Italy from Germany or The Netherlands). The rules of linear perspective were discovered and put to use by artists.

In the case of genres, the line dividing new from old is more difficult to draw than in the case of techniques, but the changes are obvious enough. In sculpture we see the rise of the free-standing statue, and more especially that of the equestrian monument and the portrait – bust.[5] In painting, too, the portrait emerged as an independent genre,

---

[2] The term comes from Kroeber (1944). Although he writes as if 'culture growth' can be measured like economic growth, his comparisons and contrasts remain suggestive.

[3] The definition (precise, if perhaps too narrow) is that of Kristeller (1955).

[4] There is no space for a serious discussion of mathematics here; see Rose (1975).

[5] On sculpture, see Pope-Hennessy (1958), Seymour (1966) and Avery (1970); on the equestrian monument, see Janson (1967).

followed rather more slowly by the landscape and the still-life.[6] In architecture, the development, or even, perhaps, the 'invention', of conscious town planning took place in the fifteenth century (Westfall, 1974). In literature, there was the rise of the comedy, the tragedy and the pastoral (whether drama or romance) (Herrick, 1960, 1965). In music, the emergence of the *frottola* and the madrigal, both types of song for several voices (Einstein, 1949; Bridgman, 1964, ch. 10). Art theory, literary theory, music theory and political theory all became more autonomous in this period.[7] In education, we see the rise of what is now called 'humanism' and was then called 'the studies of humanity' (*studia humanitatis*), an academic package which emphasized five subjects in particular, all concerned with language or morals: grammar, rhetoric, poetry, history and ethics (Kristeller, 1955, ch. 1).

Innovation was conscious, though it was sometimes seen and presented as revival. The classic statement about innovation in the visual arts is that of the mid-sixteenth-century artist-historian Giorgio Vasari, with his three-stage theory of progress since the age of the 'barbarians'. The same pride in innovations is noticeable in his description of his own work in Naples, the first frescos 'painted in the modern manner [*lavorati modernamente*]'. He makes frequent contemptuous references to what he calls the 'Greek style' and the 'German style', in other words, Byzantine and Gothic art.[8] Musicians also thought that great innovations had been made in the fifteenth century. Johannes de Tinctoris, a Netherlander living in Italy, writing in the 1470s, dated the rise of modern composers (the *moderni*), to the 1430s, adding that 'Although it seems beyond belief, there does not exist a single piece of music regarded by the learned as worth hearing which was not composed within the last forty years.'[9]

This disrespectful attitude to the past suggests the possibility that one reason for the central place of Italy in the Renaissance was the fact that Italian artists had been less closely associated with the Gothic style than their colleagues in France, Germany or England. Innovations often take place in regions where the previously dominant tradition has penetrated less deeply than elsewhere. Germany, for example, was less deeply affected by the Enlightenment than

---

[6] On the portrait, see Pope-Hennessy (1966); on the landscape, see Gombrich (1966), pp. 107–21, Turner (1966) and chapter 7, p. 00; on the still-life, see Sterling (1959) and Gombrich (1963), pp. 95–105.

[7] On art theory, see Panofsky (1924) and Blunt (1940); on literary theory, see Weinberg (1961); on political theory, see Skinner (1978).

[8] On Vasari's view of 'progress', see Panofsky (1955) and Gombrich (1960b).

[9] From the preface of *De arte contrapuncti* (1477) by Johannes de Tinctoris, discussed in Lowinsky (1966).

France, and this facilitated the German transition to Romanticism. Similarly, it may have been easier to develop a new style of architecture in Florence in the fifteenth century than in Paris or even Milan.

All the same, Renaissance Italians had not lost their reverence for tradition altogether. What they did was to repudiate recent tradition in the name of a more ancient one. Their admiration for classical antiquity allowed them to attack medieval tradition as itself a break with tradition. When, for example, the fifteenth-century architect Antonio Filarete referred to 'modern' architecture, he meant the Gothic style which he was rejecting.[10] His position was not unlike that of the rebels and reformers of late medieval and early modern Europe, who regularly claimed to be going back to the 'good old days', before certain evil customs had become established. In any case the enthusiasm for classical antiquity is one of the main characteristics of the Renaissance movement, which cultural historians have to make intelligible, whether they discuss it in terms of the affinity between the two cultures, as a means of legitimating innovation in a traditional society or as an extension to the arts of the political glamour of ancient Rome.

In architecture, this tendency to imitate the Greeks and Romans is particularly obvious. The treatise by the Roman writer Vitruvius was studied, and ancient buildings were measured, in order to learn the classical 'language' of architecture, not only the vocabulary (pediments, egg-and-dart mouldings, Doric, Ionic and Corinthian columns and so on), but also the grammar, the rules for combining the different elements. In the case of sculpture, such innovations as the portrait-bust and the equestrian statue were ancient genres revived.[11] In the case of literature, it is again easy to see how writers of comedy imitated the Romans Terence and Plautus, writers of tragedy, Seneca, and writers of epic, Virgil.

Painting and music are more intriguing cases because classical models were not available (the Roman paintings now discussed by scholars were only discovered in the eighteenth century or later). The lack of concrete exemplars did not rule out imitation on the basis of literary sources. Botticelli's *Calumny* and his *Birth of Venus*, for example, are attempts to reconstruct lost works by the Greek painter Apelles (Cast, 1981). The literary criticism of classical writers such as Aristotle and Horace was pressed into service to provide criteria for excellence in painting on the principle that 'as is poetry, so is painting'

---

[10] See Antonio Filarete, *Trattato di Architettura*, passim.

[11] On architecture, see Murray (1963) and Heydenreich and Lotz (1974). On the visual arts in general, see Dacos (1979).

(Lee, 1940). Discussions of what Greek music must have been like were based on passages in Plato or on classical treatises such as Ptolemy's *Harmonika* (Palisca, 1985).

Contemporary descriptions of changes in the arts are indispensable sources for understanding what was happening but, like other historical sources, they cannot be taken at their face value. Contemporaries generally claimed to be imitating the ancients and breaking with the recent past, but in practice they borrowed from both traditions and followed neither completely. As so often happens, the new was added to the old rather than substituted for it. Classical gods and goddesses did not drive the medieval saints out of Italian art but coexisted and interacted with them. Botticelli's Venuses are difficult to distinguish from his Madonnas, while Michelangelo modelled the Christ in his *Last Judgement* on a classical Apollo. The poets Jacopo Sannazzaro and Marco Girolamo Vida wrote epics on the birth and the life of Christ in the manner of Virgil's *Aeneid*.[12] A Renaissance prince would be as likely to read or listen to the medieval romance of Tristan as to the classical epic of Aeneas, and Ariosto's *Orlando Furioso* is a hybrid epic – romance set in the age of Roland and Charlemagne. Poliziano's pastoral drama *Orfeo* begins with the entry of Mercury, who takes over the place and function of the angel who commonly introduced Italian mystery plays.

Again, the rise of humanism did not drive out medieval scholastic philosophy (despite the deprecating remarks the humanists made about the *scholastici*). Indeed, leading figures in the Renaissance movement, such as the neoplatonist Marsilio Ficino, were well read in medieval as well as in classical philosophy. Lorenzo de'Medici, the ruler of Florence, can be found writing to Giovanni Bentivoglio, the ruler of Bologna, asking him to search the local bookshops for a copy of the commentary on Aristotle's *Ethics* by the late medieval philosopher Jean Buridan, while Leonardo da Vinci studied the work of Albert of Saxony and Albert the Great (Ady, 1937).

Realism, secularism and individualism are three features commonly attributed to the arts in Renaissance Italy. All three characteristics are problematic. In the case of the term 'realism', several different problems are involved. In the first place, although artists in a number of cultures have claimed to abandon convention and imitate 'nature' or 'reality', they have nevertheless made use of some system of conventions.[13] In the second place, since the term 'realism' was

---

[12] These examples of Renaissance 'hybridization' come from Wind (1958).

[13] The classical discussion of this problem in the case of painting is Gombrich (1960a). Other important studies of realism are Huizinga (1920), Auerbach (1946) and Wellek (1954, 1963).

coined in nineteenth-century France to refer to the novels of Stendhal and the paintings of Courbet, its use in discussions of the Renaissance encourages anachronistic analogies between the two periods. In the third place, the term has too many meanings, which need discrimination. It may be useful to distinguish three kinds of realism: domestic, deceptive and expressive.

'Domestic' realism refers to the choice of the everyday, the ordinary or the low status as a subject for the arts, rather than the privileged moments of privileged people. Courbet's stonebreakers and Pieter de Hooch's scenes from everyday Dutch life are examples of this 'art of describing' (Alpers, 1983, esp. the introduction). 'Deceptive' realism, on the other hand, refers to style, for example to paintings which produce or attempt to produce the illusion that they are not paintings. 'Expressive' realism also refers to style, but to the manipulation of outward reality the better to express what is within, as in the case of a portrait where the shape of the face is modified to reveal the sitter's character or a natural gesture is replaced by a more eloquent one.

How useful are these concepts in approaching the arts in Renaissance Italy? Expressive realism is not difficult to identify in Leonardo's *Last Supper*, say, or in the paintings of Raphael and Michelangelo; the only difficulty lies in finding a period in which works of art do not have this trait. More of an innovation in the paintings of the Italian Renaissance (as in the Flemish art of the period) is the domestic realism of the backgrounds. Carlo Crivelli's *Annunciation*, for example, lingers lovingly on carpets, embroidered cushions, plates, books and the rest of the interior decoration of the Virgin's room. Ghirlandaio's *Adoration of the Shepherds* includes, as the art historian Heinrich Wölfflin (1898, p. 218) put it, 'the family luggage – a shabby old saddle lying on the ground with a small cask of wine beside it'. It is important to see that the details are there, but also to remember that they are merely in the background. Today, we often see the details as genre paintings in miniature, and reproduce them as such. Contemporaries, on the other hand, did not have the concept of genre picture, and may well have seen the details as symbolic or as ornaments to fill up a blank space.

It is possible to find similar domestic details in the literature of the time, in the mystery plays, for example. In one anonymous play on the birth of Christ the Shepherds, Nencio, Bobi, Randello and the rest, bring food with them when they go to adore the Saviour, and eat it on stage (D'Ancona, 1872, pp. 197–8). In literature, however, unlike painting, there were genres in which domestic realism filled the foreground. There was the *novella*, for example, the short story dealing with the lives of ordinary people, a favourite Italian genre

CARLO CRIVELLI, *THE ANNUNCIATION*
Reproduced by courtesy of the Trustees of the National Gallery, London.

between Boccaccio in the fourteenth century and Bandello in the sixteenth. The comedy might portray peasant life, as in the case of the plays in Paduan dialect written and performed by Antonio Beolco *il Ruzzante* ('the jester'). Music too might attempt to recreate hunting or market scenes.

More difficult is the question of deceptive realism. From Vasari to Ruskin and beyond, the Renaissance was generally seen as an important step in the rise of more and more accurate representations of reality. At the beginning of this century, however, this notion was challenged, just at the time (surely no coincidence) of the development of abstract art. Heinrich Wölfflin, for example, suggested that 'it is a mistake for art history to work with the clumsy notion of the imitation of nature, as though it were merely a homogeneous process of increasing perfection' (Wölfflin, 1915, p. 13), while another celebrated art historian, Alois Riegl, wrote more dramatically still

DOMENICO GHIRLANDAIO, *ADORATION OF THE SHEPHERDS*
S. Trinita, Florence. Photograph from The Mansell Collection.

that 'Every style aims at a faithful rendering of nature and nothing else, but each has its own conception of nature' (quoted in Gombrich, 1960a, p. 16).

At this point the reader may well be thinking that the Renaissance discovery of linear perspective is a counter-example, but even this argument was challenged by the art historians Erwin Panofsky and Pierre Francastel, who argued that perspective is a 'symbolic form', 'a set of conventions like any other', depending on monocular vision. This was the point of Brunelleschi's famous box with a peep-hole in it, to which the viewer could put one eye and see, reflected in a mirror, a view of the Baptistery in Florence.[14]

If these arguments are valid, to talk about 'Renaissance realism' is to talk nonsense. However, Riegl's arresting formulation is in danger of unfalsifiability, of circularity. The evidence of an artist's conception of nature comes from his paintings, but the paintings are then interpreted in terms of that same conception. It seems more useful to start from the empirical fact that some societies, like some individuals, take a particular interest in the visible world, as it appears to them, and that Renaissance Italy was one of these. Wax images, often life-size and dressed in the clothes of the person they represented, were placed in churches, life- masks and death-masks were frequently made, and some artists dissected corpses in order to understand the structure of the human body.[15] The point is not that deceptive realism was the only aim of the artists of the time; it is easy to show such a statement to be false. Paolo Uccello, for example, coloured his horses according to quite different criteria. However, Vasari criticized Uccello precisely for this lack of verisimilitude, and the literary sources discussed in chapter 6 suggest that many viewers expected this kind of realism and judged paintings in terms of truth to appearances.

Another distinctive feature of the Italian culture of the Renaissance was that it was, relative to the Middle Ages, secular. The contrast should not be exaggerated. A sample study suggests that the proportion of Italian paintings that were secular in subject rose from about 5 per cent in the 1420s to about 20 per cent in the 1520s. In this case, 'secularization' only means that the minority of secular pictures grew somewhat larger.[16] In the case of sculpture, literature and music, it is

---

[14] On 'symbolic form', see Panofsky (1924–5), a formulation which echoes the philosophy of symbolic forms of his friend Cassirer (Holly (1984) ch. 5). On 'conventions', see Francastel (1950), pp. 7, 79. Brunelleschi's box is described in Manetti (1970), p. 9, and discussed in Edgerton (1975), ch. 10.

[15] On wax images, see Warburg (1966), p. 117f.

[16] The sample taken was that of dated paintings, listed in Errera (1920). The dangers of bias in the sample are discussed in chapter 7, and details of the pattern decade by decade are analysed in chapter 10.

more difficult to use quantitative methods, or to go beyond the obvious point that several of the new genres were secular: the equestrian statue, for example, the comedy and the madrigal.

If one tries to go further, conceptual problems become acute, as the case of what might be called 'crypto-secularization' illustrates. Pictures which are officially concerned with St George (say) or St Jerome seem to devote less and less attention to the saint and more and more to the background; the saints become smaller, for example. This trend suggests a possible tension between what the patrons really wanted and what they considered legitimate. The difficulty is that contemporaries did not make the sharp distinctions between the sacred and the secular that became obligatory in Italy in the late sixteenth century, following the Council of Trent. By later standards they were continually sanctifying the profane and profaning the sacred. Masses were based on the tunes of popular songs. The philosopher Marsilio Ficino like to call himself a 'priest of the Muses', and there was a 'chapel of the Muses' in the palace at Urbino. God and his vicar the pope might be addressed as 'Jupiter' or 'Apollo'. Some people, such as Erasmus (who visited Rome in 1509), were scandalized by practices such as these, but they persisted throughout the period, as chapter 9 will suggest. If we are going to discuss the Renaissance in terms of 'secularization', we should at least be aware that we are imposing later categories on the period.

A third characteristic generally ascribed to the culture of Renaissance Italy, and discussed in detail in Burckhardt's famous book on the subject, is 'individualism'. Like 'realism', 'individualism' is a term which has come to bear too many meanings (discussed on pp. 193–6 below). It will be used here to refer to the fact that works of art in this period (unlike the Middle Ages) were made in a personal style. But is this really a 'fact'? To twentieth-century observers, medieval paintings look much less like the work of different individuals than Renaissance paintings do, but this may be an illusion of the type 'all Chinese look alike' (to the non-Chinese). At all events, the testimony of contemporaries suggests that in the fifteenth and sixteenth centuries, artists and public alike were interested in individual styles. In his craftsman's handbook, Cennino Cennini advised painters 'to find a good style which is right for you [*pigliare buna maniera propia per te*]'. In his discussion of the perfect courtier and his understanding of the arts, Baldassare Castiglione suggested that Mantegna, Leonardo, Raphael, Michelanglo and Giorgione were each perfect 'in his own style [*nel suo stilo*]'. The Portuguese visitor to Italy Francisco de Hollanda made a similar point about Leonardo, Raphael and Titian:

'each one paints in his own style [*cada um pinta por sua maneira*]'.[17] In literature, the imitation of ancient models was a matter for debate, in which some protagonists, notably Poliziano, attacked the ideal of writing like Cicero, and argued the value of individual self-expression.[18] There was, of course, much imitation of classical and modern artists and writers. Indeed, it was probably the norm. The point about individualism, like secularism, is not that it was dominant, but that it was relatively new, and distinguishes the Renaissance from the Middle Ages.

So much for the apparently obvious features of Italian Renaissance culture and the need to describe them with care. Some other general characteristics of more than one art may be worth a brief mention. There was, for example, a trend towards greater autonomy, in the sense that the arts were becoming increasingly independent from practical functions (discussed in chapter 5) and from one another. Music, for example, was ceasing to depend on words. Instrumental pieces, such as the organ compositions of Andrea Gabrieli and Marco Antonio Cavazzoni, were growing longer and more important. Sculpture was becoming more independent from architecture, the statue from the niche. There are even a few sculptures, like the battle scene made by Bertoldo for Lorenzo de'Medici, which have no subject in the sense that they do not illustrate a story, and a few paintings at least which appear to be independent of religious, philosophical or literary meanings (a topic discussed in chapter 7).[19] It may well be significant that the term *fantasia* is used of pictorial and musical compositions alike in this period, to mean a work which the painter or musician has created out of pure imagination, rather than to illustrate or accompany a literary theme.

Another general characteristic of Italian culture at this time was the breakdown of compartments, the cross-fertilization of disciplines. The gap between theory and practice in a number of arts and sciences narrowed at this time, and this was a cause or consequence of a number of famous innovations. For example, Brunelleschi's box, which dramatized his discovery of the rules of linear perspective, was a contribution to optics (called *perspective* in his day) as well as to the craft of painting. The humanist Leon Battista Alberti was a man of

---

[17] Cennini, *Il libro dell' arte*, p. 15; Castiglione, *Il cortegiano*, book 1, ch. 37, adapting Cicero, *De oratore*, book 2, ch. 36; Hollanda, *Da Pintura Antigua*, p. 23. A general discussion can be found in Wittkower (1961).

[18] On this debate, see Fumaroli (1980), part 1, Greene (1982) and pp. 157 below.

[19] See Gombrich (1966), pp. 122–8 and C. Gilbert (1952). This theme is also emphasized in the Slade lectures by Charles Hope, still (1986) unpublished.

theory, a mathematician, as well as a man of practice, an architect, and each kind of study helped the other. His churches and palaces were built on a system of mathematical proportions, while he told scholars that they could learn from observing craftsmen at work. Again, Leonardo's studies of optics and anatomy were used in his paintings. Some writers on music, such as the monk Pietro Aron, a member of the papal chapel in pope Leo X's time and the author of a series of treatises known as *Toscanella*, bridged the traditional gap between the theorist of music and the player – composer. In the history of political thought Machiavelli, a sometime professional civil servant, bridged the gap between the academic mode of thought about politics, exemplified in the 'mirror of princes' tradition of treatises dealing with the moral qualities of the ideal ruler, and the practical mode of thought, which can be illustrated in the records of council meetings and in the dispatches of ambassadors.[20]

Another gap which was closing was the one between the culture of the different regions of the peninsula, as Tuscan achievements became the model for the rest. The reception of the Italian Renaissance abroad was preceded by the reception of the Tuscan Renaissance in other parts of Italy. Florentine innovations were introduced by Florentine artists, such as Masolino in Castiglione Olona (in Lombardy), Donatello in Padua and Naples, Leonardo in Milan, and so on, while the dialect of Tuscany established itself as the literary language of the entire peninsula. Marked regional variations continued to exist throughout the period; Venetian painting, for example, stressed colour where Tuscan painting stressed form (*disegno*), and Lombard architecture emphasized ornament where Tuscan architecture emphasized simplicity. However, the minor art centres, such as Siena or Emilia were gradually attracted into the orbit of the greater ones. The rise of Rome, a city which lacked a strong artistic tradition of its own but became a major centre of patronage in the early sixteenth century, encouraged an inter-regional art. Like literature, the visual arts were more Italian in 1550 than they had been a hundred or two hundred years before.[21]

---

[20] Cf. Panofsky (1953), p. 128, on 'decompartmentalization', and Chastel (1964) on 'décloisonnement'.
[21] A succinct survey of regional styles can be found in the *Encyclopaedia of World Art* under 'Italian art'.

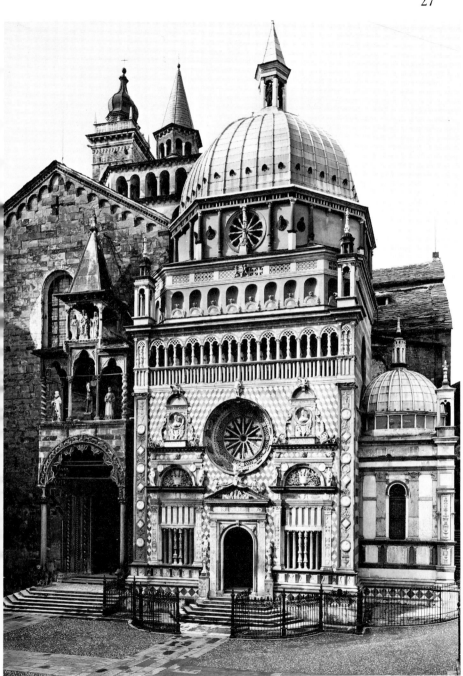

THE COLLEONI CHAPEL IN BERGAMO
Photograph from The Mansell Collection.

2

THE HISTORIANS: THE DISCOVERY OF SOCIAL AND CULTURAL HISTORY

THE problem of explaining the clustering of so many outstandingly creative individuals in this period – as in the case of ancient Greece and Rome – is one which has concerned historians since the Renaissance itself. The humanist Leonardo Bruni believed that politics was the key to the problem. Like Tacitus, he thought that the end of the Roman Republic had meant the decline of Roman culture. 'After the Republic had been subjected to the power of a single head, those outstanding minds vanished, as Tacitus says.' Conversely, he suggested (at least by implication) that the literary achievements of the Florentines were the result of their liberty.[1] A hundred years later, Machiavelli remarked that letters flourish in a society later than arms; first come the captains, then the philosophers.[2]

It was Giorgio Vasari, however, who first offered a detailed analysis of the problem. Vasari is, of course, the most indispensable source for the art history of the Italian Renaissance: a writer who was also an artist (though he lived towards·the end of the period, so that he is as far away from Masaccio as we are from the Pre-Raphaelites, and his information correspondingly second- or third-hand). We use him, as some Renaissance architects used the ruins of ancient Rome, as a quarry for raw material. However, we should remember that he was himself a serious historian. Although he was most concerned with individual achievement, Vasari found room in his lives of painters, sculptors and architects for what we might call the social factor. Impressed by the clustering of talents of the order of Brunelleschi, Donatello and Masaccio, he commented that 'It is Nature's custom, when she creates a man who really excels in some profession, often not to create him by himself, but to produce another at the same time and in a neighbouring place to compete with him.'[3]

Vasari also addressed himself, in his life of Perugino, to the

---

[1] Bruni, *Panegyric to the City of Florence*, pp. 154, 174.
[2] Machiavelli, *Istorie fiorentine*, book 5, prologue.
[3] Vasari, *life of Masaccio*. On Vasari as historian, see Gombrich (1960b) and Boase (1979).

28

problem of explaining the outsized contribution of Florence to the arts, placing into the mouth of Perugino's teacher the suggestion that three incentives were present in that city which were generally lacking elsewhere.

> The first was the fact that many people were extremely critical (because the air was conducive to freedom of thought), and that men were not satisfied with mediocre works . . . Secondly, that it was necessary to be industrious in order to live, which meant using one's wits and judgement all the time . . . for Florence did not have a large or fertile countryside round about it, so that men could not live cheaply there as they could in other places. Thirdly . . . came the greed for honour and glory which that air generates in men of every occupation.

Modern readers may find this emphasis on the air as the ultimate cause rather difficult to take seriously, but this difficulty should not prevent them from seeing that Vasari has offered explanations of what we would call an economic, social and psychological kind, in terms of challenge-and-response and the need for achievement.

It was only in the eighteenth century, however, that what contemporaries called the 'history of manners', which more or less coincides with what we describe as cultural and social history, became the object of systematic study. Voltaire, for example, tried to shift the attention of historians from wars to the arts. His *Essay on Manners* (1756, ch. 118) made the point – in language not unlike Vasari's – that the sixteenth century was a time when 'nature produced extraordinary men in almost all fields, above all in Italy'.

Enlightenment writers offered essentially two explanations for this phenomenon: liberty and opulence. Lord Shaftesbury (c. 1712, p. 129) explained the 'revival of painting' by the 'civil liberty, the free states of Italy as Venice, Genoa and then Florence'. If Gibbon had written the history of Florence which he once planned, it is likely that the relation between liberty and the arts would have been a central theme, as it was in his famous *Decline and Fall of the Roman Empire*. In any case the book he failed to write, or something like it, was produced only a few years later by the Liverpool banker William Roscoe (see Hale, 1954, ch. 4). His *Life of Lorenzo de'Medici* (1795) began as follows:

> Florence has been remarkable in modern history for the frequency and violence of its internal dissensions, and for the predilection of its inhabitants for every species of science, and every production of art. However discordant these characteristics may appear, they are not difficult to reconcile . . . The defence of freedom has always been found to expand and strengthen the mind.[6]

The liberty theme was developed still further in the *History of the Italian Republics* (1807–18) by the Swiss historian J. C. L. S. de Sismondi.

A common Enlightenment view was that liberty encouraged commerce, while commerce encouraged culture. As Charles Burney, the historian of music, put it, 'All the arts seem to have been the companions, if not the produce, of successful commerce; and they will, in general, be found to have pursued the same course . . . that is, like commerce, they will be found, upon enquiry, to have appeared first in Italy; then in the Hanseatic towns; next in the Netherlands' (Burney, 1776–89, vol. 2, p. 584). The social theorists of Scotland agreed. Adam Ferguson noted that 'the progress of fine arts has generally made a part in the history of prosperous nations'; John Millar of Glasgow pointed out that Florence led the way in 'manufactures' as well as in the arts, and Adam Smith planned to write a book about the relationship between the arts and sciences and society in general in which it is likely that – as in his *Wealth of Nations* – the city-states of Italy would have had a prominent place.[4]

The Scottish theorists dreamed of a science of society on Newtonian lines. It is not unfair to describe their model of cultural change as a mechanical one. At much the same time, an alternative, organic model was being created in Germany. J. J. Winckelmann took the important step of replacing the lives of artists, in the manner of Vasari, by a *History of Ancient Art* (1764), in which he discussed the relation between art and the climate, the political system and so on, in order to make art history 'systematically intelligible' (Winckelmann, 1764, vol. 1, p. 285f). J. G. Herder did much to develop the history of literature, which he saw as growing naturally out of particular local environments. Where the Scottish theorists had discussed cultural changes in terms of the impact of commerce, Herder saw art and society as parts of the same whole. 'As men live and think, so they build and inhabit.' In the case of Italy, he stressed the 'spirit' of commerce, of industry, of competition (Herder, 1791, book 20).[5] A similar stress on the organic unity of a given culture can be found in the *Philosophy of History* (1837, part 4, section 2) of the philosopher G. W. F. Hegel, who described the arts (like politics, law and religion) as so many 'objectifications' of spirit, the 'spirit of the age'. Discussing the Renaissance, Hegel suggested that the flowering of the arts, the revival of learning and the discovery of America were three related instances of spiritual expansion.[6]

---

[4] On eighteenth-century 'sociological' explanations of the Renaissance, see Weisinger (1950).

[5] On Herder, see Berlin (1976).

Karl Marx was also interested in the place of the Renaissance in world history. Rejecting Hegel's emphasis on consciousness ('life is not determined by consciousness, but consciousness by life'), he returned to the eighteenth-century concern with the relation between the arts and the economy, though he showed more interest than Ferguson or even Adam Smith in the precise relationship between material production and what he called 'cultural production' (*geistige Produktion*). Marx and Engels (1846, p. 430) suggested that the cultural 'superstructure' was shaped by the economic 'base', and in the case of the Italian Renaissance that 'Whether an individual like Raphael succeeds in developing his talent depends wholly on demand, which in turn depends on the division of labour and the conditions of human culture resulting from it.' A complementary point about 'supply' rather than 'demand' and the role of the individual in the history of the Renaissance was made by the Russian Marxist Plekhanov (1898, p. 53) when he wrote that 'If . . . Raphael, Michelangelo and Leonardo da Vinci had died in their infancy, Italian art would have been less perfect, but the general trend of its development in the period of the Renaissance would have remained the same. Raphael, Leonardo da Vinci and Michelangelo did not create this trend; they were merely its best representatives.'

It should by now be obvious that Jacob Burckhardt's famous study of *The Civilisation of the Renaissance in Italy*, first published in 1860 and still influential, stands in a long tradition of attempts to relate culture to society. Burckhardt's discovery of Italy was, like Winckelmann's, one of the great experiences of his life. He came from an art-loving patrician family of Basel, which was still a quasi-city-state when he was born in 1818. He was himself something of a 'universal man' who sketched, played the piano, and wrote music and poetry. Renaissance Italy was for him not unlike an idealized version of the world of his youth, as well as an escape from the modern, centralized, industrial society he hated. Himself a 'good private individual', he saw the Renaissance as an age of individualism.[7] All the same, his 'essay', as he called it, owes a good deal to his predecessors. Like Voltaire and Sismondi, he emphasized the importance for Renaissance culture of the wealth and freedom of the towns of northern Italy. Burckhardt's approach also owes something to Herder, Hegel, and perhaps Schopenhauer, despite the fact he claimed to put forward no philosophy of history, preferring to study what he called 'cross-sections' through a culture at particular moments in time. He shared

---

[6] For a vigorous, if somewhat exaggerated critique, see Gombrich (1969). Cf. Podro (1982), ch. 2.

[7] On Jacob Burckhardt, see Kaegi (1947–82), esp. vol. 3. Cf. Baron (1960).

with the philosophers a concern with the polarities of inner and outer, subjective and objective, conscious and unconscious. His study of Renaissance Italy resembles Hegel's discussion of ancient Greece in its stress on the growth of individualism and its awareness of the state as a 'work of art'. Like Herder and Hegel, Burckhardt believed that some periods, at least, should be seen as wholes, and in his *Reflections on World History* (1906, see ch. 3 in particular) he analysed societies in terms of the reciprocal interaction of three 'powers': the state, culture and religion. In so doing he made explicit his method in *The Civilisation of the Renaissance in Italy*.

One does not have to be a Marxist to be struck by the absence from both studies of a fourth 'power': the economy. Burckhardt admitted this himself. To a younger friend he wrote 14 years after the publication of his *Renaissance in Italy* that 'your ideas about the early financial development of Italy as the foundation [*Grundlage*] of the Renaissance are extremely important and fruitful. That was what my research always lacked.'[8]

What that study also lacked, as its author again admitted, was any serious discussion of Renaissance art. Burckhardt had been collecting material on the prices of paintings, and patronage, and these and other papers were found after his death with instructions that they were not to be printed. His executors were able to print three late essays on the art collector, the altar piece and the portrait. But these essays, fascinating as they are, do not fill the gap,[9] nor does the volume on the architecture of Renaissance Italy (Burckhardt, 1867), despite its occasional remarks on the functions of buildings. It is possible that the gap was left deliberately. Although he was interested in the relation between the three 'powers', each shaping and in turn being shaped by the other two, Burckhardt also believed that 'the connection of art with general culture is only to be understood loosely and lightly. Art has its own life and history.'

This last remark was made by Burckhardt in conversation with his pupil Heinrich Wölfflin, who was in a sense his intellectual heir. Wölfflin is often described as a supporter of an autonomous (or even isolationist) art history, but his approach was more subtle and somewhat ambivalent. He distinguished two approaches to innovation in the arts; the 'internalist' approach with which he is generally associated, which accounts for change in terms of an inner development, and the 'externalist' approach, according to which 'to explain a style . . . can mean nothing other than to place it in its general

---

[8] Letter to Bernhard Kugler, 21 August 1874.
[9] The essays were published in Burckhardt (1898); the unpublished manuscripts are discussed in the introduction.

historical context and to verify that it speaks in harmony with the other organs of its age' (Wölfflin, 1888, p. 79).[10] The illuminating observations on historical context which Wölfflin sometimes produced (such as the remarks on the social history of gesture, below p. 238) are enough to make one regret the self-denying ordinance by which he generally restricted himself to explanations of style in intrinsic terms. As a result, Burckhardt's intellectual heritage passed not to Wölfflin but to Aby Warburg.

Aby Warburg's life is reminiscent of more than one character in the novels of his contemporary Thomas Mann. The eldest son of a Hamburg banker, he rejected the world of business for the world of scholarship. It is hardly surprising that he should have been fascinated by the Medici. Warburg was not a pupil of Burckhardt's, but in 1892 he gave the older man his essay on Botticelli, and the generous comments on this 'fine piece of work' suggest that Burckhardt thought that this study of a painter's contacts with poets and humanists did not diverge in essentials from his own. It was a testimony, wrote Burckhardt, to 'the general deepening and many-sidedness' which research on the Renaissance had reached.[11] Warburg was indeed many-sided. He treated the history of art as part of the general history of culture, and disliked any kind of intellectual 'frontier control' as he called it. On the other hand, he was faithful to the maxim that God is to be found in the details (*'Der Liebe Gott steckt in Detail'*). To interpret the paintings of Botticelli, for example, he went to the poems of Poliziano and the philosophy of Ficino. Warburg's interests extended to social and economic history; in his own work the concept of the Florentine 'bourgeoisie' played a considerable part, while his friend the economic historian Alfred Doren dedicated to him a study of the Florentine cloth industry (Doren, 1901).[12]

Warburg's central concern was, however, with the persistence and transformation of the classical tradition. For a thorough and detailed social history of Renaissance art, it was necessary to wait for Martin Wackernagel. Wackernagel, an art historian from Basel, made a study of Florence in the period 1420–1530 which concentrated on the organization of the arts: on workshops, patrons and the art market. In other words, he focused on what (with a rather unhappy choice of term for a book published in 1938) he called the artist's *Lebensraum*, his milieu, defined as 'the whole complex of economic-material as

---

[10] On Wölfflin, see Antoni (1940), ch. 5; Podro (1982), ch. 6 and Holly (1984).

[11] Quoted in Kaegi (1933), p. 285. On Warburg, see esp. Doren (1931), Bing (1965), Gombrich (1970), Podro (1982), ch. 7 and Maikuma (1985).

[12] On his friendship with Warburg, see Doren (1931).

well as sociocultural circumstances and conditions'. Although the present study is concerned with learning, literature and music as well as the visual arts, and with Italy as a whole rather than Florence, its debt to Wackernagel is great.[13]

Another attempt was made in the 1930s to fill the gap between the social and cultural history of the Renaissance. Where Wackernagel provided a detailed social history or 'sociography', Alfred von Martin (a pupil of the Hungarian Marxist Karl Mannheim) offered a sociology. His concise, elegant essay reads like a mixture of Marx and Burckhardt, with a dash of Mannheim and the German sociologist Georg Simmel. Like Burckhardt, von Martin is concerned with the themes of individualism and the origins of modernity, but he places much more emphasis than Burckhardt on the economic basis of the Renaissance and its 'curve of development' through time. Alfred von Martin's Renaissance is a 'bourgeois revolution'. In the first part of his essay he charts the rise of the capitalist, who replaces the noble and the cleric as the leader of society. It is this social change that underlies the rise of a rational calculating mentality. In parts two and three, however, we see the bourgeois becoming timid and conservative and the individualist ideal of the entrepreneur replaced by the conformist ideal of the courtier.

It is easy to criticize this essay for its confident use of general terms like 'Renaissance man' (or indeed 'bourgeois') or for its speculations on 'the analogy of money and intellectualism' (two powerful forces which can be applied to any end) or between democracy and the representation of nude figures in art (the idea being that nakedness is egalitarian). Its defects are partly those of a pioneer, lacking sufficient case studies in the social history of culture on which to base generalizations. *The Sociology of the Renaissance* (1932) nevertheless remains a valuable corrective and complement to Burckhardt.[14]

Another study of the Renaissance in the tradition of Marx and Mannheim – despite the fact that its author studied with Wölfflin – is Frederick Antal's *Florentine Painting and its Social Background* (1947). It starts with a vivid contrast between two Madonnas, hanging side by side in the National Gallery in London, both of them painted between 1425 and 1426, one by Masaccio and the other by Gentile da Fabriano. Masaccio's is described as 'matter-of-fact, sober and clear-cut', while Gentile's is 'ornate', 'decorative' and 'hieratic'.

---

[13] On Wackernagel, see Alison Luchs's introduction to her translation of the 1938 book. For a monograph on Florentine humanism on similar lines to Wackernagel's, see Martines (1963).
[14] The introduction by W. K. Ferguson to the 1963 edition of *The Sociology of the Renaissance* offers a balanced assessment of the book.

GENTILE DA FABRIANO, *ADORATION OF THE SHEPHERDS* (DETAIL) Galleria Uffizi. Photograph from The Mansell Collection.

Antal goes on to explain the differences by the fact that the works were intended for 'different sections of the public', more exactly different social classes, with different worldviews. The 'upper middle class', whose worldview was sober, rational and 'progressive', pre-ferred the paintings of Masaccio, while those of Gentile appealed to the conservative 'feudal' aristocracy. Antal concludes that Masaccio's appearance on the Florentine scene reflected the rise of the upper middle class, and that he lacked followers because this class was assimilated into the aristocracy.[15]

It is difficult not to admire this brilliant application of Marxist theory to art history. With great intellectual economy, a few central ideas of Marx are used to generate interpretations of art and society in a specific milieu as well as at a general level. But Antal lays himself open to two serious charges. The first is that of anachronism, of applying to fifteenth-century Florence such modern terms as 'progres-sive' or even 'class' without expressing any awareness of the problems involved (some of which will be discussed in chapter 9). The second charge – and one to which von Martin must also plead guilty – is that of circularity. As Antal knows, one of Gentile da Fabriano's patrons, Palla Strozzi, was the father-in-law of one of Masaccio's patrons, Felice Brancacci. Do these two men belong to different classes? Antal modifies his thesis by arguing that the upper middle class contained a less progressive section which borrowed a feudal ideology from the aristocracy. How do we distinguish the more progressive section of the upper middle class from the rest? By looking at the paintings they commissioned.

The most powerful critique of the Marxist approach has come from Sir Ernst Gombrich in what was originally a review of a social history of art by Arnold Hauser (1951) (like Antal, a Hungarian refugee). Gombrich (1963) distinguishes two senses of the phrase 'social history of art'. The first sense he defines as the study of art 'as an institution' or as 'an account of the changing material conditions under which art was commissioned and created'. The second sense of the social history of art is described by Gombrich as social history reflected in art, and dismissed.[16]

It is indeed dangerous to assume that art 'reflects' society in a direct way, but the phrase 'art as an institution' is also somewhat ambi-guous. It may refer to Wackernagel's *Lebensraum*; in other words, to the world of the workshop and the patron, to what sociologists call a

---

[15] Assessments of Antal's work include Meiss (1948) and Renouard (1950).

[16] More recent Marxist approaches to the Renaissance include Batkin (1978) and Heller (1979). More subtle Marxist or near-Marxist approaches to art history include Clark (1973) and Barrell (1980).

'microsocial' approach. Much valuable work on the social history of Renaissance art has been done along these lines, from Wackernagel to Gombrich's own study (1966) of Medici patronage and Margot and Rudolf Wittkower's (1963) study of artists. The social history of Italian literature has been approached along similar lines, following the pioneering study of Renaissance writers by Carlo Dionisotti (1967).

The problem remains whether the study of 'the changing material conditions under which art was commissioned and created' should be limited to the immediate milieu or extended to society as a whole. It is obviously illuminating to consider the relationship between paintings and the art patronage of the time but many historians will want to go further and ask what sociologists call 'macrosocial' questions about the relationship of art patronage to other social institutions and to the state of the economy. Some historians have indeed asked this kind of question about the Italian Renaissance and come up with rather different answers, some stressing economic factors, like Robert Lopez, and others politics, like Hans Baron.

Lopez, whose particular interest is the economic history of Genoa (his native city), has argued that the fourteenth and fifteenth centuries were a period of economic recession for Europe in general and Italy in particular. He is well aware of the difficulties this recession theory creates for the conventional view of the economic preconditions of the Renaissance. The 'superstructure' seems to be out of phase with the 'base'. He firmly rejects any attempt to explain away the discrepancy by suggesting that culture lags behind the economy. 'Cultural lags, as everybody knows, are ingenious elastic devices to link together events which cannot be linked by any other means . . . Personally, I doubt the paternity of children who were born two hundred years after the death of their fathers . . . the Renaissance . . . was conditioned by its own economy and not by the economy of the past.' What Lopez does is to turn the conventional view upside down and propound a theory of 'hard times and investment in culture'. Struck by the fact that medieval Italy had a booming economy and small churches, while medieval France had great cathedrals and a less successful economy, he puts forward the hypothesis that the cathedrals ate up capital and labour which could have gone into economic growth. Conversely, Renaissance merchants may have had more time to spare for cultural activities because they were less busy in the office. The value of culture 'rose at the very moment that the value of land fell. Its returns mounted when commercial interest rates declined.' It is not clear how seriously, how literally we are to take the notion of 'investment' here, and we shall have to return to the

problem in chapter 4. However, it is plain that the prosperity theory
of culture now has a serious competitor (Lopez, 1952, 1953).[17]

A more political explanation of the Renaissance has been put
forward by Hans Baron, a scholar who grew up during the Weimar
Republic and remains committed to republican values. His study of
Florence and the 'crisis' of the early Italian Renaissance (Baron, 1955)
notes the important changes in ideas which took place in the years
around 1400. 'By then, the civic society of the Italian city-states had
been in existence for many generations and was perhaps already past
its prime', thus ruling out any simple social explanation of intellectual
change. Instead, he offers a political explanation, returning to the
traditional theme of liberty dear to Shaftesbury, Roscoe and Sismondi, but placing more stress on self-consciousness and offering a close
analysis of key political events. Baron argues that about the year
1400, Florentines suddenly became aware of their collective identity
and of the unique characteristics of their society. This awareness led
them to identify with the great republics of the ancient world, Athens
and Rome, and this identification with antiquity led in turn to major
changes in their culture. Baron explains the rise of Florentine
self-consciousness as a response to the threat to the city's liberty from
the ruler of Milan, Giangaleazzo Visconti, who made an unsuccessful
attempt to incorporate Florence into his empire. To become aware of
one's ideals, there is nothing like fighting for them.

The value of Baron's approach, like that of Lopez, lies in what it
has added to the common store rather than in sweeping away all
previous accounts of the Renaissance. Baron's emphasis on political
events, for example, does not make full sense without some consideration of underlying structures. Why, for instance, did Florence resist
Milan when other city-states capitulated?

At a more general level, microsocial and macrosocial approaches
should be taken as complementary rather than contradictory. Each
has its own dangers and defects. The macrosocial approach runs the
risk of what has been called 'Grand Theory' – too little information,
too much interpretation, too rigid a framework. This approach tends
to give the impression that 'social forces' (which take on a life of their
own) act on 'culture' in a crudely direct way. The microsocial
approach, on the other hand, runs the opposite danger of
hyperempiricism – description rather than analysis, too many facts,
too little interpretation (cf. Mills, 1959, chs 1–3).

There seems to be a case for a pluralistic approach which attempts

---

[17] For criticisms of this theory, see Cipolla (1963–4) and Burke (1978).

to test the broader theories, old and new, and to weave empirical studies into a general synthesis. To do this, and in particular to link microsocial to macrosocial approaches, is in fact the aim of this book. It is not concerned, like the sociology of art, with cross-cultural generalization (apart from the comparisons and contrasts offered in the last few pages). Nor is it as sharply focused on the particular as historical monographs tend to be. It deals essentially with styles, attitudes, habits and structures which were typical of a particular society over a few generations – Italy in the fifteenth and early sixteenth centuries. Regional variation, discussed in the next chapter, remains in the background. The Venetian cultural achievement of the period, for example, long received considerably less than its due, partly for accidental reasons. In the sixteenth century, a Venetian (perhaps the patrician Marcantonio Michiel) collected material on the lives of painters, but this Venetian Vasari did not complete his enterprise, let alone publish it, thus robbing posterity of material necessary to counter the real Vasari's Tuscan bias. An equivalent of Wackernagel's book on Florence, planned earlier this century, also remained unpublished and incomplete. It is only recently that studies of the social history of the arts in Venice in this period have begun to appear in sufficient numbers to make possible serious comparisons and contrasts with Florence.[18]

I have tried to avoid giving the Florentines more than their share of the limelight; indeed, only a quarter of the artists and writers discussed in the next chapter came from Tuscany.[19] The primary aim of this book, however, is not so much to redress any regional imbalance or even to explore the cultural differences between different parts of Italy, as to present a general picture against which to measure regional variation. In a similar way, the discussion of change within the period (within each section and in chapter 10) has been made relatively brief, in order to free the maximum space for the description and analysis of structures, for explaining how what might be called the 'art system' worked, and in what ways it was related to other activities in the society. In other words, pluralistic as it is, this study does not claim to offer all the possible social interpretations of the Renaissance. In any case, the social approach is only one of a number of possible avenues to the arts.

---

[18] See Logan (1972), Howard (1975), Rosand (1982), Foscari and Tafuri (1983), Tafuri (1985) and King (1986).
[19] The artists to be studied were drawn, as the Appendix explains, from the region-by-region account of the Italian Renaissance given in the *Encyclopaedia of World Art*.

Part II

The Arts in their Milieu

3

ARTISTS AND WRITERS

RECRUITMENT

L ET us begin by assuming that artistic and other creative abilities are randomly distributed among the population. In conditions of perfect opportunity, a cultural elite, that is, the people whose creative abilities are recognized in that society, would be in all other respects a random sample of the population. In practice this never happens. Every society erects obstacles to the expression of the creativity of some groups, and Renaissance Italy was no exception. The 600 painters, sculptors, architects, humanists, writers, 'composers' and 'scientists' studied in this chapter (and described for simplicity's sake as 'artists' and 'writers' or 'the creative elite') are in many ways untypical of the Italian population.[1]

To begin with the most spectacular example of bias. One 'variable' in the survey of artists and writers appears to have been almost invariable: their sex. Only three out of the 600 are women: Vittoria Colonna, Veronica Gambara and Tullia d'Aragona. All are poets, and all come at the end of the period. This bias is not, of course, uniquely Italian or confined to this period, whether it is to be explained psychologically (male creativity as a substitute for inability to bear children) or sociologically (women's abilities being suppressed in a male-dominated society). It is interesting to discover that when the social obstacles are a little less heavy than usual, women artists and writers make their appearance. For example, the daughters of artists sometimes paint. Tintoretto's daughter Marietta is known to have painted portraits, though nothing which is certainly by her has

---

[1] For the composition of this group, see the Appendix. The choice of the 600 is necessarily somewhat arbitrary, though no more arbitrary than the choice of named individuals in other studies of the Renaissance. The terms 'architect', 'composer' and 'scientist' are convenient but problematic. The emergence of the architect, as opposed to the master mason, was taking place in this very period (Ettlinger, 1977). Although the word *compositore* existed in this period, men whom we call 'composers' were more commonly described as 'musicians'. The term 'scientist' is a convenient anachronism to avoid the circumlocution 'writer in physics, medicine, etc.' As for *artista*, although Michelangelo uses the term in the modern sense, in the early fifteenth century it meant a university student of the seven liberal arts (p. 54 below). No references will be given for information about individual artists derived from Thieme–Becker (1907–50), about humanists from Cosenza (1952) or about musicians from Groves (1980). Nor will page references be given to Vasari, since the lives are short and the editions are many.

survived.[2] Vasari tells us that Uccello had a daughter, Antonia, who 'knew how to draw' and became a Carmelite nun. Nuns sometimes worked as miniaturists, like Caterina da Bologna, better known as a saint. There was also a sculptress active in Bologna, Properzia de'Rossi, whose life was written by Vasari, with appropriate references to such gifted women of antiquity as Camilla and Sappho.[3]

In the case of women writers, it is easy to extend the list to include the poets Gaspara Stampa, Laura Terracina and Laura Battiferri. All six women flourished at the end of our period, towards the middle of the sixteenth century. Their emergence may well be a result of the increasing importance of Italian (as opposed to Latin) literature, and to the opening up of literary society. Recent research has also uncovered a small group of women who were interested in humanism. The most important of these learned ladies were Laura Cereta, Cassandra Fedele, Isotta Nogarola and Alessandra della Scala. They attracted some attention at the time, but they also had to face male ridicule and, whether they married or became nuns, their studies generally came to a premature end (Jardine, 1983, 1985).

Even among adult males, however, the creative elite is far from a random sample. It is, for example, geographically biased. If we divide Italy into seven regions, we find that about 26 per cent of the elite came from Tuscany, 23 per cent from the Veneto, 18 per cent from the States of the Church, 11 per cent from Lombardy, 7 per cent from south Italy, 1.5 per cent from Piedmont and 1 per cent from Liguria. Another 7 per cent came from outside Italy altogether (leaving 5.5 per cent unknown). If we compare these figures with those for the populations of these seven regions, we find that four regions (Tuscany, the Veneto, the States of the Church and Lombardy, in that order) produced more than their share of artists and writers, while the other three, from Piedmont to Sicily, were culturally underdeveloped.[4] It is also clear that on these criteria, Tuscany is well ahead of the others.

Another striking regional variation concerns the proportion of the elite practising the visual arts. In Tuscany, the Veneto and Lombardy the visual arts are dominant, while in Genoa and southern Italy the

---

    [2] Tietze-Conrat (1934) attempts some identifications.
    [3] Since this book was first published, womens' history has become established, and the creative women of the Renaissance are receiving serious attention, for example in Kelly (1977). On painters, see Greer (1979).
    [4] Tuscany had 10 per cent of the population and 26 per cent of the elite; the Veneto, 20 and 23 per cent; the States of the Church, 15 and 18 per cent; Lombardy, 10 and 11 per cent. On the other hand, south Italy had 30 per cent of the population and 7 per cent of the elite; Piedmont, 10 and 1.5 per cent; Liguria, 5 and 1 per cent. For statistics on writers alone, see Bec (1983), p. 247.

writers are more important.[5] In other words, the region in which he (or occasionally she) is born appears to effect not only the chances of an individual's entering the creative elite, but also the part of it he enters.

Chances of becoming a successful artist or writer (or at least of entering the select 600) were also affected by the size of the community in which an individual was born. Some 13 per cent of Italians, living in towns of 10,000 or more people, formed the reservoir from which at least 60 per cent of the elite were drawn.

Rome's poor contribution deserves emphasis. Only four of our artists and writers were born in Rome: the humanist Lorenzo Valla, the architect–painter Giulio Pippi ('Giulio Romano'), the sculptor Gian Cristoforo Romano and the painter Antoniazzo Romano. It is true that Rome was no more than the eighth city in Italy at this period, but Ferrara, which was smaller, produced 15 members of the elite, and even tiny Urbino produced 7.[6] The importance of Rome in the Renaissance was as a centre of patronage which attracted creative individuals from other parts of Italy.

It is only to be expected that sculptors and architects tended to come from regions where stone was plentiful and suitable for carving and building. In Tuscany, Isaia da Pisa did indeed come from Pisa, near the white marble of the west coast, while four major sculptors (Desiderio da Settignano, Antonio and Bernardo Rossellino, and Bartolommeo Ammannati) were all born in Settignano, a village near Florence with important stone quarries. Michelangelo was put out to nurse there with a stonecutter's wife, and later joked about sucking in his love of sculpture with his nurse's milk. Lombardy, with 10 per cent of the elite, had 22 per cent of the sculptors and 25 per cent of the architects, as well as much of the best stone. Domenico Gaggini and Pietro Lombardo, founders of whole dynasties of sculptors and architects, both came from the area around Lake Lugano. A third region rich in sculptors and architects as well as in stone was Dalmatia, beyond the frontiers of Italy but not far away and with economic links to Venice in particular. Luciano Laurana the architect and Francesco Laurana the sculptor both came, in all probability, from the Dalmatian town of La Vrana, while the famous sculptor

---

[5] Tuscany, 60 per cent visual (95 to 62); the Veneto, 55 per cent (75 to 62); Lombardy, 70 per cent (45 to 19); south Italy, 58 per cent non-visual (24 to 17); while the Genoese have four humanists to one artist.

[6] Urbino had a population of less than 5,000, but it included the historian Polidore Vergil, the mathematician Commandino, the composers M. A. Cavazzoni and his son Girolamo, and the painters Genga, Santi and Raphael. The architect Bramante was born nearby.

Ivan Duknovic came from Trogir and the architect-sculptor Juraj Dalmatinac came from Sibenik.

These Dalmatians are a reminder of the importance of the foreign artists and writers who worked in Italy, 41 of them altogether. Twenty-one musicians, mostly Flemings like Guillaume Dufay, Josquin des Près, Heinrich Isaak and Adriaan Willaert (Bridgman, 1964, ch. 7). There were some Greek humanists, notably Janos Argyropoulos, Georgios Gemistos Plethon, and Cardinal Bessarion. There were a few Spaniards, including the poet Benedetto Gareth from Barcelona, the painter Jacomart Baçó from Valencia, and the composer Ramos de Pareja.

Some of the most distinguished Italian artists and writers in Italy were 'foreign' in another sense; that is, born outside the city in which they did most of their work. The humanist Leonardo Bruni, famous for his eulogy of the city of Florence, came from Arezzo; the philosopher Ficino, from Figline in the Valdarno; Leonardo da Vinci from Vinci, a village in Tuscany; the humanist Poliziano from Montepulciano. Giorgio Merula, Giorgio Valla and Marcantonio Sabellico were three non-Venetian humanists who spent considerable time in Venice. The most famous Venetian painters were not in fact from Venice itself; Giorgione was born in the small town of Castelfranco, Titian in Pieve di Cadore. It is possible that as outsiders they were freer from the pressures of local cultural traditions and so found it easier to innovate.

The creative elite appears to have been biased socially as well as geographically. A note of caution has to be sounded because the father's occupation in 57 per cent of the group is unknown. All the same, the remaining 43 per cent do tend to come from a fairly restricted social milieu. The majority of the Italian population at this time was made up of peasants or agricultural labourers, but only seven members of the elite are known to have had fathers from this class: two humanists, Bartolommeo della Scala and Giovanni Campano; one engineer–sculptor, Mariano Taccola; and four painters; fra Angelico, Andrea del Castagno, Andrea Sansovino and Domenico Beccafumi. Of the remaining artists and writers, 114 were children of artisans and shopkeepers, 84 were noble and 48 the children of merchants and professional men. In fact, the artists tended to be the children of artisans and shopkeepers, while the writers tended to be the children of nobles and professional men; the contrast is a dramatic one.[7]

Since at least 96 artists came from artisan or shopkeeper families, it may be worth attempting to subdivide this group. It turns out that the nearer a craft is to painting or sculpture, the higher the chance of the craftsman's son becoming an artist. In 26 cases there was no connection with the arts; the father was a tailor for example, or a poultry-seller. In 34 cases there was an indirect connection with the arts; the father was a carpenter, a mason, a stonecutter and so on. In 36 cases, the artist was the son of an artist, as Raphael was, for example. It is clear that the arts ran in families. The Bellini family of Venice included the father, Jacopo; his more famous sons, Gentile and Giovanni; and his son-in-law, Mantegna. The Lombardo dynasty has already been mentioned; the founder, Pietro, his sons Tullio 1 and Antonio 1, and their descendants. In the case of the Solaris, sculptors in Milan and elsewhere, there were at least five generations of artists, including four members of the creative elite.

The sheer number of these artist families deserves emphasis. Think of an artist of the Italian Renaissance; the odds are roughly 50–50 that he had relatives practising the arts.[8] Masaccio, for example: his brother Giovanni was a painter, and Giovanni had two sons, a grandson and a great-grandson who were also painters. Titian had a brother and a son who were artists. Tintoretto had two artist sons as well as his daughter Marietta.

What is the significance of these artist dynasties? The Victorian scientist Francis Galton (1869) quoted some of these examples to support his views on the importance of 'hereditary genius'. However, a sociological explanation is at least as plausible as a biological one. In Renaissance Italy painting and sculpture were family businesses, like grocery or weaving. There is evidence to suggest that some artist fathers hoped that their sons would follow them into the craft; two of them at least named their children after famous artists of antiquity. The painter Sodoma called his son 'Apelles'; the boy died young. The architect Vincenzo Seregni, equally hopeful, called his son 'Vitruvio'; the boy survived to become an architect like his father. Guild regulations encouraged family businesses by reducing entry fees for the relatives of masters. The statutes of the painters' guild at Padua, for example, laid down that an apprentice should pay two lire to enter the guild unless he was the son, brother, nephew or grandson of a master, in which cases the price was halved. A master was also allowed to take a relative as an apprentice without charge (Gaye, 1839–40, vol. 2, p. 43f). The contrast between the visual arts on one side and literature and learning on the other supports the sociological

---

[7] The known fathers of painters, sculptors and architects include 96 artisans and shopkeepers compared to 40 nobles, professional men or merchants. The known fathers of writers, humanists and scientists include 7 artisans and shopkeepers compared to 95 nobles, professional men and merchants. Cf. Bec (1983), pp. 248–9.

[8] Some 48 per cent of the artists in the creative elite are known to have artist relatives.

against the biological explanation of artist dynasties. Nearly half the artists in the creative elite are known to have had artist relatives. In the case of literature and learning, however, which was not organized on family lines, the proportion sinks to just over a quarter.[9] The difference between the two groups indicates the strength of social forces.

The significance of this information about the geographical and social origins of artists and writers is that it helps to explain why the arts flourished in Italy. It is unlikely that social forces can produce great artists, but it is plausible to suggest that social obstacles can thwart them. If that is the case, it follows that art and literature flourish in those places and periods in which able men and women are least frustrated. In early modern Europe, including Italy, talented males faced two major obstacles, placed at the opposite ends of the social scale and discriminating respectively against the able sons of nobles and of peasants.

In the first place, a talented but well-born child might be unable to become a painter or a sculptor because his parents considered these manual or 'mechanical' occupations beneath him. In his lives of artists, Vasari tells several stories about parental opposition. For example, he says that when Brunelleschi's father found that young Filippo had artistic inclinations, he was 'greatly displeased' because he had wanted the boy to become either a notary like himself or a physician like his great- grandfather.[10] Again, we learn that Baldovinetti's family had long been merchants and that young Alesso became interested in art 'more or less against the will of his father, who would have liked him to have gone into business'. In the case of Michelangelo, the son of a patrician, Vasari comments that his father 'probably' thought Michelangelo's interest in art unworthy of their old family; but another pupil of Michelangelo claimed that Michelangelo's father and uncles hated art and thought it shameful that their boy should practise it (Condivi, 1964, p. 24).

At the other end of the social scale, it was difficult for the sons of peasants to become artists and writers because they could not easily acquire the necessary training, if indeed they knew that such occupations even existed. Scala the humanist was a miller's son, but millers were relatively well off. The painter fra Angelico and the humanist Giovanni Antonio Campano climbed the traditional ladder for poor men's sons; they entered the Church.[11]

---

[9] The exact figures are 48 per cent and 27 per cent, respectively.

[10] However, the life of Brunelleschi attributed to Manetti and written some 60 years closer to the events records that Filippo's father made no objection, 'as he was a man of discernment'.

Of four sons of peasants who became artists, stories were told which sound like folktales. Of the great fourteenth-century painter Giotto we learn that he was set to mind the sheep but was discovered by the artist Cimabue, who just happened to be passing, drawing on a rock with a piece of stone.[12] In the case of Andrea del Castagno, we are told that 'he was taken from keeping animals by a Florentine citizen who found him drawing a sheep on a rock, and brought him to Florence' (Frey, 1892, pp. 21–2). Vasari adds –perhaps to flatter his own Medici patron – that this citizen was a member of the Medici family. He tells a similar story about Domenico Beccafumi, who was observed by a landowner 'drawing with a pointed stick in the sand of a little stream as he was keeping his sheep', and taken to Siena, and another about Andrea Sansovino, who 'kept cattle like Giotto, drawing in the sand and on the ground the beasts which he was watching', before he too was discovered and taken to Florence for training. These reworkings of the old myth of the birth and childhood of the hero do not have to be taken too literally. What they illustrate are contemporary perceptions of the poor boy with talent.[13] Yet something almost as dramatic must have happened for these boys to have become artists, and in the case of the architect Palladio, life seems to have imitated art. There is documentary evidence that his father, a poor man, apprenticed his son to a stone-carver at Padua. The boy ran away to Vicenza, where his gifts were noticed by the humanist nobleman Gian Giorgio Trissino, on whose house he was working (Puppi, 1975, ch. 1).

Unlike the sons of nobles and peasants, the sons of artisans did not run such a high risk of discouragement and frustration, and many of them would have been used to thinking in a plastic manner from childhood, having watched their fathers at work. The conclusion seems inescapable that for the visual arts to flourish in this period, a concentration of artisans was necessary, in other words an urban environment. In the fifteenth and sixteenth centuries, the most highly urbanized regions in Europe were in Italy and The Netherlands, and these were indeed the regions from which most of the major artists came (on The Netherlands, see chapter 10).

The most favourable environment for artists to grow up in seems to have been a city which was orientated towards craft–industrial production, like Florence, rather than towards trade or services, like Naples or Rome. It was only when Venice turned from trade to

---

[11] On Campano, see D'Amico (1983), pp. 14–15.
[12] The story is told by Ghiberti (1947), p. 32, followed by Vasari.
[13] For a good analysis of this type of story, see Kris and Kurz (1934), ch. 2.

A BUST OF FILIPPO BRUNELLESCHI, FLORENCE CATHEDRAL.
Photograph from The Mansell Collection.

industry, at the end of the fifteenth century, that Venetian art caught up with that of Florence.

The predominance of the sons of nobles and professional men in literature, humanism and science is not difficult to explain. A university education was much more expensive than an apprenticeship. It seems to have been as difficult for the son of an artisan to become a writer, humanist or scientist as for a peasant's son to become an artist. There are five known cases. The humanist Guarino of Verona was the son of a smith; the physician Michele Savonarola (father of the more famous friar) was the son of a weaver; the poet Burchiello, the son of a carpenter; while the professional writers Pietro Aretino and Antonfrancesco Doni were the sons of a shoemaker and a scissors-maker respectively. In other words, from the social point of view the creative elite was not one group but two, a visual group recruited in the main from artisans and a literary group recruited from the upper classes (the composers, whose social origins are rarely known, were in any case mostly foreigners).

However, the major innovators in the visual arts were often untypical of the group in their social origin. Brunelleschi, Masaccio and Leonardo were all the sons of notaries, while Michelangelo was the son of a patrician. Socially as well as geographically it was the outsiders, those with least reason to identify with local craft traditions, who made the greatest contribution to the new trends.

TRAINING

Training, like recruitment, suggests that artists and writers belonged to two different cultures, the cultures of the workshop and the university.

The painter Carlo da Milano is described in a document as 'a doctor of arts', while another painter, Giulio Campagnola, was a page at the court of Ferrara; but in the overwhelming majority of cases, painters and sculptors were trained, like other craftsmen, by apprenticeship. At the beginning of our period, the process of apprenticeship was described as follows:

> To begin as a shop-boy studying for one year, to get practice in drawing on the little panel; next, to serve in the shop under some master, to learn how to work at all the branches which pertain to our profession; and to stay and begin the working up of colours; and to learn to boil the sizes, and grind the *gessos* [the white ground used in painting]; and to get experience in gessoing *anconas* [panels with mouldings], and modelling and scraping them; gilding and stamping; for the space of a good six years. Then to get experience in painting, embellishing with mordants, making cloths of gold, getting practice in working on the wall, for six more years, drawing all the time, never leaving off, either on holidays or on workdays.[14]

Thirteen years' training is a long time, and it is probably a counsel of perfection. The statutes of the painter's guild at Venice required a minimum apprenticeship of only five years, followed by two years as a journeyman, before a candidate could submit his 'masterpiece' and

---

[14] Cennini, *Il libro del'arte*, p. 65. Cf. Cole (1983), esp. ch. 2; on Florence, see Wackernagel (1938), ch. 12; on Venice, see Tietze (1939)

become a master painter with the right to open his own shop. All the same, painters were required to perform a wide variety of tasks in a variety of media (wooden panels, canvas, parchment, plaster, and even cloth, glass and iron), and it is scarcely surprising to find that they often started young. Andrea del Sarto was seven when he began his apprenticeship. Titian was nine, Mantegna and Sodoma ten. Paolo Uccello was already one of Lorenzo Ghiberti's shop-boys when he was 11. Michelangelo was 13 when he was apprenticed to Ghirlandaio, and Palladio the same age when he began work as a stone-carver. Child labour was common enough in early modern Europe. From the contemporary point of view, Botticelli and Leonardo left things a little late, for Botticelli was still at school when he was 13, while Leonardo was not apprenticed to Verrocchio until he was 14 or 15. Artists did not have time for many years at school and most of them probably learned no more than a little reading and writing. Arithmetic, taught at the so-called 'abacus school' (Gold-thwaite, 1972), was considered an advanced subject leading to a commercial career. Brunelleschi, Luca della Robbia, Bramante and Leonardo were probably exceptional among artists in attending schools of this kind.

Apprentices generally formed part of their master's extended family. Sometimes the master was paid for providing board, lodging and instruction; Sodoma's father paid the considerable sum of 50 ducats for a seven-year apprenticeship (on the purchasing power of the ducat, see p. 218 below). In other instances, however, it was the master who paid the apprentice, at higher rates as the boy grew more highly skilled. Michelangelo's contract with the Ghirlandaio work-shop laid down that he was the receive six florins in the first year, eight in the second and ten in to third.

The fact that apprentices sometimes took their master's name, as in eighteenth-century Japan, is a reminder of the importance of the master by whom an artist was trained. Jacopo Sansovino and Domenico Campagnola were not the sons but the pupils of Andrea Sansovino and Giulio Campagnola. Piero di Cosimo took his name from his master Cosimo Rosselli. It is in fact possible to identify whole chains of artists, each the pupil of the one before. Bicci di Lorenzo, for example, taught his son Neri di Bicci, who taught Cosimo Rosselli, who taught Piero di Cosimo, who taught Andrea del Sarto, who taught Pontormo, who taught Bronzino. The differences in individual style in these examples shows that the Florentine system of cultural transmission was far from producing a traditional art. Again, Gentile da Fabriano taught Jacopo Bellini, who taught his sons Gentile (named after his old master) and Giovanni (who had a whole host of pupils, traditionally said to have included Giorgione and Titian).

A few workshops seem to have been of central importance for the art of the period: Lorenzo Ghiberti's, for example, in which the pupils included Donatello, Michelozzo, Uccello, Antonio Pollaiuolo, and possibly Masolino, and Verrocchio's, which included not only Leonardo da Vinci but also Botticini, Domenico Ghirlandaio, Lorenzo di Credi and Perugino. But the most important workshop in the whole period was probably that of Raphael, in which the pupils and assistants included Giulio Romano, Gianfrancesco Penni, Polidoro da Caravaggio, Perino del Vaga, and Lorenzo Lotti (to be distinguished from Lorenzo Lotto).

An important part of the training of painters was the study and copying of the workshop collection of drawings, which served to unify the shop style and to maintain its traditions. A humanist described the process in the early fifteenth century: 'When the apprentices are to be instructed by their master . . . the painters follow the practice of giving them a number of fine drawings and pictures as models of their art.'[15] Such drawings formed an important part of a painter's capital, and might receive a special mention in wills, as they do from Cosimo Tura of Ferrara in 1471. Designs might be lettered in code because they were considered trade secrets, as in the case of a notebook from Ghiberti's studio (Prager and Scaglia, 1970, p. 65f). It is possible that as deliberate individualism in style came to be prized more highly (above p. 25), workshop drawings lost their importance. Vasari tells us that Beccafumi's master taught him by means of 'the designs of some great painters which he had for his own use, as is the practice of some masters unskilful in design', a comment which suggests that the practice was dying out.

For humanists and scientists (and to a lesser extent, writers, for 'writer' was a role played by amateurs), the equivalent of an apprenticeship was a university education. There were 13 universities in Italy in the early fifteenth century: Bologna, Ferrara, Florence, Naples, Padua, Pavia, Perugia, Piacenza, Pisa, Rome, Salerno, Siena and Turin. Of these universities, the most important in this period was Padua, where 52 members of the elite were educated, 17 of them between 1500 and 1520. The growth of the university was encouraged by the Venetian government, in whose territory Padua lay. They increased the salaries of the professors, forbade Venetians to go to other universities, and made a period of study at Padua a

---

[15] Gasparino Barzizza, quoted by Baxandall (1965), p. 183n. The drawings of the period have been studied by Ames-Lewis (1981, ch. 4) and Ames-Lewis and Wright (1983).

prerequisite for office. It was convenient to have a university outside the capital. Lodgings were cheap, and the prosperity which the students brought with them helped to secure the loyalty of a subject town. Padua also attracted students from other regions; of the 52 humanists and writers who attended the university, about half were born outside the Veneto. Students of scientific subjects ('natural philosophy', as it was called, and medicine) were particularly attracted to Padua. Of the 53 'scientists' in the creative elite, at least 18 studied there.[16]

The next most popular university among the elite was Bologna, with 26 students. The senior university of Italy, Bologna had been through a decline, but it was reviving in the fifteenth century. Next came Ferrara, with 12 members of the elite. It had an international reputation for low fees; a sixteenth-century German student wrote that Ferrara was commonly known as 'the poor man's refuge [*miserorum refugium*]' (Rashdall, 1936, vol. 2, p. 54). Pavia (which serviced the state of Milan as Padua did Venice); Pisa (which serviced Florence); Siena, Perugia and Rome each accounted for about half a dozen of the elite. It is a pleasure to add that two of them (John Hothby and Paul of Venice) were Oxford men. Their colleges are not known.

Students tended to go to university younger than they do now; the historian Francesco Guicciardini was fairly typical in going up to Ferrara when he was 16. They began by studying 'arts', in other words the seven liberal arts, divided into the more elementary, grammar, logic and rhetoric (the *trivium*), and the more advanced, arithmetic, geometry, music and astronomy (the *quadrivium*), and proceeded to one of the three higher degrees in theology, law or medicine. The curriculum was the traditional medieval one, and officially nothing changed during the period. However, it is well known that what is taught at university – let alone what is studied – does not always correspond to what is on the curriculum. Recent research on British universities in the sixteenth and seventeenth centuries, based on the notes taken by students, has shown that a number of new subjects, including history, had been introduced unofficially (Kearney, 1970). No equivalent study of Italian universities has yet been made, but one may suspect that history, poetry and ethics (three of the 'humanities' which were not among the seven

---

[16] Since this book first appeared, there has been something of a boom in the history of universities in Italy and elsewhere, with the work of Denley (1981, 1983), Schmitt (1975) and Verde (1973–7). On Padua, see the essay by Desroussilles in Arnaldi and Pastore Stocchi (1981).

THE TRAINING OF A HUMANIST AT UNIVERSITY, FROM C. LANDINO, *FORMULAIO DI LETTERE E DI ORATIONI VOLGARI CON LA PREPOSTA*, FLORENCE
Reproduced by kind permission of the Trustees of the Bodleian Library, Oxford.

liberal arts) were at least as important in practice as any part of the *quadrivium*.

In some ways, university students resembled apprentices. The disputation by means of which the bachelor became 'master of arts' was the equivalent of the craftsman's 'masterpiece'. A master of arts had the right to teach his subject, which was something like setting up shop on his own. However, teaching and learning, oral as well as written, took place in Latin, the symbol of a separate learned culture. Spies (*lupi* or 'wolves') ensured that the students spoke Latin even among themselves, and those who broke the rule were fined. Another obvious difference between apprentices and university students was the expense of training. It has been calculated that in Tuscany at the beginning of the fifteenth century, it cost about 20 florins a year to keep a boy at a university away from home, a sum which would have kept two servants (Martines, 1963, p. 117). In addition, a new recruit to the doctorate would be expected to lay on an expensive banquet for his colleagues. The doctorate of civil law at Pisa which Guicciardini took in 1505 cost him 26 florins. Even the 'poor man's refuge', Ferrara, was really the standby of the not so very well off.

Architects and composers need to be considered apart from the rest. Architecture was not recognized as a separate craft, so there was no guild of architects (as opposed to masons) and no apprenticeship system. Consequently, the men who designed buildings during this period had one curious characteristic in common, that they had been trained to do something else. Brunelleschi, for example, was trained as a goldsmith, Michelozzo and Palladio as sculptors or stone-carvers, and Antonio da Sangallo the elder as a carpenter, while Leon Battista Alberti was a university man and a humanist. There were, however, opportunities for informal training. Bramante's workshop in Rome was the place where Antonio da Sangallo the younger, Giulio Romano, Peruzzi and Raphael learned how to design buildings; its importance in the history of architecture is something like that of Ghiberti's workshop in Florence a hundred years earlier. Some famous architects, such as Tullio Lombardo and Michele Sammicheli, learned their trade from relatives.[17]

Composers, as we call them, were trained as performers. A number of them went to choir school in their native Netherlands; Josquin des Près, for example, was a choirboy at St Quentin. The Englishman Hothby taught music as well as grammar and arithmetic at a school attached to Lucca cathedral which presumably catered for choirboys. Music (meaning the theory of music) was part of the arts course in

---

[17] On the training of architects, see Ackerman (1954).

WOODCUT OF ADRIAAN WILLAERT, *MUSICA NOVA*, 1559
Photograph from The Mansell Collection.

universities, and several composers in the elite had degrees; Guillaume Dufay was a bachelor of canon law, and Johannes de Tinctoris a doctor in both law and theology. There was no formal training in composition, but informally the circle of Joannes Ockeghem, in The Netherlands, was the equivalent of the workshops of Ghiberti and Bramante. Ockeghem's pupils – to mention only those who worked in Italy – included Alexander Agricola, Antoine Brumel, Loyset Compère, Gaspaer van Weerbecke, and probably also Josquin des Près. From Josquin there runs a kind of apostolic succession of master–pupil relationships which links the great Netherlanders to sixteenth-century Italian composers and the Italians to the major seventeenth-century Germans. Josquin taught Jean Mouton, who taught Adriaan Willaert, a Netherlander who went to Venice and taught Andrea Gabrieli, who, at the end of our period, taught his nephew Giovanni Gabrieli, who taught Heinrich Schütz.[18]

To sum up. In Italy at this time there were two cultures and two systems of training: manual and intellectual, Italian and Latin, workshop-based and university-based. Even in the cases of architecture and music it is not difficult to identify the ladder which a particular individual has climbed. The existence of this dual system raises certain problems for historians of the Renaissance. If artists were such 'early leavers', how did they acquire the familiarity with classical antiquity that is revealed in their paintings, sculptures and buildings? And has the famous 'universal man' of the Renaissance any existence outside the vivid imaginations of nineteenth-century historians?

Contemporary writers on the arts were well aware of the relevance of higher education. Ghiberti, for example, wanted painters and sculptors to study grammar, geometry, arithmetic, astronomy, philosophy, history, medicine, anatomy, perspective and 'theoretical design'.[19] Alberti wanted painters to study the liberal arts, especially geometry, and also the humanities, notably rhetoric, poetry and history.[20] The architect Antonio Averlino, who took the Greek name Filarete ('lover of virtue'), wanted the architect to study music and astrology, 'For when he orders and builds a thing, he should see that it is begun under a good planet and constellation. He also needs music so that he will know how to harmonize the members with the parts of a building.'[21] The ideal sculptor, according to Pomponio Gaurico, who wrote a treatise on sculpture as well as practising the art, should

---

[18] On musical education, see Bridgman (1964), ch. 4.
[19] Ghiberti, I commentari, p. 2.
[20] Alberti, On Painting and Sculpture, book 3, p. 94f.
[21] Filarete, Treatise on Architecture, book 15, p. 198.

AGOSTINO VENEZIANO'S ENGRAVING OF BACCIO BANDINELLI'S
'ACADEMY' IN ROME
Reproduced by permission of the Ashmolean Museum, Oxford.

be 'well-read' (*literatus*) as well as skilled in arithmetic, music and geometry.[22]

Did real artists conform to this ideal? It used to be thought that the education many of them missed by leaving school early was provided for them in institutions called 'academies' (on the model of the learned societies of the humanists and ultimately of Plato's Academy at Athens), notably in Florence, centring on the sculptor Bertoldo; in Milan, around Leonardo da Vinci; and in Rome, in the circle of the Florentine sculptor Baccio Bandinelli, whose pupils were portrayed studying by candlelight. However, there is no hard evidence of the formal training of artists in institutions of this kind until the foundation of the Accademia di Disegno in Florence in 1563, the model for the academic system set up in seventeenth-century France, eighteenth-century England and elsewhere.[23]

However, it should not be assumed that artists' workshops of the

---

[22] Gauricus, *De sculptura*, p. 52f.
[23] Pevsner (1940), ch. 1 gives the traditional view. Vasari's famous account of Bertoldo's academy has been questioned by Chastel (1961), p. 19f.

Renaissance were empty of literary or humanistic culture. There was a tradition that Brunelleschi was 'learned in holy scripture' and 'well-read in the works of Dante' (Frey, 1892, p. 31). Some artists are known to have owned books; the brothers Benedetto and Giuliano da Maiano, for example, Florentine sculptors, owned 29 books between them in 1498. More than half of the books were religious: among them a Bible, a life of St Jerome and a book of the miracles of Our Lady. Among the secular books there were the two Florentine favourites, Dante and Boccaccio, as well as an anonymous history of Florence. Classical antiquity was represented by a life of Alexander and Livy's history of Rome (Cendali, 1926, p. 182f). The intellectual interests of the brothers revealed in this collection, traditional in orientation but with some tincture of the new learning, are not unlike those of Florentine merchants earlier in the century (Bec, 1967; cf. Bec, 1984). Artists with books like these in their possession were clearly interested in the classical past, and not only in its art, although that kind of interest can also be documented from inventories. At the time of his death in 1500, the Sienese painter Neroccio de'Landi owned several pieces of antique marble sculpture, together with 43 plaster casts of fragments (Coor, 1961, p. 107).

The most conspicuous absence from the library of Benedetto and Giuliano da Maiano is classical mythology. There is no copy of Ovid's *Metamorphoses* or Boccaccio's *Genealogy of the Gods*. Artists with such a library as theirs would have been more at home with religious paintings and sculptures than with the mythological paintings demanded by some patrons. One wonders whether Botticelli, who was of the same generation, city and social origin as the da Maianos, had a collection of books very different from theirs. If not, then the role of a patron or his adviser must have been crucial in the creation of paintings such as the *Birth of Venus* or the so-called *Primavera*, and conversations are likely to have formed an important part of an artist's education (cf. p. 109 below).

That modest collection of books needs to be set in time. In 1498, printing had been established in Italy for a generation. It is unlikely that an artist could have amassed 20 manuscripts early in the fifteenth century. On the other hand, in the next century larger libraries are not uncommon. Leonardo da Vinci, sneered at in his own day as a 'man without learning' (*omo sanza lettere*), turns out to have had 116 books in his possession at one point, including three Latin grammars, some of the Fathers of the Church (Augustine, Ambrose), some modern Italian literature (the comic poems of Burchiello and Luigi Pulci, the short stories of Masuccio Salernitano), and treatises on anatomy, astrology, cosmography and mathematics (Reti, 1968, p. 81f).

It would be foolish to take Leonardo as typical of anything, but there is a fair amount of evidence about the literary culture of sixteenth-century artists. The study of their handwriting offers some clues. In the fifteenth century, they tended to write in the manner of merchants, a style which was probably taught at abacus school. In the sixteenth century, however, Raphael, Michelangelo and others wrote in the new italic style.[24] A few of them, including Michelangelo, Pontormo and Paris Bordone, are known to have gone to grammar school. The painter Giulio Campagnola and the architect fra Giovanni Giocondo both knew Greek as well as Latin.[25] A few artists acquired a second reputation as writers. Michelangelo's poems are famous, while Bramante, Bronzino and Raphael all tried their hands at verse. Cennini, Ghiberti, Filarete, Palladio and the Bolognese architect Sebastiano Serlio all wrote treatises on the arts. Cellini and Bandinelli wrote autobiographies, while Vasari is better known for his lives of artists than for his own painting, sculpture and architecture. It is worth adding that Vasari was able to bridge the two cultures by the happy accident of powerful patronage which gave him a double education, a training in the humanities from Pierio Valeriano as well as an artistic training in the circle of Andrea del Sarto (Boase, 1979).

These examples are impressive, but it is worth underlining the fact that they do not include all distinguished artists. Titian, for example, is absent from the list: it is unlikely that he knew Latin. In any case, the examples do not add up to the 'universal man' of the Renaissance. Was he fact or fiction? The ideal of universality was indeed a contemporary one. One character in the dialogue *On Civil Life* by the fifteenth-century Florentine humanist Matteo Palmieri remarks that 'A man is able to learn many things and make himself universal in many excellent arts [*farsi universale di più arti excellenti*].'[26] Another Florentine humanist, Angelo Poliziano, wrote a short treatise on the whole of knowledge, the *Panepistemon*, in which painting, sculpture, architecture and music have their place.[27] The most famous exposition of the idea comes in count Baldassare Castiglione's famous *Courtier* (1528), in which the speakers expect the perfect courtier to be able to fight and dance, paint and sing, write poems and advise his prince. Did this theory have any relation to practice? The careers of Alberti (humanist, architect, mathematician and even athlete), Leonardo and Michelangelo are dazzling testimony to the existence of the universal man, and another 15 members of the elite practised

---

[24] A point made by Armando Petrucci in a lecture to the Warburg Institute in 1968.
[25] Cf. Dempsey (1980) on the later sixteenth century.
[26] Palmieri, *La vita civile*, book 1, p. 43.
[27] One of the few discussions of this is in Summers (1981), ch. 17.

three arts or more, among them Brunelleschi, Ghiberti and Vasari.[28]
The humanist Paolo dal Pozzo Toscanelli (a friend of Alberti and
Brunelleschi) also deserves a place in this company since his interests
included mathematics, geography and astronomy (de Santillana,
1966).

About half of these 18 universal men were Tuscans; about half had
fathers who were nobles, professional men or merchants; and no less
than 15 of them were, among other things, architects. Either
architecture attracted universal men or it encouraged them. Neither
possibility is surprising, since architecture was a bridge between
science (since the architect needed to know the laws of mechanics),
sculpture (since he worked with stone) and humanism (since he
needed to know the classical vocabulary of architecture). Apart from
Alberti, these many-sided men belong to the tradition of the non-
specialist craftsman rather than that of the gifted amateur. The theory
and the practice of the universal man seem to have coexisted without
much contact. The greatest of all, Michelangelo, did not believe in
universality. At the time he was painting the ceiling of the Sistine
Chapel, he wrote to his father complaining that painting was not his
job (*non esser mia professione*). He created masterpieces of painting,
architecture and poetry, while continuing to protest that he was just a
sculptor.

THE ORGANIZATION OF THE ARTS

For painters and sculptors, the fundamental unit was the workshop,
the *bottega*; a small group of men producing a wide variety of objects
in collaboration, a great contrast to the specialist, individualist artist
of modern times. Although distinctions were sometimes drawn
between painters of panels and frescos, on the one hand, and painters
of furniture, on the other, one still finds Botticelli painting *cassoni*
(wedding chests) and banners; Cosimo Tura of Ferrara painting horse
trappings and furniture; and the Venetian Vincenzo Catena painting
cabinets and bedsteads. Even in the sixteenth century, Bronzino
painted a harpsichord cover for the duke of Urbino. To deal with this
wide variety of commissions, masters often employed assistants as

---

[28] I am distinguishing only seven arts: painter, sculptor, architect, writer, humanist,
scientist and composer, a classification which tends to play down the many-sidedness of the
elite rather than exaggerate it. The 18 men who practised three arts or more are Alberti;
Silvestro Aquilano; Bramante; Brunelleschi; Filarete; Ghiberti; Giovanni Giocondo;
Francesco di Giorgio; Leonardo; Piero Ligorio; Guido Mazzoni; Michelangelo; Alessandro
Piccolomini; Serlio; Tebaldeo; Vasari; Vecchietta; Zenale.

STUCCO RELIEF SHOWING RAPHAEL'S WORKSHOP (DETAIL)
Musei Vaticani.

well as apprentices, particularly if they worked on a large scale or
were much in demand, like Ghirlandaio, Perugino or Raphael. It is
reasonably certain that Giovanni Bellini employed at least 16 assistants in the course of his long working life (c. 1460–1516), and he
may have used many more. Some of these 'boys' (garzoni) as they
were called – irrespective of age – were hired to help with a particular
commission, and the patron might guarantee to pay their keep, as the
duke of Ferrara promised Tura in 1460 in contracting for the painting
of a chapel (cf. Chambers, 1970b, nos 7, 11, 15). Others worked for
their master on a permanent basis, and they might specialize. In
Raphael's workshop, for example, which might be better described as
'Raphael Enterprises', Giovanni da Udine concentrated on animals
and grotesques (Marabottini, 1968).

The workshop was often a family affair. A father, like Jacopo
Bellini, would train his sons in the craft. The garzoni were probably
treated as members of the family, and might marry their master's
daughter, as Mantegna and others did. When Jacopo died he be-
queathed his sketchbooks and unfinished commissions to his eldest
son Gentile, who took over the shop. Giovanni Bellini succeeded his

brother Gentile, and was succeeded in turn by his nephew Vittore Belliniano.[29] The signing of paintings used to be taken to be a mark of 'Renaissance individualism'. However, it has been argued that when a painting is signed by the head of a workshop it does not mean that he painted it with his own hand. It may even mean the reverse; the point is to declare that the work meets the standards of the shop (Tietze, 1939).

Not all master painters could afford to set up shop on their own. Like other small masters (dyers, for example), painters sometimes shared expenses for rent and equipment. Usually, though not always, they acted as a trading company and pooled expenses and receipts (Procacci, 1960). Giorgione, for example, was in partnership with Vincenzo Catena. An association of this kind had the advantage of offering a kind of insurance against illness and defaulting clients. There may also have been a division of labour inside the shop.

These habits of collaboration make it easier to understand how well- known artists could work on the same paintings, together or consecutively. In the Ovetari Chapel at Padua, for example, four artists worked on the frescos in pairs: Pizzolo with Mantegna, and Antonio da Murano with Giovanni d'Allemagna. Pisanello finished a picture of St John the Baptist begun by Gentile da Fabriano. This practice continued into the sixteenth century. Pontormo made two paintings from cartoons by Michelangelo, while Michelangelo agreed to finish a statue of St Francis by Pietro Torrigiani. This system of collaboration obviously militated against deliberate individualism of style, and helps explain why this individualism emerged only slowly.

Sculptors' workshops were organized in a similar way to those of painters. Donatello was in partnership with Michelozzo, while the Gaggini and Solari dynasties furnish obvious examples of family businesses. Assistants were all the more necessary, since statues take longer to make and because the head of the shop might have to arrange for marble to be quarried in order to carry out a particular commission, with the problem that if it turned out badly, as Michelangelo complains in his letters, hundreds of ducats might be wasted and it might be difficult to prove to the client that the expenditure had been necessary or even that it had taken place at all.[30] The workshop of Bernardo Rossellino was one in which there was considerable division of labour, on 'apparently arbitrary' lines (Schutz, 1977, p. 11).

---

[29] On the persistence of the family workshop in Venice, see Rosand (1982), p. 7f.
[30] On sculptors' partnerships, see Caplow (1974). On the quarries of Carrara, see Klapisch-Zuber (1969). Cf. Chambers (1970)b, no. 2 on the problems of Jacopo della Quercia, which in cluded paying duty on Istrian stone.

Architecture was, of course, organized on a larger scale with a more elaborate division of labour. Even a relatively small palace like the Ca D'Oro, still to be seen on the Grand Canal in Venice, had 27 craftsmen working on it in 1427. There were carpenters; two main kinds of mason, respectively concerned with hewing and laying stone; unskilled workmen, to carry materials; and perhaps foremen. Co-ordination was therefore a problem. As Filarete put it, a building project is like a dance; everyone must work together in time. The man who ensured coordination was sometimes called the *architetto*, sometimes the *protomaestro* or chief of the master masons. It is likely that the two names reflect two different conceptions of the role, the old idea of the senior craftsman and the new idea of the designer. In any case, considerable administrative work was involved. Besides designing the building, someone had to appoint and pay the workmen and arrange for the supply of lime, sand, brick, stone, wood, ropes and so on. All this work could be organized in a number of different ways. In Venice, building firms were small because master masons were not allowed to take more than three apprentices each. When a large building was needed, it was common for an entrepreneur (*padrone*) to contract for the whole work and then subcontract pieces of it to different workshops.[31] At the other extreme, at St Peter's in the 1520s and 1530s, there was only one workshop with a large staff including an accountant (*computista*), two surveyors (*mensuratori*) and a head clerk (*segretario*), as well as masons and other workmen. Filarete recommends an agent (*commissario*) as middleman between the architect and the craftsmen. Alberti seems to have followed this system and employed at least three artists in this way; Matteo de'Pasti as his agent in Rimini, Bernardo Rossellino as his agent in Rome, and Luca Fancelli as his agent in Mantua and Florence.

This division of labour has created problems for art historians as it doubtless did for the agents. It is difficult enough to assess individual responsibility for particular paintings and statues, and still harder, in the case of a building, to know whether patron, architect, agent, master mason or mason was responsible for a given detail. The difficulty is increased by the fact that it was not yet customary for the architect to give his men measured drawings to work from. Many of the instructions were given *a bocca*, by word of mouth (Manetti, 1970, p. 77). If we know something about Alberti's intentions, it is because he did not stay in Rimini while the church of S. Francesco was being built, but designed it by correspondence, some of which has survived. On one occasion the agent, Matteo de'Pasti, was apparently

---

[31] On Venice, see Wyrobisz (1965); on Florence, see Goldthwaite (1980), part 2.

THE ARCHITECT FILARETE LEADING HIS APPRENTICES
From the doors of St Peter's, Rome. Rev. da Fabbrica di S. Pietro in Vaticano.

thinking of altering the proportions of some pilasters, but Alberti
wrote to stop him. A letter from Matteo to the client, Sigismondo
Malatesta, explains that a drawing of the façade and of a capital had
arrived from Alberti, and that it had been shown to 'all the masters
and engineers'. The problem was that the drawing was not completely
consistent with a wooden model of the building which Alberti had
previously provided. 'I hope to God that your lordship will come in
time, and see the thing with your own eyes.' Later on, another
craftsman working on the church wrote to Sigismondo for permission
to go to Rome and talk to Alberti about the vaulting.[32]

The fact that architecture was such a cooperative enterprise must
have acted as a brake on innovation. Since craftsmen were trained by
other craftsmen, they learned fidelity to tradition as well as to
techniques. When executing a design which broke with tradition, they
would be likely, if they were not supervised very closely, to 'normal-
ize' it, in other words to assimilate it to the tradition from which the
designer was deliberately diverging. Michelozzo's design for the
Medici Bank at Milan was executed by Lombard craftsmen in a local
style (a fragment of this building may still be seen in the museum of
the Castello Sforzesco). A small detail, but a significant one, is the
difference in proportions between capitals made by Florentine craftsmen for Brunelleschi when he was on the spot, and one made in 1430
while he was away (Saalman, 1958).

There seems to be a relationship between the development of a new
architectural style and the rise of a new kind of designer, the architect
who, like Alberti, had not been trained as a mason. A parallel with
shipbuilding may be illuminating. In fifteenth-century Venice, ships

---

[32] Ricci (1924), p. 588f; cf. Wittkower (1949), p. 29f. Alberti's letter to Matteo is
translated in Chambers (1970b), pp. 181–3.

were designed by senior ship carpenters, the nautical equivalent of master masons. In the sixteenth century, they were challenged by an amateur. The role of Alberti was played by the humanist Vettor Fausto, who designed a ship (which was launched in 1529) on the model of the ancient quinquereme (Lane, 1934; Concina, 1984, p. 108f).

The larger unit of organization for painters, sculptors and masons, but not architects, was the guild. Guilds had several functions. They regulated standards of quality, and relations between clients, masters, journeymen and apprentices. They collected money from subscriptions and bequests, and lent or gave some of it to members who were in need. They organized festivals in honour of the patron of the guild, with religious services and processions. In some cities, such as Milan (Motta, 1895), painters had a guild of their own, often under the patronage of St Luke, who was supposed to have painted a portrait of the Virgin. Elsewhere they formed part of a larger guild, such as that of the papermakers in Bologna or that of the physicians and apothecaries in Florence (though Florentine painters did have a social guild of their own, the Company of St Luke).

For a more vivid impression of the activities of a guild, we may look at the fifteenth-century statutes of one of them, the 'brotherhood' or *fraglia* of the painters of Padua (Gaye, 1839–40, vol. 2, p. 43f). The officers of the guild were a bursar, two stewards, a notary and a dean. There were several social and religious activities in which participation was compulsory. On certain days in the year the guild marched in procession with 'our gonfalon', and absentees were fined. There was a rota for visiting sick members, and encouraging them to confess and communicate, and fines for non-attendance at funerals. Alms were given to the poor and to lepers. There were also arrangements for the relief of needy members. A poor master had the right to sell a piece of work to the guild, which the bursar would try to sell 'as best he could' (*ut melius poterit*). Other guilds lent money; Botticelli, for example, received a loan from the Company of St Luke in Florence. The Paduan statutes also required masters to keep apprentices for three years at least, and forbade them to make overtures to the apprentices of other masters 'with gifts or blandishments' (*donis vel blandimentis*). There were regulations for the maintenance of standards; candidates aspiring to be masters were examined in the usual way, and houses were inspected to see if work was being 'falsified' (*si falsificetur aliquod laborerium nostre artis*). Standards and fair prices were also maintained by the common practice of calling in artists to evaluate the work of others – artistic judgement by one's peers – in cases of dispute with the client.[33] Finally, there was the restrictive side of the guild's activities. The Padua statutes forbade members to give or sell to non- members anything pertaining to the craft. They laid down that no work was to be brought from another district to sell in Padua, and three days only were allowed for the transit of such 'alien' work through the territory of the guild.

In Venice too the guild or *arte* seems to have had a strong territorial imperative. When Albrecht Dürer visited Venice in 1506, he commented on the suspicion or sensitivity to competition of the painters there: 'They have summoned me before the magistrates three times, and I have had to pay four florins to their guild.'[34] It has been suggested that when the Tuscan painter Andrea del Castagno was working in Venice in the middle of the fifteenth century, he had to be supervised by a less gifted artist, Giambono, simply because the latter was a Venetian (Muraro, 1961).

In Florence, however, guilds did not have so much power. The Florentine government would not allow them to force all craftsmen to join. Some artists, like Botticelli, entered a guild only at the end of their career. As a result 'foreigners' could come and work in Florence. This more liberal policy, which exposed local tradition to stimuli from outside, may help to explain Florence's cultural lead.

Writers, humanists, scientists and musicians had no guilds and no workshops. The nearest analogy to the guild in their world was the university (a term which simply meant 'association' and was sometimes used in the period to refer to guilds of painters). However, the analogy between students and apprentices, tempting as it is in some respects, is also misleading. Most of the students did not go to university to learn how to be professors, but looked forward to careers in Church and state. The students had more power in Italian universities than apprentices had in guilds. It was thanks to a petition

---

[33] This was a new development in the fifteenth century; see Conti (1979), p. 151f.
[34] Dürer, *Schriftlicher Nachlass*, vol. 1, p. 41f.

from the students from the university of Pisa, for example, that one of their teachers, the scientist Bernardo Torni, had his salary raised. The university was not geared to the production of books by the dons. Their job was lecturing, and their books were something of a sideline.

If humanists and scientists had their universities, writers had no form of organization at all. Writing was something a man did, more or less in his spare time, whereas a soldier, diplomat or bishop was what he really *was*. Hence it was a little easier for women to become writers than to practise as painters or sculptors.

There were, however, full-time poets who made a living from this occupation. I hesitate to use such a modern term as 'professional' because these singers of tales or *cantastorie*, improvisers of epic poetry, like Cristoforo Altissimo (who died about 1515), or Bernardo Accolti (1458–1535), who wandered from one court to another, were the survivals in Renaissance Italy of a culture we tend to associate with heroic ages like Homeric Greece.[35]

In other words, the production of literature was not yet an industry in fifteenth-century Italy, although it was becoming one in the mid-sixteenth century, as it was to be in eighteenth-century France and England. The reproduction of literature, on the other hand, was certainly industrialized. Of course, some people who needed particular books simply copied them by hand, while others asked someone else to do the copying for them (as Coluccio Salutati, the chancellor of Florence, asked the young humanist Poggio Bracciolini), and in these cases no formal organization of production was needed. However, in fifteenth-century Italy the production of manuscripts had become commercialized and standardized. It was in the hands of *stationarii*, a word from which the modern English 'stationer' is derived, and a term which referred in those days both to booksellers and to organizers of *scriptoria*, workshops for producing manuscripts. The term *stationarius* had two meanings because the same man tended to perform the two functions, publishing and retail distribution.

The most famous *stationarius* of the Renaissance is the Florentine Vespasiano da Bisticci, who has immortalized himself by writing biographies of his customers. These biographies give the impression of a highly organized system for the copying of manuscripts, reminiscent of the Rome of Cicero and his friend the 'publisher' Atticus. For example, Vespasiano explains how he built up a library for Cosimo de'Medici by engaging 45 scribes who were able to complete 200 volumes in 22 months. What is impressive in this case is not the speed of the individual copyist (since five months per volume seems rather

---

[35] On the singers of tales, see Lord (1960).

slow, unless the volumes were large ones, or the quality unusually high), but the fact that a man (or at any rate Cosimo, the uncrowned ruler of Florence) could go to a bookseller and place an order for 200 volumes which would be delivered within two years. One wonders how the actual writing was organized; whether works which were much in demand were ever copied by 10 or 20 scribes writing from dictation, or whether the whole industry was organized on a 'putting-out' basis, with each scribe turning up at the bookseller's every few months to collect supplies of vellum and the volume to be copied, and returning to his house to write. The latter method seems likely in view of the fact that scribe was often a part-time occupation, paid at piece-work rates (by the 'quintern'). Vespasiano employed as scribes men who were primarily notaries or priests.[36]

From the mid-fifteenth century onwards, this copying system had to compete with the mass production of books which were 'written' mechanically (as early printed books sometimes describe themselves). In 1465, two German clerics called Sweynheym and Pannartz arrived at the Benedictine monastery of Subiaco, a few miles east of Rome, and set up a press there, the first in Italy. Two years later they moved to Rome itself. It has been estimated that in five years they produced 12,000 volumes, a number which Vespasiano would have had to find 1,000 scribes to equal in the time. It is clear that the new machine was a formidable competitor. By the end of the century, some 150 presses had been founded in Italy. It is hardly surprising that Vespasiano, who had for the new method something of the contempt a skilled wheelwright may have felt for the horseless carriage, gave up bookselling in disgust and retired to his country estate to relive the past.

Other scribes were rather more adaptable. Some became printers themselves, like Domenico de'Lapi and Taddeo Crivelli, who produced the famous Bologna Ptolemy in 1477. Early printed books often look rather like manuscripts, down to the illuminated initials. Similarly the printers, a new occupation, stepped into the shoes of the *stationarii*. Like their predecessors, the printers tended to unite roles which in the twentieth century we tend to distinguish, those of producing books and selling them. They soon added a third, that of 'publisher', that is, an individual who issues under his imprint and takes responsibility for books which were in fact printed by someone

---

[36] See Vespasiano, *Vite di uomini illustri*, especially the life of Cosimo de'Medici. On him, see de la Mare (1965), who notes that although one or two illuminators worked in Vespasiano's shop, it was too small to be a proper *scriptorium*, and that Vespasiano's letters to scribes show that manuscripts were copied for him elsewhere. Cf. Martini (1956) and Petrucci (1983a).

else. For example, the colophon of the illustrated edition of Ovid's *Metamorphoses* produced in Venice in 1497 declares that it was printed by Zoare Rosso (otherwise known as Giovanni Rubeo) 'at the instance of' Lucantonio Giunti. Printers sometimes exercised a fourth role as well, that of merchants in commodities other than books. After all, who could be sure that the new product was not going to go out of fashion?[37]

The effects of the invention of printing on the organization of literature were as diverse as they were shattering. In the first place, it was a disaster to scribes and *stationarii* who were not prepared to adapt themselves and begin a new career. In the second place, the expansion of book production led to the creation of new occupations which helped support creative writers. As libraries became bigger, there was a greater need for librarians. Several members of the creative elite were in fact occupied in this way. The grammarian Giovanni Tortelli was the first Vatican librarian (to the so-called 'humanist pope', Nicholas V), and the post was later held by the humanist Bartolommeo Platina. The poet– scholar Angelo Poliziano was librarian to the Medici (Branco, 1983). The Venetian poet–historian Andrea Navagero was librarian of the Marciana, while the philosopher Agostino Steuco was librarian to the Venetian cardinals Marino and Domenico Grimani.[38]

Another new occupation dependent on the rise of printing was that of corrector for the press, a useful part-time occupation for a writer or scholar. Platina worked as corrector for Sweynheym and Pannartz in Rome, while the humanist Giorgio Merula was corrector to the first press to be established in Venice, that of Johan and Windelin Speyer. By the sixteenth century, printers and publishers had begun to ask writers to edit books, to translate them and even to write them, a new form of literary patronage which led to the rise of *poligrafo* or professional writer in Venice towards the middle of the sixteenth century. The most famous of this group of professionals was Pietro Aretino, who made even his 'private' letters saleable (Larivaille, 1980). Around Aretino's sun circulated lesser planets (not to say Grub Street hacks) such as his secretary Niccolò Franco; his sometime friend and later enemy Anton Francesco Doni; Giuseppe Betussi; Lodovico Dolce; Ludovico Domenichi; Girolamo Ruscelli; and Fran-cesco Sansovino, son of the artist Jacopo.[39] The firm of Giolito at Venice, which concentrated on books that were popular rather than

---

[37] This was still a worry in the late sixteenth century. See Tenenti (1957), a study of the younger Lucantonio Giunti. On the fifteenth century, see Lowry (1979), esp. ch. 1.

[38] On libraries public and private, see Petrucci (1983b).

[39] On Franco and Doni, see Grendler (1969a); on Sansovino, see Grendler (1969b).

scholarly at a time when this was still unusual, seems to have been a pioneer in its use of professional writers. Betussi and Dolce were both in Giolito service, editing, translating, writing and (as hostile critics pointed out), plagiarizing (Quondam, 1977). Even at the end of our period, however, the professional writer was only just beginning to emerge.

Music resembled literature in that reproduction was organized but production was not. Churches had their choirs, towns their drummers and pipers, and courts had both, but the role of composer was scarcely recognized. Although the word *compositore* sometimes occurs, the more common term is the more vague *musico*, which makes no disinction between someone who invents a tune and someone who plays it (Bridgman, 1964, ch. 2). In their own day, all the 49 composers in the creative elite were viewed as writers on the theory of music, or as singers, or as players of instruments, as some of their names, like Alfonso della Viola and Antonio degli Organi, may remind us.

An important feature of the organization of the arts in different places and times is the relative opportunity (or need) for mobility. About 25 per cent of the creative elite are known to have done a great deal of travelling. Some moved about because they were successful enough to receive invitations from abroad, like the painter Jacopo de'Barbari, who worked in Nuremberg, Naumburg, Wittenberg, Weimar, Frankfurt-on-Oder and Malines. Others, on the contrary, seem to have travelled because they had little success in any one place, like Lorenzo Lotto, who worked in Venice, Treviso, Bergamo, Rome, Ancona and Loreto. Architects were hardly ever sedentary. Humanists and composers tended to be more mobile than painters and sculptors, presumably because their services were required in person, while painters and sculptors could always dispatch their work abroad while remaining at home themselves. One good example of a mobile humanist is Pomponio Leto, whose career took him not only to Salerno, Rome and Venice, but also to Germany and even Muscovy. However, he is easily surpassed by Francesco Filelfo, who visited Germany, Hungary, Poland and Constantinople, and when in Italy worked in Padua, Venice, Vicenza, Bologna, Siena, Milan, Pavia, Florence and Rome.[40]

The theme of the wandering scholar, often emphasized, has provoked a sceptical reaction. 'It can probably be shown', writes one historian, 'that every itinerant humanist like Aurispa, Panormita, or the youthful Valla had his stay-at-home counterpart in humanists like

---

[40]   On transient foreign humanists in Venice, see King (1986), p. 220f.

Andrea Giuliano, Francesco Barbaro and Carlo Marsuppini' (Martines, 1963, p. 97). So far as the creative elite is concerned, however, the balance tips in favour of the wanderers: 58 compared to 43.[41]

Printers also travelled widely, like Simon Bevilacqua, who worked in Venice, Saluzzo, Cuneo, Novi Ligure, Savona and Lyons during the decade 1506–15. If humanists and printers were often on the road from year to year, actors, singers of tales and pedlars of books (not to mention students in vacation) travelled from day to day. There may also have been some artists in this class, for the fifteenth-century painter Dario da Udine is described in a document as *pictor vagabundus*.

Another important aspect of the organization of the arts is the extent to which they were full-time or part-time, amateur or professional occupations. It has already been suggested that painting, sculpture and music were usually professional and full-time occupations; that writing was usually amateur and part-time; and that architects usually practised another art besides architecture. What I here call a 'scientist' was a man whose professional description would usually have been 'teacher' or 'physician' (22 out of the 53, including Giovanni Marliani, more distinguished in physics than in physic). Scholars were usually professional teachers, and at least 45 out of the 178 writers and humanists in the elite taught in universities or schools or were engaged as private tutors (Poliziano to Piero de'Medici, Matteo Bandello to the Gonzagas). However, it is possible to point to amateurs (or at any rate non-academics) like the civil servant Leonardo Bruni; the merchant Cyriac of Ancona; the printer Aldo Manuzio; the statesman Lorenzo de'Medici; and the noblemen Giovanni Pico della Mirandola and Pietro Bembo. These exceptions are numerous and important enough to make one a little uncomfortable with Paul Kristeller's famous definition of the humanist as a teacher of the humanities.[42] It should be added that if some humanists, notably Vittorino da Feltre and Guarino of Verona, treated teaching as a vocation, others considered it a fate to be cursed. 'I, who have until recently enjoyed the friendship of princes', wrote one of them sadly in 1480 'have now, because of my evil star, opened a school.'[43]

The Church remained an important source of part-time employ-

---

[41] Of 103 humanists in the elite, 1 classify 14 as extremely sedentary; 29 as fairly sedentary; 12 as fairly mobile; 46 as extremely mobile, while 2 individuals are impossible to classify for lack of information.

[42] See Kristeller (1955), ch. 1, a salutary reaction against some extremely vague conceptions of the humanist.

[43] Acciarini to Poliziano, quoted in Usmiani (1957), p. 19.

ment for writers (22 members of the elite), humanists (22 more) and composers (20), not to mention 7 scientists (such as Paul of Venice), 6 painters (of whom the most famous are fra Angelico and fra Bartolommeo), and one architect (fra Giovanni Giocondo of Verona).[44]

Another common employment for writers and humanists was that of secretary; their rhetorical skills were in high demand. Leonardo Bruni, Poggio Bracciolini and Bartolommeo della Scala were made chancellors of Florence for their skill in writing persuasive letters; the humanists Antonio Loschi and Pier Candido Decembrio performed similar services for the Visconti of Milan; while the poets Benedetto Chariteo and Giovanni Pontano were secretaries of state in Naples. Other writers were more like private secretaries: Masuccio Salernitano, best known for his prose fiction, was secretary to prince Roberto Sanseverino, while the poet Annibale Caro served various members of the Farnese family.[45]

In a few cases, artists and writers pursued occupations which are somewhat surprising, not to say bizarre. The painter Mariotto Albertinelli was at one time an innkeeper (like Jan Steen in seventeenth-century Leiden). The painter Niccolò dell'Abbate, like the humanists Platina and Calcagnini, was a soldier. Another painter, Giorgio Schiavone, sold salt and cheese. Giorgione's partner Catena seems to have sold drugs and spices, while Giovanni Caroto of Verona kept an apothecary's shop; this combination of art and drugs may be explained by the fact that some apothecaries sold artists materials. The Fogolino brothers combined their work as painters with that of spying for the Venetians in Trento. Antonio Squarcialupi kept a butcher's shop as well as playing the organ and composing. Domenico Burchiello was a barber as well as a comic poet. Mariano Taccola was a notary as well as a sculptor and an engineer. The dramatists Giovanni Maria Cecchi and Anton Francesco Grazzini were respectively a wool merchant and an apothecary.[46] These occupations warn us not to attribute too high a status to the artists and writers of the Renaissance.

THE STATUS OF THE ARTS

The status associated with the roles of artist and writer was problematic. The problem was a special case of the more general difficulty

---

[44] There is an important discussion of clerical writers in the sixteenth century in Dionisotti (1967).

[45] On humanists as secretaries in Venice, see King (1986), p. 294f.

of accommodating in the social structure, as the division of labour progressed, all roles other than those of priest, knight and peasant–those who prayed, fought and worked–the 'three orders' officially recognized in the Middle Ages (Duby, 1979; Niccoli, 1979). If the status of an artist was ambiguous, so was that of a merchant. And just as Italians, in some regions at least, had gone further towards the social acceptance of the merchant than most other Europeans had, so it was in Italy that the status of the artist seems to have been at its peak. In the discussion that follows, the evidence of high status comes first, then the evidence of contempt and, finally, an attempt to reach a balanced conclusion.

Artists regularly declared that they had or ought to have a high status. Cennini at the beginning of the period and Leonardo towards the end both compared the painter with the poet, on the grounds that painter and poet alike use their imagination, their *fantasia*. Another point in favour of the high status of painting, and one which reveals something of Renaissance assumptions or mentalities, was that the painter could wear fine clothes while he was at work. As Cennini put it: 'Know that painting on panel is a gentleman's job, for you can do what you want with velvet on your back.' And Leonardo: 'The painter sits at his ease in front of his work, dressed as he pleases, and moves his light brush with the beautiful colours . . . often accompanied by musicians or readers of various beautiful works.'[47] In his treatise on painting, Alberti offered several more arguments which recur during the period, such as the argument that painters need to study liberal arts such as rhetoric and mathematics and the argument from antiquity–that in Roman times works of art fetched high prices, while distinguished Roman citizens had their sons taught to paint, and Alexander the Great admired the painter Apelles.

Some people who were not artists seem to have accepted the claim that painters were not ordinary craftsmen. The humanist Guarino of Verona wrote a poem in praise of Pisanello, while the court poet of Ferrara dedicated a Latin elegy to Cosimo Tura, and Ariosto praised Titian in his *Orlando Furioso* (more exactly, he inserted the praise of Titian into the 1532 edition of his poem). St Antonino, archbishop of Florence, noted that whereas in most occupations the just price for a piece of work depends essentially on the time and materials employed, 'Painters claim, more or less reasonably, to be paid the salary of their art not only by the amount of work, but more in proportion

---

[46] That Grazzini actually practised as an apothecary has been questioned by Plaisance (1974), p. 82n.
[47] Cennini, *Il libro dell'arte*, vol. 2; Leonardo da Vinci, *Literary Works*, ed. J. P. Richter. Oxford, 1939.

to their application and greater expertness in their trade.'[48] When the ruler of Mantua gave Giulio Romano a house, the deed of gift opened with a firm statement of the honour due to painting: 'Among the famous arts of mortal men it has always seemed to us that painting is the most glorious [*praeclarissimus*] . . . we have noticed that Alexander of Macedon thought it of no small dignity, since he wished to be painted by a certain Apelles' (Hartt, 1958, doc. 69).

A few painters achieved high status according to the criteria of the time, notably by being knighted or ennobled by their patrons. Gentile Bellini was made a count by the emperor Frederick III, Mantegna by pope Innocent VIII, and Titian by the emperor Charles V. The Venetian painter Carlo Crivelli was knighted by prince Ferdinand of Capua; Sodoma by Pope Leo X; Giovanni da Pordenone by the king of Hungary. For the patron it was a cheap way of rewarding service, but for the artist the honour was real enough. Some painters held offices which conferred status as well as income. Giulio Romano held an office at the court of Mantua, while the painters Giovanni da Udine and Sebastiano del Piombo held office in the Church. (Sebastiano's nickname, 'the lead', was a reference to his office as Keeper of the Seal.) Other painters held high civic office. Luca Signorelli was one of the priors of Cortona; Perugino, one of the priors of Perugia; Jacopo Bassano, consul of Bassano; Piero della Francesca, a town councillor of Borgo San Sepolcro.

Again, a few painters are known to have become rich. Pisanello inherited wealth, but Mantegna, Perugino, Cosimo Tura, Raphael, Titian, Vincenzo Catena of Venice and Bernardino Zenale of Treviso all seem to have become rich by their painting. Wealth gave them status, and the prices they commanded show that painting was not held cheap.

The testimony of Albrecht Dürer carries considerable weight. On his visit to Venice he was impressed by the fact that the status of artists was higher than in his native Nuremberg, and he wrote home to his friend the humanist patrician Willibald Pirckheimer, 'Here I am a gentleman, at home a sponger [*Hie bin ich ein Herr, doheim ein Schmarotzer*).'[49] In Castiglione's famous dialogue, one of the speakers, Count Lodovico da Canossa, declares that the ideal courtier should know how to draw and paint. A few sixteenth-century Venetian patricians, such as Daniele Barbaro, actually did.[50]

There is similar evidence for the status of sculptors and architects. Ghiberti's programme of studies for sculptors, and Alberti's for

---

[48] Quoted and discussed in C. Gilbert (1959.

[49] Dürer, Letter to Pirckheimer, 13 October 1506, *Schriftlicher Nachlass*, vol. 1, p. 41f.

[50] Castiglione, *Il cortegiano*, book 1, ch. 49; on Barbero see Dolce, *Aretino*, p. 106f.

TITIAN, *PORTRAIT OF GIULIO ROMANO*
Private Collection.

architects, imply that these occupations are on a level with the liberal arts. Alberti advised architects to build only for men of quality, 'because your work loses its dignity by being done for mean persons'.[51] The patent issued in 1468 by Federigo di Montefeltro, the

---

[51] Ghiberti, *I commentari*, 2, suggests that the sculptor should study ten subjects he calls 'liberal arts': grammar, geometry, philosophy, medicine, astrology, perspective, history, anatomy, design and arithmetic.

ruler of Urbino, on behalf of Luciano Laurana declares that architecture is 'an art of great science and ingenuity', and that it is 'founded upon the arts of arithmetic and geometry, which are the foremost of the seven liberal arts' (Chambers, 1970b, no. 104). A papal decree of 1540, freeing sculptors from the need to belong to the guilds of 'mechanical craftsmen', remarked that sculptors 'were prized highly by the ancients', who called them 'men of learning and science' (*viri studiosi et scientifici*) (Steinmann, 1905, vol. 2, p. 754). Some sculptors, Andrea il Riccio of Padua for example, had poems addressed to them. Some were ennobled. The king of Hungary, Matthias Corvinus, not only made Giovanni Dalmata a nobleman, but gave him a castle as well. Charles V made Leone Leoni and Baccio Bandinelli knights of Santiago. Ghiberti's work made him rich enough to be able to buy an estate complete with manor house, moat and drawbridge. Other prosperous sculptors and architects include Brunelleschi, the brothers da Maiano, Bernardo Rossellino, Simone il Cronaca of Florence, Giovanni Amadeo of Pavia, and, among the wealthiest of all, Titian. The houses of artists are a sign of their rising status; in particular the palaces of Mantegna and Giulio Romano at Mantua, and of Raphael in Rome (cf. Coni, 1979, p. 206f).

Composers of the period sometimes compared themselves to poets. Johannes de Tinctoris, who had impeccable credentials as an academic theorist of music, dedicated his treatise on modes to two practitioners, Ockeghem and Busnois, an unusual thing to do since the conventional view was that theory was the master and practice (composition no less than performance) merely the servant. A number of composers were treated with honour in Italy at this time, although it is not easy to decide whether this was a tribute to their composi- tions or their performances (if indeed such a distinction was taken seriously at all). The humanists Guarino of Verona and Filippo Beroaldo wrote epigrams in praise of the lutenist Piero Bono, and medals were struck in his honour. Ficino and Poliziano wrote elegies on the death of the organist Squarcialupi, while Lorenzo de'Medici composed his epitaph and had a monument to him erected in the cathedral in Florence. Lorenzo's son pope Leo X made the lutenist Gian Maria Guideo a count, while Philip the Handsome of Burgundy did the same for the Italian singer–composer Marbriano da Orto. The elaborate preparations made for the arrival of Jakob Obrecht in Ferrara show how highly he was prized by Duke Ercole d'Este. At the court of Mantua in the time of Ercole's daughter Isabella, Marchetto Cara and Bartolommeo Tromboncino were honoured members of a musical circle. In Venice, Willaert, master of St Mark's chapel, died rich, while Gioseffe Zarlino, another master of St Mark's, had medals struck in his honour by the Republic and ended his days as a bishop (Anthon, 1946; Bridgman, 1964, ch. 2; Lowinsky, 1966).

A number of humanists also achieved high status. In the case of Florence, it has been argued that humanists belonged to the top 10 per cent of Florentine families. Leonardo Bruni, Poggio Bracciolini, Carlo Marsuppini, Giannozzo Manetti and Matteo Palmieri, for example, were all wealthy men. Bruni, Poggio and Marsuppini all held the high office of chancellor of Florence, while Palmieri held office at least 63 times and Manetti had a distinguished career as a diplomat and a magistrate. Of these five, three were born into the upper class, while Bruni (the son of a grain dealer) and Poggio (the son of a poor apothecary) entered it through their own efforts. All five made good marriages. Finally, Bruni, Marsuppini and Palmieri were all given splendid state funerals.[52]

In case Florence was not typical, it may be useful to take a brief look at 25 humanists who were born outside Tuscany and active in the fifteenth and early sixteenth centuries.[53] Of these 25, at least 14 had fathers from the upper classes, while only three are definitely of humble origin (Guarino, Vittorino and Platina). Two were ennobled: Filelfo by King Alfonso of Aragon, Nifo by both pope Leo X and Charles V. Three were famous university teachers: the lawyer Andrea Alciati, the philosopher Pietro Pomponazzi, and the literary critic Sperone Speroni. The Venetians Ermolao Barbaro and Andrea Navagero had distinguished political careers as senators and ambassadors. Angelo Decembrio, Antonio Loschi, Mario Equicola and Giovanni Pontano all held high administrative or diplomatic posts at the courts of Milan, Mantua and Naples. By worldly standards, almost all of them seem to have had successful careers.

There is, however, another side to the picture. Artists and writers were not respected by everyone. Some members of the elite whose achievements have been recognized by posterity had a difficult time of it in their own age. Three social prejudices against artists retained

---

[52] Martines (1963), a study of 45 humanists in the period 1390–1460.

[53] The first edition of this book listed 32, including some Greeks. The 25 are as follows: Andrea Alciati, from Alzate in Lombardy; Ermolao Barbaro, from Venice; Filippo Beroaldo, from Bologna; Flavio Biondo, from Forlì in the Papal States; Angelo Decembrio, from Lombardy; Mario Equicola, from Caserta; Bartolommeo Fazio, from La Spezia in Liguria; Francesco Filelfo, from Tolentino, near Ancona; Guarino Veronese; Pomponio Leto, from Lucania; Antonio Loschi, from Vicenza; Pietro Martire d'Anghiera, from Lombardy; Andrea Navagero, from Venice; Agostino Nifo, from Calabria; Antonio Panormita, from Palermo; Giovanni Pico, from Mirandola; Bartolommeo Platina, from Cremona; Pietro Pomponazzi, from Mantua; Giovanni Pontano, from Ponte in Umbria; Sperone Speroni, from Padua; Giorgio Valla, from Piacenza; Lorenzo Valla, from Rome; Maffeo Vegio, from Lodi; Pietro Paolo Vergerio the elder, from Capodistria; Vittorino da Feltre, from the Veneto.

their power in this period. Artists were considered ignoble because their work involved manual labour, because it involved retail trade and because they lacked learning.

To use a twelfth-century classification still current in the Renaissance, painting, sculpture and architecture were not 'liberal' but 'mechanical' arts. They were also dirty; a nobleman would not like to soil his hands using paints. The argument from antiquity, which Alberti had used in defence of artists, was actually double-edged, since Aristotle had excluded craftsmen from citizenship because their work was mechanical, while Plutarch had declared in his life of Pericles that no man of good family would want to become a sculptor like Phidias (Mondolfo, 1954). Leonardo's vigorous protest against views like these is well known: 'You have set painting among the mechanical arts! . . . If you call it mechanical because it is by manual work that the hands represent what the imagination creates, your writers are setting down what originates in the mind by manual work with the pen.' He might have added the example of fighting sword in hand. Even Leonardo, however, shared the prejudice against sculptors : 'The sculptor produces his work by . . . the labour of a mechanic, often accompanied by sweating which mixes with the dust and turns into mud, so that his face becomes white and he looks like a baker.'[54]

The second point commonly made against artists was that they made a living from retail trade, so that they deserved the same low status as cobblers and grocers. Noblemen, on the other hand, were ashamed to take money for their work. Giovanni Boltraffio, a Lombard nobleman and humanist who also painted, usually worked on a small scale, perhaps because he intended his pictures to be gifts for his friends, and his epitaph emphasized his amateur status. Leonardo threw this accusation, too, back into the faces of the humanists: 'If you call it mechanical because it is done for money, who fall into this error . . . more than you yourselves? If you lecture for the schools, do you not go wherever you are paid the most?'[55] In practice, a distinction was often drawn between being on the payroll of a prince, which could happen to the best people, and keeping a shop. Michelangelo insisted strongly on this distinction: 'I was never a painter or a sculptor like those who set up shop for that purpose. I always refrained from doing so out of respect for my father and brothers.[56] In a similar manner Vasari, after years in Medici service,

---

[54] Adapted from Leonardo da Vinci, *Literary Works*, ed. J. P. Richter. Oxford, 1939.
[55] Ibid., p. 91.
[56] Michelangelo, Letter of 2 May 1548, *Carteggio*: Ramsden's translation.

was able to refer with contempt to a minor painter, in his life of Perino del Vaga, as 'One of those who keep an open shop and stand there in public, working at all sorts of mechanical tasks.'

The third prejudice against the visual arts was that artists were 'ignorant'; in other words, that they lacked a certain kind of training (in theology and the classics, for example) that had a higher esteem than the training which they had received and their critics had not. When cardinal Soderini was trying to excuse Michelangelo's flight from Rome (below p. 107), he told the pope that the artist 'has erred through ignorance. Painters are all like this both in their art and out of it.' It is a pleasure to record that Julius did not share this prejudice. He told Soderini roundly that 'You're the ignorant one, not him!' (Condivi, 1964, p. 45).

Although a few artists, already mentioned, became rich by means of their art, many remained poor. Their poverty was probably as much the cause as the result of prejudices against the arts. The Sienese painter Benvenuto di Giovanni declared in 1488 that 'The gains in our profession are slight and limited, because little is produced and less earned' (Coor, 1961, p. 10). Vasari made a similar point: 'The artist today struggles to ward off famine rather than to win fame, and this crushes and buries his talent and obscures his name'. Vasari's comment might be dismissed as special pleading, inconsistent with what he says elsewhere (let alone with his own wealth). Benvenuto's remarks, on the other hand, come from his tax return, which he knew would be subject to checking. The same goes for Verrocchio, whose return for 1457 claims that he was not earning enough to keep his firm in hose (*non guadagniamo le chalze*) (Mather, 1948). Botticelli and Neroccio de'Landi went into debt. Lotto was once reduced to trying to raffle 30 pictures, and he was only able to dispose of seven of them.

Humanists too did not always make fortunes and they were not invariably respected. The Greek scholar Janos Argyropoulos is said to have been so poor at one time that he was forced to sell his books. Bartolommeo Fazio had an up-and-down career, at one time a school teacher in Venice and Genoa, at another a notary in Lucca, before he landed a safe and well-paid job as secretary to Alfonso of Aragon. Bartolommeo Platina worked in a variety of occupations – soldier, private tutor, press-corrector, secretary – before becoming Vatican librarian. Angelo Decembrio was at one time a school master in Milan, Pomponio Leto in Venice and Francesco Filelfo in several different towns. Jacopo Aconcio was at one time a notary, at another secretary to the governor of Milan, at another trying his luck in England.

These humanists were the distinguished ones. To calculate the status of the group as a whole, it is also necessary to consider the less important ones. Ideally, if the evidence permits, a study should be made of the careers of all the students of the humanities. Until such a study is published, it is difficult to do more than guess at the status of humanists. My own guess would be that there was a considerable gap between the few stars and the less successful majority, even if a small-town teacher or impoverished corrector for the press might enjoy a status higher than that of a successful but 'ignorant' artist. Musicians, whose low status was lamented by Alberti, seem to have been in a similar position. For every lutenist who was rewarded by a patron as generous as pope Leo X, there must have been many who were poor, since there were few Italian courts, and still fewer honourable positions outside them.

In summing up, it is tempting to take the easy way out and to close on a note of 'on the one hand . . . on the other'. However, it is possible to make a few more precise points, three at least. As in the case of training, so in status the creative elite formed two cultures, with literature, humanism and science enjoying more respect than the visual arts and music. All the same, to choose the humanities as a career was to take a considerable risk. Many were trained but few were chosen. In the second place, Renaissance artists were an example of what sociologists call 'status dissonance'. Some of them achieved high status, others did not. According to some criteria, artists deserved honour; according to others, they were just craftsmen. Artists were in fact respected by some of the noble and powerful, but they were despised by others. The status insecurity which naturally resulted may well explain the touchiness of certain individuals, such as Michelangelo and Cellini. In the third place, the status of both artists and writers was probably higher in Italy than elsewhere in Europe; higher in Florence than in other parts of Italy; and higher in the sixteenth century than it had been in the fifteenth. By the middle of the sixteenth century it was no longer extraordinary for artists to have some knowledge of the humanities; the distinction between the two cultures was breaking down.[57] The social mobility of painters and sculptors is symbolized if not confirmed by the appearance of the term 'artist' in more or less its modern meaning.

ARTISTS AS SOCIAL DEVIANTS

If the artist was not an ordinary craftsman, what was he? He could if he wanted imitate the style of life of a nobleman, a model suitable for those endowed with wealth, self-confidence and the ability to behave like something out of Castiglione's *Courtier*. A number of artists, mainly sixteenth-century ones, are described in these terms in Vasari's *Lives*. An obvious example is Raphael, who was in fact one of Castiglione's friends. Other instances of the artist as gentleman include Giorgione; Titian; Vasari's kinsman Signorelli; Filippino Lippi, described as 'affable, courteous and a gentleman'; the sculptor Gian Cristoforo Romano (who makes an appearance in *The Courtier*); and a small number of others, including, of course, Vasari himself. All the same, the artist who adopted this role still had to face the social prejudice against manual labour which has just been described. For those who were no longer content to be ordinary craftsmen, yet lacked the education and poise necessary to pass as gentlemen, a third model was developed in this period (how self-consciously, it is hard to say); that of the eccentric or social deviant.

At this point distinctions are necessary. Vasari and others have recorded a number of highly dramatic stories about artists of the period who killed or wounded men in brawls (Cellini, Leone Leoni and Francesco 'Torbido' of Venice) or committed suicide (Rosso, Torrigiani). Others were described by contemporaries as 'sodomites' (Leonardo, 'Sodoma'). The significance of these stories is difficult to assess. The evidence is insufficient to determine whether these artists were what they were described as being, and even if they were, we cannot conclude from a few cases that artists were more likely than other social groups to kill others or themselves or to love members of the same sex (Wittkower, 1963).

There is a much richer vein of contemporary comment about a more significant kind of eccentricity associated with artists: irregular working habits. In one of the stories of Matteo Bandello, who was in a good position to know, there is a vivid description of Leonardo's way of working, which stresses his 'caprice' (*capriccio, ghiribizzo*).[58] Vasari makes similar comments about Leonardo, and tells a story in which the artist justifies his long pauses to the duke of Milan with the argument that 'Men of genius sometimes accomplish most when they work the least; for they are thinking of designs [*inventioni*]'. The key concept here is a relatively new one, 'genius' (*genio*), which turned the eccentricity of artists from a liability into an asset.[59] Patrons had to learn to put up with it. On one occasion the marquis of Mantua, explaining to the duchess of Milan why Mantegna had not produced a particular work on time, made the resigned remark that 'usually

---

[57] On the education of artists in the later sixteenth century, see Dempsey (1980).
[58] Bandello, *Novelle* (1554), novella 58, dedication.
[59] On the idea of genius, see Zilsel (1926). Cf. Klibansky et al. (1964).

these painters have a touch of the fantastic [*hanno del fantasticho*]'
(Chambers, 1970b, no. 61). Other clients were less tolerant. Vasari
remarked of the painter Jacopo Pontormo that 'What most annoyed

PALMA VECCHIO, *PORTRAIT OF A POET*
Reproduced by courtesy of the Trustees of the National Gallery, London.

GIULIO ROMANO, THE PALAZZO DEL TE, MANTUA
Detail of frieze with slipped triglyphs. Photograph by James Austin.

other men about him was that he would not work save when and for whom he pleased and after his own fancy.' Composers – or their patrons – posed similar problems. When the duke of Ferrara wanted to hire a musician, he sent one of his agents to see – and hear – both Heinrich Isaak and Josquin des Près. The agent reported that 'It is true that Josquin composes better, but he does it when he feels like it, not when he is asked.' It was Isaak who was hired (van der Straeten, 1882, p. 87; see below p. 112).

In the case of other artists, their eccentricity took the form of doing too much work rather than too little, and neglecting everything but their art. Vasari has a series of such stories. Masaccio, for example, was absent-minded (*persona astratissima*); 'Having fixed his mind and will wholly on matters of art, he cared little about himself and still less about others . . . he would never under any circumstances give a thought to the cares and concerns of this world, nor even to his clothes, and was not in the habit of recovering his money from debtors.' Again, Paolo Uccello was so fascinated by his 'sweet' perspective that 'He remained secluded in his house, almost like a hermit, for weeks and months, without knowing much of what was going on in the world and without showing himself.'[60] Vasari also gives a vivid account of the 'strangeness' of Piero di Cosimo, who was absent-minded, loved solitude, would not have his room swept, and could not bear children crying, men coughing, bells ringing or friars chanting (is his attempt to preserve himself from distraction really so 'strange'?).

The fact that Masaccio, in early fifteenth-century Florence, is presented as uninterested in money is a trait worth emphasis. A still more conspicuous contempt for wealth is shown by Donatello, of whom 'It is said by those who knew him that he kept all his money in a basket, suspended from the ceiling of his workshop, so that everyone could take what he wanted whenever he wanted.'[61] This looks very much like a conscious rejection of the fundamental values of Florentine society. Why Donatello should have rejected these values emerges from another story of Vasari's, about a bust made by the sculptor for a Genoese merchant, who claimed to have been overcharged because the price worked out at more than half a florin for a day's work.

---

[60] Masaccio died in 1428, Uccello in 1475. Vasari could have learned about them from the oral traditions of the artists of Florence, but in Masaccio's case this would have been more than a hundred years after the event. Readers can make their own assessment of the reliability of information transmitted orally over such a period.

[61] The story is best known from Vasari, but I quote a version current 50 years nearer Donatello's day from Gauricus, *De sculptura*, p. 53.

Donatello considered himself grossly insulted by this remark, turned on the merchant in a rage, and told him that he was the kind of man who could ruin the fruits of a year's toil in the hundredth part of an hour; and with that he suddenly threw the bust down into the street where it shattered into pieces, and added that the merchant had shown he was more used to bargaining for beans than for bronzes.

Whether the point was Donatello's or Vasari's, the moral is clear; works of art are not ordinary commodities, and artists are not ordinary craftsmen to be paid by the day.

One is reminded of what the Attorney-General said to Whistler about his *Nocturne*, and the artist's reply: "The labour of two days then is that for which you ask 200 guineas?" "No: I ask it for the knowledge of a lifetime". The point still needed to be made in 1878. However, the question was very much alive in Renaissance Italy. The archbishop of Florence recognized, as we have seen (p. 75) that artists claimed with some justification to be different from ordinary craftsmen. Francisco de Hollanda, a Portuguese in the circle of Michelangelo, argued still more forcefully that 'Works of art are not to be judged by the amount of useless labour spent on them but by the worth of the skill and mastery of their creator [*lo merecimento do saber e da mão que as faz*].'[62]

The same idea, that the artist is not an ordinary craftsman, may well underlie the behaviour of Pontormo (again according to Vasari) when he rejected a good commission and then did something 'for a miserable price'. He was showing the client that he was a free man. Artistic eccentricity carried a social message.

---

[62] de Hollanda' *Da Pintura Antigua*, 59 (3rd dialogue).

4

Patrons and Clients

Why do you think there was such a great number of capable men in the past, if
not because they were well treated and honoured by princes?
Filarete, *Trattato di Architettura*
I cannot live under pressures from patrons, let alone paint.
Michelangelo, *Carteggio*

YSTEMS of patronage differ. It may be useful to distinguish five
main types. First, the household system: a rich man takes the
artist or writer into his house for some years, gives him board,
lodging and presents, and expects to have his artistic and literary
needs attended to. Second, the made-to-measure system: again, a
personal relationship between the artist or writer and his patron
('client' might be a better term in this case), but a temporary one,
lasting only until the painting or poem is delivered. Third, the market
system, in which the artist or writer produces something 'ready-made'
and then tries to sell it, either directly to the public or through a
dealer. This third system was emerging in Italy in the period, although
the first two types were dominant. The fourth and fifth types had not
yet come into existence: the academy system (government control by
means of an organization staffed by reliable artists and writers), and
the subvention system (in which a foundation supports creative
individuals but makes no claim on what they produce).[1]

This chapter is concerned with two problems: first, with discovering what kinds of people gave artists commissions, and why they did
so, secondly, with assessing the extent to which it was the patron or
client, rather than the artist or writer, who determined the shape and
content of the work. In the background lurks the more elusive
question to which the epigraphs above allude. Was the patronage
system encouraging or discouraging to artists and writers? In other
words, did the Renaissance happen in Italy because of the system or
in spite of it?[2]

---

[1] Edwards (1968) distinguishes four types; I have divided his 'personalized' system into
two.
[2] On art patronage, see Burckhardt (1898); Wackernagel (1938), part 2; Chambers
(1970)b; Baxandall (1972), pp. 3–14; Logan (1972), ch. 8; and Settis (1978). On music,
Bridgman (1964), ch. 1, and Fenlon (1980).

WHO ARE THE PATRONS?

Patrons may be classified in various ways. The division into ecclesiastical and lay is a simple and useful one, at least at first sight, contrasting the monks of San Pietro in Perugia (say), for whom Perugino painted an altarpiece of the Ascension, with Lorenzo de Pierfrancesco de'Medici (not the famous Lorenzo, but his cousin), for whom Botticelli painted the *Primavera*. The Church was traditionally the great patron of art, and this is the obvious reason for the predominance of religious paintings in Europe over the very long term (from the fourth century or thereabouts to the seventeenth). In Renaissance Italy, however, it is likely that most religious paintings were commissioned by laymen. They might order the painting for a church (for their family chapel, for example); Palla Strozzi asked Gentile da Fabriano to paint his *Adoration of the Magi* to hang in the Strozzi Chapel in the church of Santa Trinità in Florence. Lay people might also commission religious paintings to hang in their own homes. The Medici did this, for example, as we know from the inventory of the contents of their palace (Müntz, 1888). Just as the laity asked for religious works, so the clergy commissioned paintings with secular subjects, such as the *Parnassus* which Raphael painted for Julius II in the Vatican. It would be interesting to know whether the laity were more likely to commission secular works, or whether the gradual secularization of painting reflected a secularization of patronage, but the evidence is too fragmentary to allow such questions to be answered.

A second way of classifying patrons is to distinguish public from private. The guild patronage of early fifteenth-century Florence is particularly well known. The wool guild, the Arte della Lana, was responsible for the upkeep of the cathedral, which involved new commissions; one to Donatello for a statue of the prophet Jeremiah, another to Michelangelo for his *David*. The cloth guild, the Calimala, was responsible for the Baptistery, and so it was this guild which commissioned Ghiberti to make the famous doors. The lesser guilds as well as the greater placed statues on the façade of the church of Orsanmichele; Donatello's *St George*, for example, was commissioned by the armourers. The guilds were interested in paintings as well as sculptures. In 1433, the linen guild commissioned fra Angelico to paint a Madonna for their guildhall.[3]

Another kind of corporate patron, still more important if one takes

---

[3] Baron (1938) stresses the importance of Florentine civic patronage. On Venice, see Humfrey and Mackenney (1986). Documents 20–30 in Chambers (1970b) deal with guilds.

the whole period and the whole of Italy into account, was the religious fraternity (discussed in chapter 9). The fraternity was in effect a social and religious club, usually attached to a particular church, which might perform works of charity and might also act as a bank. The patronage of the Venetian fraternities, known as *scuole*, was particularly lavish. The huge pictures of St Ursula which Vittore Carpaccio painted in the 1490s were designed for the hall of the guild dedicated to that saint, a small guild with a mixed membership of men and women, nobles and commoners (Molmenti and Ludwig, 1903).[4] Still more important was the patronage of the six *scuole grandi*, including S. Giovanni Evangelista, for whom Gentile Bellini painted a number of large pictures, and S. Rocco, whose Tintorettos may still be viewed in the hall of the fraternity. Indeed, their expenditure on building and pageants was so great as to provoke criticism from contemporaries who considered that all this magnificence was at the expense of the poor charity to whom was the original purpose of these organizations (Pullan, 1971, p. 119f).

The patronage of fraternities was important not just in Venice but all over Italy, as the paintings of Vecchietta and Battista Dossi remind us. Leonardo's *Virgin of the Rocks* was commissioned by a fraternity, that of the Conception of the Virgin in the church of S. Francesco at Milan. It was the fraternity of Corpus Christi at Urbino which commissioned Justus of Ghent's *Institution of the Eucharist*, as well as Uccello's *Profanation of the Host*. The importance of organizations like these in the history of art is that they made possible the participation in patronage of people who did not have the money to commission works individually. One would love to know what discussions went on before a particular artist or subject was chosen. It is intriguing to find that in 1433 the Florentine Board of Works for the Cathedral (the *Operai del Duomo*), delegated their authority to one man to work out details of a commission to Donatello. Was this because the Board was unable to agree? Would groups have been more conservative in their tastes than individuals, as they have generally been over the past couple of centuries, or is this assumption anachronistic?

Another kind of corporate patron was the state, whether republic or principality. It was the Signoria, the government of Florence, which commissioned Leonardo's *Battle of Anghiari* and its companion piece, Michelangelo's *Battle of Cascina*. In Venice there existed an official position of Protho, or architect to the Republic (held by Jacopo Sansovino among others), and a quasi-official

---

[4] On the *scuole* more generally, see Pullan (1971, 1981).

LORENZO VECCHIETTA, *THE CONFRATERNITY*
Pinacoteca, Siena.

position of painter to the Republic (offered to Dürer on one occasion, and held by Giovanni Bellini and by Titian) (Logan, 1972, p. 181f; Howard, 1975; Hope, 1980, p. 98).

However, one painter alone could not cope with all the state's commissions. In 1495 there were nine painters, including Giovanni Bellini and Alvise Vivarini, working on battle scenes to decorate the Hall of the Great Council in the Doge's Palace. The problems of patronage by committee emerge clearly from the documents referring to a battle scene by Titian for the same place. In 1513 Titian petitioned the Council of Ten to be allowed to paint it, with the help of two assistants. A resolution accepting the offer was carried (10 votes to 6); Bellini protested. In March 1514 the decree was revoked (14 votes to 1) and the assistants were struck off the payroll; Titian protested. In November, the revocation was revoked (9 votes to 4), and the assistants reappeared on the payroll. Then it was reported that three times as much money had been spent as need have been, and all arrangements were cancelled. Titian agreed to accept a single assistant, and his offer was accepted in 1516, but the battle painting was still unfinished in 1537 (Lorenzi, 1868, pp. 157–65; Chambers, 1970b, nos 42–3).

In the case of princes it is often hard to decide whether patronage is public or private, or indeed, whether the patron personally commissioned all the works of art executed on his behalf. What is clear is that the style of princely patronage differed a great deal from that of guilds, fraternities or committees. It was not the delays but the impatience of the patron which was usually the problem for the artist working for a prince. 'We want you to work on some paintings which we wish to have made, and we wish you, as soon as you have received this, to drop everything, jump on your horse and come here to us', wrote the duke of Milan to the Lombard painter Vicenzo Foppa. The same ruler commanded painters to work night and day to decorate the Castello Sforzesco, and a contemporary chronicle tells a story of a room painted 'in a single night'. His successor was equally demanding and on one occasion resolved, as he put it, 'to have our ballroom at Milan painted immediately with stories, at all possible speed' (Malaguzzi-Valeri, 1902; Chambers, 1970b, nos 96–100).

Alfonso d'Este of Ferrara was a man of the same stamp. When Raphael kept him waiting, Alfonso sent him a message: 'Let him beware of provoking our anger.' When Titian failed to produce a painting on time in 1519, Alfonso instructed his agent 'To tell him instantly, that we are surprised that he should not have finished our picture; that he must finish it whatever happens or incur our great

BATTISTA DOSSI, *MADONNA WITH SAINTS AND THE CONFRATERNITY*
Galleria Estense, Modena.

displeasure; and that he may be made to feel that he is doing a bad turn to one who is in a position to resent it.'[5]

Another impatient patron was Federico II, marquis of Mantua. For example, he wrote to Titian in 1531 asking for a picture of St Mary Magdalen, 'and above all, let me have it quickly'. (Titian sent it in less than a month.) When Giulio Romano and his assistants failed to decorate the Palazzo del Te with sufficient speed, the marquis wrote that 'We are not amused that you should again have missed so many dates by which you had undertaken to finish.' Giulio replied obsequiously that 'The greatest pain I can receive is when Your Excellency is angry ... if it is pleasing to you, have me locked up in that room until it is done.' This seems a far cry from Federico's flattering comparison of his painter to Apelles (above p. 76), unless Alexander the Great treated his painters in the same way (Hartt, 1958, vol. 1, pp. 74–5; original text in D'Arco, 1842, appendix).

Perhaps the most important distinction is the one with which this chapter began, between patrons, generally princes, who took artists into their service on a more or less permanent basis (Leonardo in Milan, Mantegna in Mantua and so on), and clients who merely commissioned a single work. From the artist's point of view, in so far as it is possible to reconstruct it, each system had its advantages and disadvantages. Permanent service at court gave the artist a relatively high status, without the social taint of shop-keeping (above p. 80). It also meant relative economic security; board and lodging and presents of clothes, money and land. When the prince died, however, the artist might lose everything. When the duke of Florence, Alessandro de'Medici, was murdered in 1537, Giorgio Vasari, who had been in the duke's service, found his hopes 'blown away by a puff of wind'. Another disadvantage of the system was its servitude. At the court of Mantua, Mantegna had to ask permission to travel or to accept outside commissions. It was not possible to avoid the demands of patrons as easily as those of temporary clients. The great danger for a court artist (from posterity's point of view, if not from his own) was that of turning into a glorified odd-job man.

Two examples should make the danger clear. When Cosimo Tura entered the service of Borso d'Este, duke of Ferrara, he earned his regular salary not only from pictures but by painting furniture, gilding caskets and horse trappings, and designing chair backs, door curtains, bed quilts, a table service, tournament costumes and so on. At the court of Lodovico Sforza of Milan, Leonardo was similarly occupied in miscellaneous projects. He painted the portrait of the

---

[5] Adapted from the translations in Crowe and Cavalcaselle (1881), pp. 183–4.

ANDREA DEL CASTAGNO, *THE YOUTHFUL DAVID* (painted shield)
1942.9.8, National Gallery of Art, Washington; Widener Collection.

duke's mistress, Cecilia Gallerani; he decorated the interior of the Castello Sforzesco; he worked on 'the horse', an equestrian monument to the duke's father; he designed costumes and stages for court festivals; and he was employed as a military engineer. One might say that at least he went to Milan with his eyes open, since the draft of the letter he wrote to the duke asking to be taken into his service has survived, and listed what he could do in the way of designing bridges, mortars and chariots, ending 'in the tenth place' that he could also paint and sculpt. All the same it is a judgement on Ludovico that we remember Leonardo at Milan for two works, neither of them for the duke (though he may have arranged the first commission); the *Last Supper* was painted for a monastery, the *Virgin of the Rocks* for a fraternity (Kemp, 1981, p. 78f).

The disadvantages of courts as a milieu for artists should not be exaggerated. Republics too commissioned temporary decorations on festive occasions, and to regret this is perhaps only the bias towards the permanent of an age of museums. All the same, there remains an impression that court artists were more likely than others to have to dissipate their energies on the transient and the trivial, like the court mathematicians in seventeenth-century Versailles, concerned with the hydraulics of fountains or with the probable outcomes of royal games of cards.

When an artist kept a shop, on the other hand, he had less economic security and a lower social status, but it was easier for him to evade the commission he did not want, as Giovanni Bellini seems to have done in the case of a request from Isabella d'Este (below p. 108). Clients too might offer artists a variety of odd jobs, but some workshops were so organized that different members could specialize. It is hard to say how important this freedom of working was to artists, but it may be significant that when Mantegna was appointed court painter in Mantua, in 1459, he lingered in Padua, as if the decision to leave had been a difficult one (Chambers, 1970b, nos 59–60). Whether individual artists cared about their freedom or not, the difference in working conditions seems to be reflected in what was produced. The major innovations of the period took place in Florence and Venice, republics of shop-keepers, and not in courts.

Another distinction between patrons is that between rich and poor. How widely diffused was the habit of commissioning artists? Architecture and sculpture were expensive, but the possibility that people with modest incomes commissioned paintings cannot be dismissed. The documents are almost entirely concerned with upper-class patronage, but those are the documents most likely to survive.

There are casual references in Vasari to artisan clients, such as the mercer and the joiner who commissioned Madonnas from Andrea del Sarto, and the tailor who commissioned Pontormo's first recorded work. What we do not know is whether this situation was at all common, as it was in the Dutch Republic in the seventeenth century.[6]

It may be useful to distinguish three main motives for art patronage in the period: piety, prestige and pleasure (see also chapter 5). A fourth has been suggested, but it is probably anachronistic: investment. If investment in works of art means buying them on the assumption that they will be worth more in the future, then it is difficult to find evidence for it before the eighteenth century.[7] 'The love of God', on the other hand, is frequently mentioned in contracts with artists; and if piety had not been an important as well as a socially acceptable motive for patrons, it would be difficult to explain the predominance of religious paintings and sculptures in the period. Prestige was also a socially acceptable motive, above all in Florence. It is not infrequently mentioned in contracts. When the *Operai del Duomo* of Florence commissioned twelve apostles from Michelangelo, for example, they referred to the 'fame of the whole city' and its 'honour and glory'. When Giovanni Tornabuoni commissioned frescos for his family chapel in Santa Maria Novella, he referred openly to the 'exaltation of his house and family', and ensured that the family coat of arms was prominently displayed (Chambers, 1970b, no. 107). The most extraordinary example of the desire for prestige, however, is surely the tabernacle commissioned by Piero de'Medici for the church of the Annunziata in Florence, and inscribed 'the marble alone cost 4,000 florins [*Costo fior. 4 mila el marmo solo*]' (Wackernagel, 1938, p. 239n). This classic example of nouveau-riche exhibitionism makes one wonder whether – as seems to have been the case in eighteenth-century Venice – rising families saw art patronage as a way of showing the world that they had reached the top, and whether they were more active as patrons than families already established (Haskell, 1963, p. 249f).

The prestige acquired by art patronage might be of political value to a ruler. Filarete, who had of course an axe to grind, or rather, a palace to build, argued this case and tried to demolish the economic argument that buildings were too expensive:

---

[6] Wackernagel (1938), p. 6 notes the existence of artisan clients.

[7] See Lopez (1953); and contrast Burke (1978). For economic arguments for art as investment, see Goldthwaite (1980), p. 397f.

Magnanimous and great princes, and republics as well, should not hold
back from building great and beautiful buildings because of the
expense. No country was ever impoverished nor did anyone ever die
because of the construction of buildings ... In the end when a large
building is completed there is neither more nor less money in the
country but the building does remain in the country or city together
with its reputation or honour.[8]

Machiavelli too saw the political use of art patronage and suggested
that 'a prince ought to show himself a lover of ability, giving
employment to able men and honouring those who excel in a
particular field.'[9]

The third motive for patronage was 'pleasure', a more or less
discriminating delight in paintings, statues and so on, whether as
objects in their own right or as a form of interior decoration. It has
often been suggested that this motive was more important as well as
more self- conscious in Renaissance Italy than it had been anywhere
in Europe for a thousand years (Alsop, 1982). This is likely enough,
although the 'more' cannot be measured; all that can be done is to
quote examples of the trend.

   Filarete, for example, stressed the pleasure in building for its own
sake, 'a voluptuous pleasure as when a man is in love'. The more the
patron sees the building, the more he wants to see it, and he loves to
talk to everyone about it – typical lover's behaviour. The names of
some villas of the period suggest that they were playthings: *Schifanoia*
(Avoid Boredom) at Ferrara; *Casa Zoiosa* (Happy House) at Mantua.
According to the bookseller Vespasiano da Bisticci, who did not go
out of his way to praise the visual arts, two of his prominent clients,
Federico of Urbino and Cosimo de'Medici, took a keen personal
pleasure in sculpture and architecture. To hear Federico talk to a
sculptor, 'one would have thought it his trade', while Cosimo was so
much interested in architecture that his advice was sought by those
who intended to build. The correspondence of Isabella d'Este leaves
the impression that the reason she commissioned paintings was
simply to have them. She was not the only patron to think in this way.
Isabella failed to acquire two Giorgiones because they had been
commissioned by two Venetian patricians 'for their own enjoyment'
(Chambers, 1970b, no. 91). There seems to have been a circle of
patrician collectors in Venice at this time, including Taddeo Contarini
and Gabriele Vendramin, a well-known art-lover in whose house the
famous *Tempest* could be seen in 1530 (Settis, 1978, p. 129f).

---

[8] Filarete, *Treatise on Architecture*, p. 106.
[9] Machiavelli, *Prince*, ch. 21.

LEONARDO DA VINCI, *ISABELLA D'ESTE*
Musée du Louvre, cliché des Musées Nationaux, Paris.

This desire to acquire works of art for their own sake is found above all in individuals who have something else in common: a humanist education. After Gianfrancesco Gonzaga, marquis of Mantua, engaged Vittorino da Feltre to teach his children, they grew up to become patrons of the arts, and so did Federico of Urbino, who also studied with Vittorino. Similarly, the children of the ruling house of Este at Ferrra became patrons of the arts after they had been educated by Guarino of Verona. As a child, Lorenzo de'Medici had a humanist tutor, Gentile Becchi. Gabriele Vendramin moved in a social circle which included humanists of the calibre of Ermolao Barbaro and Bernardo Bembo (Logan, 1972, p. 157). Although humanists did not always respect artists, the study of the humanities seems to have encouraged a taste for pictures and statues.[10]

PATRONS V ARTISTS

This section is concerned with the relationships between patrons and artists; with cooperation and conflict, with each group's expectations of the other and, above all, with the problem of the extent of the patron's influence, or the patron's adviser's influence, on particular paintings, statues and so on.

How did artists acquire patrons or clients, or patrons acquire artists? When artists heard that projects were in the air, they might approach the patron directly or through an intermediary. For example, in 1438 the painter Domenico Veneziano wrote to Piero de'Medici that 'I have heard that Cosimo [Piero's father] has decided to have an altarpiece painted, and wants a magnificent work. This pleases me a great deal, and it would please me still more it it were possible for me to paint it, through your mediation [*per vostra megianita*]' (Gaye, 1839, vol. 1, p. 136; Chambers, 1970b, no. 46). In 1474, there was news in Milan that the duke wanted a chapel painted at Pavia. The duke's agent complained that 'all the painters of Milan, good and bad, asked to paint it, and trouble me greatly about it' (Ffoulkes and Maiocchi, 1909, p. 300f). Again, in 1488, Alvise Vivarini petitioned the doge to let him paint something for the Hall of the Great Council in Venice as the Bellinis were doing, and in 1515, as we have seen, Titian made a similar request (Chambers, 1970b, nos 41–2).

In these cases, as in many other matters, friendships, equal and unequal, counted for a great deal. Art patronage was part of a much larger patron–client system, discussed in chapter 9. The importance

---

[10] Cf. Baxandall (1965), and the discussion of the humanist adviser below (p. 109).

AGNOLO BRONZINO, *UGOLINO MARTELLI*
Gemäldegalerie Staatliche Museen Preussischer Kulturbesitz, Berlin.

of friends and relations may be illustrated from the careers of two sixteenth-century Tuscan artists, Giorgio Vasari and Baccio Bandinelli. Vasari came to work for Ippolito and Alessandro de'Medici because he was a distant relative of their guardian, Cardinal Silvio Passerini. After his hopes had been 'blown away', as we have seen, by the death of duke Alessandro, Vasari managed to enter the permanent service of his successor Cosimo. Bandinelli also had a family connection with the Medici in the sense that his father had worked for them before their expulsion from Florence in 1494. After their restoration in 1513, Baccio introduced himself to the brothers Giovanni (soon to become pope Leo X) and Giuliano, offered them a gift, and received commissions in return. Bandinelli also worked for Giulio de'Medici, who became pope Clement VII. He expected the commission to make the tombs of both Medici popes and visited Cardinal Salviati so often to arrange this that he was mistaken for a spy and nearly assassinated (Boase, 1979: Vasari, life of Bandinelli).

It is less easy to discover how patrons chose particular artists. The less expert sometimes asked advice of others, such as Cosimo de'Medici (as we have seen) or his grandson Lorenzo the Magnificent. It was Lorenzo, for example, who recommended the sculptor Giuliano da Maiano to prince Alfonso of Calabria. Some patrons seem to have chosen between rival offers on financial grounds, others for stylistic reasons. The duke of Milan's agent, in the case of the chapel quoted above, chose the artists who offered to do the work for 150 rather than for 200 ducats. Twenty years later, however, a memorandum from the papers of the new duke of Milan, Ludovico Sforza, attempted to distinguish between Botticelli, Filippino Lippi, Perugino and Ghirlandaio on the grounds of style (Chambers, 1970b, no. 95, cf. p. 143 below).

Formal competitions for commissions also took place on occasion, especially in Florence and Venice, which is what one might have expected from republics of merchants. The most famous of these competitions are surely the ones for the Baptistery doors in Florence in 1400 (in which Ghiberti defeated Brunelleschi), and for the cupola of Florence Cathedral (in which it was Brunelleschi's turn to win), but there are many other examples. In 1477, for instance, Verrocchio defeated Piero Pollaiuolo for the commission for the tomb of cardinal Forteguerri (Gaye, 1839, vol. 1, p. 256; Chambers, 1970b, no. 51). In 1491, there was a competition for designs for the façade of the cathedral in Florence. In 1508, Benedetto Diana won and Vittore Carpaccio lost a commission from the Venetian Scuola della Carità. In Venice, incidentally, even the organists at San Marco were appointed only after a competition.

Now that the patron and the artist have been introduced to each other, we may consider their relative influence on the finished product. The testimony of contemporaries suggests that the influence of the patron was considerable. The term 'made' [*fecit*) continued to be used of patrons, as it had been in the Middle Ages. Filarete described the patron as the father of the building, the architect as the mother. Titian told Alfonso duke of Ferrara that he was:

> convinced that the greatness of art amongst the ancients was due to the assistance they received from great princes content to leave to the painter the credit and renown derived from their own ingenuity in commissioning pictures . . . I shall, after all, have done no more than give shape to that which received its spirit – the most essential part – from Your Excellency (Crowe and Cavalcaselle, 1881, p. 181).

He was, of course, flattering the duke, but the different forms taken by flattery in different periods provide valuable evidence for social historians.

More precise evidence about the relative importance of patrons and artists and the expectations of both parties is provided by the scores of surviving contracts, which concentrate on six issues. In the first place come materials, an important question because of the expense of the gold and lapis lazuli used for paintings, or the bronze and marble for sculpture. Sometimes the patron provided the materials, sometimes the artist did so. Contracts often specified that the materials employed be of high quality. Andrea del Sarto promised to use at least 5 florins' worth of azure on a Virgin Mary, while Michelangelo promised that the marble for his famous *Pietà*, begun in 1501, should be 'new, pure and white, with no veins in it' (Shearman, 1965, doc. 30). The emphasis on materials is a clue to what the client thought he was buying. Leonardo's contract for *The Virgin of the Rocks* gives a ten-year guarantee; if anything was to need repainting within that period, it was to be at the expense of the artist. One wonders whether Leonardo gave a similar guarantee in the case of his flaky *Last Supper*.

Secondly, there was the question of price, including the currency (large ducats, papal ducats and so on). Sometimes the money was paid on completion, sometimes in instalments while the work was in progress. Alternatively, the price might not be fixed in advance; either the artist declared his readiness to accept what the patron thought good to offer, or the work would be valued by other artists, as it was in cases of dispute (Chambers, 1970b, nos 123–7). Payments in kind were sometimes included. Signorelli's contract for frescos in Orvieto cathedral gave him the right to a sum of money, to gold and azure, to lodgings and a bed. After negotiations, he raised the offer to two beds.

Thirdly, there was the question of delivery date, vague or precise, with or without sanctions if the artist did not keep his word. A Venetian state commission to Giovanni Bellini stated that the paintings should be finished 'as quickly as possible'. In 1529, Beccafumi was given 'a year, or eighteen months at most' to finish a picture. Other clients were more precise, or more demanding. In 1460, fra Lippo Lippi promised a painting by September of that year, and if he failed to produce it, the client was given the right to ask someone else to finish it. On 25 April 1483, Leonardo promised to deliver *The Virgin of the Rocks* by 8 December. Michelangelo's contract of 1501 for 15 statues laid down that he was not to make any other contracts which would delay the execution of this one. (It is perhaps surprising that academic publishers do not make this stipulation today.) Raphael was given two years to paint an altarpiece, with a large fine (40 ducats, over half the price) if he failed to meet the deadline. The contract which Andrea del Sarto made in 1515 to paint an altarpiece within a year contained the clause 'that if he did not finish the said picture within the said time, the said nuns would have the right to give the said commission to someone else [*dictam tabulam alicui locare*].

Fourthly, there was the question of size. This is surprisingly often left unspecified, perhaps an indication of sixteenth–century vagueness about measurements, although in many cases the fact that a fresco was painted on a particular wall, or a statue made from the client's block of marble or to fit a particular niche would have made precision unnecessary. However, Michelangelo promised in 1514 to make his *Christ Carrying the Cross* 'life size'. Andrea del Sarto agreed to make his altarpiece of 1515 at least 3 braccia wide and 3½ braccia high. Isabella d'Este, who wanted a set of matching pictures for her study, enclosed a thread in her letter commissioning Perugino so that he would get the measurements right.

Fifthly, the question of assistants. Some contracts were made with groups of artists rather than individuals. Others mention assistants, usually to specify the responsibility for paying them. Some specify that the artist signing the contract should produce all or part of the work with his own hand. Raphael, for example, promised to paint with his own hand the figures in his altarpiece of the coronation of the Virgin. Perugino and Signorelli, however, promised to paint only the figures 'from the waist up', in their frescos in Orvieto Cathedral.

The final question, crucial to posterity, of what actually went into the picture has been left till last because it does not loom large in the contracts themselves. On occasion, the subject is spelled out in words, sometimes in detail, but on other occasions rather briefly. Elaborate details were laid down for Domenico Ghirlandaio by Giovanni Tornabuoni in the Santa Maria Novella frescos which have already been mentioned. Domenico and the others were to paint the right-hand wall of the chapel with seven specified scenes from the life of the Virgin. The painters also promised 'in all the aforesaid histories . . . to paint figures, buildings, castles, cities, mountains, hills, plains, rocks, garments, animals, birds and beasts . . . just as the patron wants, if the price of materials is not prohibitive [*secundum tamen taxationem colorum*]' (Chambers, 1970b, no. 107).

A more common formula in contracts was to give a relatively brief description of the iconographical essentials. On some occasions the description of even these essentials in legal Latin seems to have been too much for the notary, and the document suddenly lapses into Italian. The Ghirlandaio frescos were to be 'as they say in the vernacular, frescoed [*ut vulgariter dicitur, posti in frescho*]'. A 1429 contract for a church at Loreto asks for the Virgin 'with her son in her lap, according to custom [*secondo l'usanza*]', an interestingly explicit demand on a painter to follow tradition. It was often simpler to refer to a sketch, plain or coloured, or a model (Chambers, 1970b, nos 5, 68, 86, 101, 113, 137 etc). When the duke of Milan was having his chapel painted in 1474, his agent sent him two designs to choose from, 'with cherubs or without' (cherubs cost extra), and asked for the designs back 'to see, when the work is finished, whether the azure was as fine as was promised' (Chambers, 1970b, no. 99). Alternatively, the client sent the sketch to the artist (as Isabella d'Este did when commissioning Perugino), or asked for something along the lines of a painting by someone else which had taken his or her fancy. A contract for a Crucifixion between a painter called Barbagelata and the Confraternity of St Bridget at Genoa (1485) required the figures to be painted in the same manner and quality 'as those which are painted in the altarpiece of St Dominic for the late Battista Spinola in the church of the said St Dominic, made and painted by master Vincent of Milan [Vincenzo Foppa]' (ffoulkes and Maiocchi, 1909).

Besides these descriptions and drawings, there may be more or less precise references to the initiative of the artist or, more often, to the wishes of the patron. Tura contracted with the duke of Ferrara to paint the chapel of Belriguardo 'with the histories which please his said Excellency most'. When the monks of San Pietro in Perugia contracted with Perugino for an altarpiece, the predella was to be 'painted and adorned with histories according to the desire of the present abbot'. Isabella left Perugino a restricted area of freedom: 'you may leave things out if you like, but you are not to add anything

PIETRO PERUGINO, *BATTLE OF LOVE AND CHASTITY*
Museé du Louvre, cliché des Musées Nationaux, Paris.

of your own' (Chambers, 1970b, no. 76). Michelangelo, on the other hand, late in the period but still exceptionally, seems usually to have got his own way. The contract for *Christ Carrying the Cross* says simply that the figure should be posed 'in whatever attitude seems good to the said Michelangelo', while the commission for a work never finished which was at one point Hercules and Cacus, at another Samson and a Philistine, describes the transfer of a block of marble to the sculptor, 'who is to make from it a figure together or conjoined with another, just as it pleases the said Michelangelo' (Tolnay, 1954).

Contracts, however valuable their testimony to the relationships between artists and clients, do not tell the whole story. They offer evidence of intentions, and historians, however interesting they find intentions, also want to know whether things went according to plan.

In some cases we can be sure that they did not. In the case of Andrea del Sarto's *Madonna of the Harpies*, for example, both contract and painting have survived, but there are serious discrepancies between them. The contract refers to two angels; they do not appear in the finished painting. The contract refers to St John the Evangelist: in the painting he has turned into St Francis. Such alterations may well have been negotiated with the client; we do not know. They are none the less a warning not to take one kind of evidence too seriously (Shearman, 1965, doc. 30 and pp. 47–51). The most effective way to discover the true balance of power between artists and patrons in this period is surely to study the open conflicts between them, conflicts which made manifest the tensions inherent in the relationship. Although the evidence for these conflicts is fragmentary, a coherent picture does at least appear to emerge.

There were two main reasons for conflicts between artists and patrons at this time. The first, which need not detain us, was money. It was a special instance of the general problem of getting clients of high status to pay their debts. Mantegna, Poliziano and Josquin des Près were driven to remind their patrons of their obligations by pictorial, literary and musical means respectively.

The second reason for conflict, which reveals a good deal more about the relationship between culture and society in this period, concerns the works themselves. What happened when the artist did not like the patron's plan, or the patron was dissatisfied with the result? Here are some examples. In 1436 the *Operai del Duomo* of Florence commissioned Paolo Uccello to paint the equestrian portrait of Sir John Hawkwood on the cathedral wall, but a month later they ordered the picture to be destroyed 'because it is not painted as it should be [*quia non est pictus ut decet*]'. One wonders what experiments in perspective Uccello had been trying out (Poggi, 1909). Again, Piero de'Medici objected to certain small seraphs in a fresco by Benozzo Gozzoli, who wrote to say that 'I'll do as you command; two little clouds will take them away' (Gaye, 1839, vol. 1, p. 191; Chambers, 1970b, no. 49).

In other cases, the conflict seems to have reached deadlock. Vasari tells a story about Piero di Cosimo painting a picture for the Foundling Hospital in Florence. The client, who was the director of the hospital, asked to see the picture before it was finished; Piero refused. The client threatened not to pay; the artist threatened to destroy the painting. Again, Julius II, the irresistible force, and Michelangelo, the immovable object, came into conflict over the Sistine ceiling. Before he had finished Michelangelo left Rome in secret and returned to Florence. Vasari's explanation for Michelangelo's flight was 'that the pope became angry with him because he would not allow any of his work to be seen; that Michelangelo distrusted his own men and suspected that the pope . . . disguised himself to see what was being done.' Why did Piero and Michelangelo object to their work being seen before it was finished? Some artists today are touchy about laymen looking over their shoulder; but there may have been something more to these cases than that. Suppose an artist did not want to treat a subject in the way that the client wanted. A possible tactic would be to hide the picture from him until it was finished, hoping that he would accept a *fait accompli* rather than wait for another version. For another Sistine ceiling the pope would have had to wait quite a while.

Giovanni Bellini was another painter who did not easily submit to the will of others. The humanist Pietro Bembo described him as one 'whose pleasure is that sharply defined limits should not be set to his style, being wont, as he says, to wander at his will in paintings [*vagare a sua voglia nelle pitture*]'. Isabella d'Este asked him for a mythological picture. It appears that he wanted neither to paint such a picture nor to lose the commission, so he used delaying tactics, while hinting, via the agents Isabella used in her dealings with artists, that another subject might not take so long. As one of the agents told her, 'If you care to give him the liberty to do what he wants, I am absolutely sure that Your Highness will be served much better.' Isabella knew when to give way gracefully, and replied that 'If Giovanni Bellini is as reluctant to paint his history as you say, we are content to leave the subject to him, provided that he paints some history or ancient fable.' In fact, Bellini was able to beat her down still further, and she ended by accepting a Nativity (Chambers, 1970b, nos 64–72).

In this last case, the history of events leads us to the history of structures. The fact that Bellini kept a shop, and that he was in Venice while Isabella was at Mantua, probably helped him to get his way. Had he been attached to the court, the outcome of the conflict would probably have been very different. Isabella seems to have learned this lesson, and soon afterwards she took Lorenzo Costa into her permanent service.

These examples of conflict are some of the most celebrated and best- documented ones. They are not a sufficient basis for generalization. However, there is other evidence to suggest that the balance of power between patron and artist was changing in this period in the artist's favour, allowing a greater individualism of style. As the status of artists rose, patrons made fewer demands. To Leonardo, Isabella made concessions from the start; 'We shall leave the subject and the time to you' (Chambers, 1970b, nos 85–90). Again, a famous letter to

Vasari from the poet Annibale Caro acknowledges the freedom of the artist by comparing the two roles: 'For the subject matter [*invenzione*] I place myself in your hands, remembering . . . that both the poet and the painter carry out their own ideas and their own schemes with more love and with more diligence than they do the schemes of others.' It is unfortunate that he was to follow this compliment with fairly precise instructions for an Adonis on a purple garment, embraced by Venus.

Caro also drew up a detailed programme for the decoration of the palace for the Farnese family at Caprarola (Gombrich, 1972, pp. 9–11, 23–5; cf. Robertson, 1982). He was, in other words, a humanist adviser, an intellectual middleman between patron and client. The hypothesis of the humanist adviser – Poliziano in this case – was put forward by Aby Warburg (1966), pp. 36, 43) when discussing the mythological paintings of Botticelli. Since artists, as we have seen, generally lacked a classical education, they must have needed advice when required to paint scenes from ancient history or mythology. There is, in fact, evidence of such advice being given on a few occasions.

In the earliest known case the subject was not classical but biblical: in 1424, the Calimala guild of Florence asked the humanist Leonardo Bruni to draw up a programme for the 'Gates of Paradise', the third pair of doors for the Baptistery in Florence. Bruni chose 20 stories from the Old Testament. However, the sculptor, Ghiberti, claimed in his memoirs to have been given a free hand, and the Bruni programme was not followed, for the doors illustrate only ten stories (Krautheimer and Krautheimer-Hess, 1956, p. 169f; Chambers, 1970b, no. 24).

In Ferrara in the mid-fifteenth century, the humanist Guarino of Verona suggested a possible programme for a painting of the Muses for the marquis, Leonello d'Este (Baxandall, 1965). Later in the century, the court librarian, Pellegrino Prisciani, was concerned with the programme of the famous astrological frescos in the Palazzo Schifanoia in Ferrara, painted by Francesco del Cossa (Warburg, 1932, pp. 249–69; 1966, pp. 242–72). In the Medici circle in the later fifteenth century, there is more indirect evidence for the advice of two humanists, the poet–philologist Angelo Poliziano and the philosopher Marsilio Ficino, on the programme of Botticelli's *Primavera*, the meaning of which still divides scholars.[11] According to his pupil Condivi, the young Michelangelo made his relief of *The Battle of the Centaurs* at the suggestion of Poliziano, 'who explained the whole

---

[11] Besides Warburg, see Gombrich (1972) and Dempsey (1968).

myth to him from beginning to end [*dichiarandogli a parte per parte tutta la favola* (Condivi, 1964, pp. 28–9).

Another milieu in which there is firm evidence of humanist advisers is the court of Mantua in the early sixteenth century. When Isabella d'Este planned a series of pagan 'fantasies' for her study and grotto, it was to the humanists Pietro Bembo and Paride da Ceresara that she turned for advice. It was Paride who provided the programme for the *Battle of Love and Chastity* which Isabella, as we have seen, commissioned from Perugino (Chambers, 1970b, nos 76, 80).

It would not be difficult to add to these examples, particularly for the sixteenth century. One thinks of the humanist bishop, Paolo Giovio, planning the decoration of the Medici villa at Poggio a Caiano (Zimmermann, 1976), or the poet Annibale Caro doing the same, as noted above, for the Farnese at Caprarola. Whether they were called in by artists or patrons, and whether their advice was taken seriously or not, classical scholars, and more rarely theologians, were involved in the planning of pictorial and sculptural programmes. They helped artists to cope with the sudden demand for classical mythology and ancient history which workshop traditions had not trained artists to provide.[12]

ARCHITECTURE, MUSIC AND LITERATURE

Architecture needs to be considered separately because architects did not work with their hands. They provided nothing but the programme, so that in cases where patrons took an active interest, their role was diminished. Filarete's treatise presents a picture, no doubt a wish-fulfilment, of a prince who accepts the plans of his architect with enthusiasm. In practice, however, patrons often wanted to interfere, or at least to intervene, in the building process. Some of them studied treatises on architecture. Alfonso of Aragon, for example, asked for a copy of Vitruvius when the plans for a triumphal arch at Naples were being discussed. Federigo of Urbino owned a copy of Francesco di Giorgio's treatise on architecture, presented by the author (Heyden-reich, 1967; Clough, 1973). Ercole d'Este borrowed Alberti's treatise on architecture from Lorenzo de'Medici before deciding how to rebuild his palace. A panegyric on Cosimo de'Medici describes him as wanting to build a church and a house in his own way (*more suo*) (Brown, 1961; cf. Gombrich, 1966; Jenkins, 1970). As for Cosimo's grandson Lorenzo, he went so far as an amateur architect as to

---

[12] For a more sceptical view of the importance of the humanist adviser, see Hope (1981) and Robertson (1982).

submit a design for the competition for the façade of Florence Cathedral in 1491. The judges were unable to choose either the design of the effective ruler of Florence or that of any other competitor, so the façade was left unbuilt.

In the case of music, it was the performers who were the recipients of patronage, and on a permanent basis, precisely because their performances were ephemeral. There were three main types of patron: Church, city and court (Bridgman, 1964, ch. 2).

The church was a great patron of singers, although not a particularly generous one. They were needed for masses and other parts of the liturgy, and they were needed all the time, as were organists. Choirmasters included men we now remember as composers, such as Giovanni Spataro, choirmaster at the church of San Petronio at Bologna from 1512 to 1541.

Cities also took musicians into their permanent service. Trumpeters, for example, were in demand for civic events such as state visits or major religious festivals. The best civic posts were in Venice. The church of San Marco was the doge's chapel, and so its choirmaster was a civic (in other words a political) appointment. The post was created in 1491 for a Frenchman, Pierre de Fossis. When he died, the forceful doge Andrea Gritti forced through the appointment of an outsider, the Netherlander Adriaan Willaert, against considerable opposition. The musical importance of sixteenth-century Venice may owe something to the relative munificence of its civic patronage.

Court patronage was the least secure of the three main types, but it offered the possibility of the greatest rewards. Some princes took a great interest in their chapels: Galeazzo Maria Sforza of Milan, for example, Ercole d'Este of Ferrara or pope Leo X. When the duke of Milan decided, in 1472, to found a choir, he spared no effort to make it a good one. He wrote to his ambassador in Naples with instructions to persuade some of the singers there to move to Milan. He was to talk to them and to make promises of 'good benefices and good salaries', but in his own name, not the duke's; 'Above all, take good care that neither his royal majesty nor others should imagine that we are the cause of those singers being taken away.' Presumably a diplomatic incident might have followed this discovery. By 1474 the duke had acquired a certain 'Josquino', perhaps Josquin des Près. He continued to take a great interest in his chapel choir, which had to follow him to Pavia, Vigevano and even outside the duchy. As for Alfonso of Aragon, he even took his choir with him when he went hunting! (Motta, 1887).

Isabella d'Este was interested in music as well as painting, and two major composers of *frottole* (songs for several voices) were active at her court, Marchetto Cara and Bartolommeo Tromboncino (Fenlon, 1980, p. 15f). A still greater interest in music was taken by pope Leo X. He played and composed himself (a canon composed by him still survives). His enthusiasm was well known, and when news arrived that Leo had been elected pope, many of the marquis of Mantua's singers left for Rome. The most distinguished composers in Leo's service were Elzéar Genet, who was in charge of the music for the papal chapel; Costanzo Festa, who was famous for his madrigals; and the organist Marco Antonio Cavazzoni. The contemporary anecdotes of Leo's generosity to musicians have been confirmed from the papal accounts. He had more than 15 musicians in his private service in 1520. He paid the famous lutenist Gian Maria Giudeo 23 ducats a month, and made him a count into the bargain.

A fourth kind of patronage should not be forgotten. It was possible for musicians to make careers in the service of private individuals. Willaert, for example, organized concerts for a Venetian lady, Pollissena Pecorina, and a nobleman, Marco Trivisano (Einstein, 1958, pp. 39–49). The organist Cavazzoni was at one time in the service of the humanist Pietro Bembo.

In all these cases, it is difficult to say whether musicians were hired because they could sing or play well or because they could compose or invent. There is a little evidence of interest in the activity of invention. Some compositions were dedicated to individuals or written in their honour. For example, a certain Cristoforo da Feltre wrote a motet on the election of Francesco Foscari as doge of Venice in 1423. Heinrich Isaak, who spent the decade 1484–94 in Florence, wrote an instrumental piece, 'Palle, palle', presumably for the Medici, since it refers to their rallying- cry and their device, and he also set to music Poliziano's lament for the death of Lorenzo the Magnificent. New compositions were required for court festivals; Costanzo Festa, for example, wrote the music for the wedding, in 1539, of Cosimo de'Medici, duke of Tuscany, and Eleonora of Toledo.

What patrons wanted from musicians emerges most vividly from a letter to Ercole d'Este, duke of Ferrara, written by one of his agents about 1500. The duke was trying to make up his mind which of two candidates to hire, Heinrich Isaak or Josquin des Près.

> Isaak the singer . . . is extremely rapid in the art of composition, and besides this he is a man . . . who can be managed as one wants . . . and he seems to me extremely suitable to serve your lordship, more than Josquin, because he gets on better with his colleagues, and would make new things more often; it is true that Josquin composes better, but he does it when he feels like it, not when he is asked; and he is demanding 200 ducats, and Isaak will be satisfied with 120. (Van der Straeten, 1882, p. 87.)

RAPHAEL, *LEO X*
Galleria Pitti, Florence. Photograph from The Mansell Collection.

In other words, the fact that Josquin 'composes better' is recognized, but it is not the most important consideration. The social historian could hardly ask for a more revealing document about the workings of patronage.

In the case of literature and learning, patronage was less necessary because so many writers were amateurs with private means and so many scholars were academics. Patronage was most necessary when it was least likely, when a writer was poor, young and unknown and wanted to study. In some cases, aid was forthcoming. Lorenzo de'Medici, for example, made it possible for Poliziano to study, while Landino was financed by a notary and Guarino by a Venetian nobleman. The Greek cardinal Bessarion, who was a generous and discerning patron of scholars such as Flavio Biondo, Poggio Bracciolini and Bartolommeo Platina, also financed the studies of his compatriot Janos Lascaris. If Alfonso I of Aragon knew of boys who were poor but able (so his official biographer, the humanist Antonio Panormita, informs us), he paid for their education. At Ferrara, Duke Borso d'Este paid for the food and clothes of poor students at the university. However, these examples are not many and one wonders how many promising careers came to nothing for lack of patronage of this kind.

For humanists, it was possible to make a career in the service of the Church or the state. This was in part because particular popes (Nicholas V, for example, or Leo X) and princes (such as Alfonso I) appreciated their achievements, and in part because their skills, notably the art of writing an elegant and persuasive Latin letter, were needed in administration. The chanceries of Rome and Florence in particular were staffed by humanists.[13]

For writers who were already established, court patronage was often forthcoming because princes were interested in fame and believed that poets had it in their gift. It might, however, take a gift for intrigue as well as for literature to defeat rival candidates for a particular post. Augustus, as Horace and Virgil had known, could only be approached through Maecenas, and on occasion in Renaissance Italy, Maecenas could only be approached through intermediaries, 'Mecenatuli' as Panormita contemptuously called them. His own search for patronage led him up several blind alleys before eventual success (Sabbadini, 1916; cf. Ryder, 1976b). He tried Florence, dedicating a poem to Cosimo de'Medici as early as 1425; he tried Mantua, only to discover that having Vittorino da Feltre, they needed no more humanists; he tried Verona, via Guarino, with

---

[13] On Rome, see D'Amico (1983), p. 29f; on Florence, see Garin (1959).

similar results. Finally, thanks to the help of the archbishop, he obtained the post of court poet at Milan.

For an actual or aspiring court poet, an obvious move – following Virgil's precedent – was to write an epic about the prince. Thus the humanist Francesco Filelfo wrote a *Sforziad* to celebrate the ruling house of Milan. Federico of Urbino had his *Feltria*, and Borso d'Este his *Borsias*, the first of a series of epics for a ruling house which became the patrons of Boiardo, Ariosto and Tasso. Ariosto made his hero and heroine Ruggiero and Bradamante ancestors of the house of Este. In the third canto, modelled on the sixth book of Virgil's *Aeneid*, Merlino prophesies that the golden age will return in the reign of Ariosto's patron Alfonso I.

Court historians were also in demand and for similar reasons. Alfonso of Aragon commissioned works of history from the rival humanists Lorenzo Valla and Bartolommeo Fazio (see Soria, 1956). Lodovico Sforza commissioned a history of Milan from a nobleman, Bernardino Corio.[14] Machiavelli's *History of Florence* was commissioned by the Medici pope Clement VII, and dedicated to the pope by his 'humble slave'. Republics were also aware of the value of official history. The Venetian government, for example, commissioned histories from the humanist Marcantonio Sabellico and the patricians Andrea Navagero and Pietro Bembo (Cozzi, 1963; Gilbert, 1970)

Rulers might also act as patrons of natural science for practical reasons. Leonardo da Vinci went to the court of Milan, as we have seen, as a military engineer rather than an artist. Pandolfo Petrucci, lord of Siena, was the patron of the engineer Vannoccio Biringuccio. Fra Luca Pacioli, who wrote on mathematics, attracted the patronage of the dukes of Milan and Urbino (Rose, 1975). As a friar, however, he did not depend on patrons. Since most 'scientists' made their living through university teaching or the practice of medicine, they did not depend on patrons either.

Less directly useful works might also be commissioned by patrons who had a taste for literature or a liking for particular authors. Cosimo de'Medici gave the philosopher Marsilio Ficino a farm in the Tuscan countryside at Careggi and encouraged him to translate Plato and other ancient authors. Poliziano wrote a poem to celebrate a famous joust in which Giuliano de'Medici, the brother of Lorenzo the Magnificent, had taken part. Like painters and musicians, poets might have to help provide the entertainment at festivals. When Poliziano was in Mantuan service, he wrote his famous drama *Orfeo* to order

---

[14] Corio's history, *Storia di Milano*, was reprinted in 1978.

for a wedding. He also wrote begging poems to Lorenzo de'Medici describing how his clothes had worn out. The verse request was a conventional literary genre, but its existence is a reminder of the importance of patronage for the culture of the time and the life of the individual writer.

As in the case of painters, court patronage offered writers status. It also offered protection, which might well be necessary. The poet Serafino of Aquila, for example, left the service of cardinal Ascanio Sforza to live in Rome without a patron. However, his satirical verses provoked an attempt to assassinate him. When he recovered, 'considering that to be without a protector was dangerous and shameful', Serafino went back to the cardinal.[15]

Despite the examples of official historians of Venice, there was virtually no civic patronage for writers. Their choice was limited to the Church, the court or the occasional private individual, like the patrician Alvise Cornaro of Padua, who encouraged the dramatist Angelo Beolco 'il Ruzzante' to write his plays, and had them collected and published (Mortier, 1930, pp. 5–19; Logan 1972, p. 111). Some Venetian patricians, such as Francesco Barbaro and Bernardo Bembo (the father of Pietro Bembo, and himself a writer of distinction) regarded the patronage of scholars as a duty (King, 1986, p. 54f). The Church offered the greatest security, and so we find such writers as Alberti, Poliziano and Ariosto, who are difficult to see as career clergymen, trying to get benefices (Dionisotti, 1967) Castiglione, the complete courtier, ended his life as a bishop, and his friend Pietro Bembo as a cardinal.

The difficulty of depending on patronage for a living can be illustrated from the career of Aretino, who began life as the son of a shoemaker. He attracted the attention first of the rich and cultivated banker Agostino Chigi, then of cardinal Giulio de'Medici, and later of Federico Gonzaga, marquis of Mantua and of the *condottiere* Giovanni de'Medici. Multiplying patrons increased Aretino's freedom but increased the risk of loss of favour. So Aretino changed his strategy. In 1527 he moved to Venice, where, despite accepting protection from doge Andrea Gritti and gifts from a number of noblemen, he was more or less his own master (Larivaille, 1980). That he was able to do this depended not only on his own remarkable talents for writing and self-advertisement, but also on the rise of the market.

---

[15] V. Calmeta's life of Serafino, prefixed to the 1505 edition of his poems: Serafino dell'Aquila, *Opere*. Venice.

TITIAN, *PIETRO ARETINO*

THE RISE OF THE MARKET

In the long run, the invention of printing led to the decline of the literary patron, and to his or her replacement by the publisher and the anonymous reading public. In this period, however, the new system coexisted with the old and interacted with it. It is possible to find instances of the commercialization of patronage (the dedication of a book in the hope of an instant reward in cash) and even of multiple dedications. Matteo Bandello dedicated each story in his collection to a different individual, and although some of the dedicatees were friends of his, they were in most cases members of noble families such as the Farnese, the Gonzaga and the Sforza, from whom he doubtless expected a return. Printers also looked for patrons. When Aldo Manuzio published his famous octavo edition of Virgil in 1501, he had several copies printed on vellum, as if they were manuscripts, and distributed to important people such as – once again – Isabella d'Este.

With the rise of the market in literature it is possible to find examples of successful printer–businessmen, such as the Giolito and the Giunti families.[16] The printed book, originally viewed as a manuscript 'written' by machine, came to be regarded as a commodity standardized in size and price. The catalogue issued by the Venetian printer Aldo Manuzio in 1498 is the first to give prices, while the Aldine catalogue of 1541 is the first to use the terms 'folio', 'quarto'. etc (Mosher, 1978). The sales of the new commodity were boosted by means of advertisements, in prose or verse, placed by the printer at the end of one book to recommend the reader to go to his shop for another. Ariosto's *Orlando Furioso*, for example, contained the advertisement: 'Whoever wants to buy a *Furioso*, or another work by the same author, let him go to the press of the Bindoni twins, the brothers Benedetto and Agostino' (Venezian, 1921, p. 121). One finds printers, such as Gabriele Giolito, employing professional authors, such as Lodovico Dolce, to write, translate and edit for them. This is how the Venetian 'Grub Street', just off the Grand Canal, came into existence in the middle of the sixteenth century (see above p. 71; cf. Quondam, 1977). At much the same time, the mid-sixteenth century, came the rise of the commercialized newsletter, or *avviso*, which flourished in Rome in particular, and of the 'professional theatre' (the literal translation of the famous term *commedia dell'arte*).

In the visual arts, too, we find the rise of the market system, in

---

[16] On the Gioliti, see Quondam (1977); on the Giunti, see Tenenti (1957).

which customers bought works 'ready-made', sometimes through a middleman. This art market coexisted with the more important and better-known personalized system of patrons and clients. Examples of the sale of uncommissioned works of art go back at least as far as the fourteenth century. The demand for Virgins, Crucifixions or St John the Baptists was sufficiently great for workshops to be able to produce them without a particular customer in mind, although they might be left unfinished in order to accommodate special requirements. Some merchants dealt in works of art as in other commodities: the 'merchant of Prato' Francesco Datini, for instance.[17] Cheap reproductions of famous sculptures were already being manufactured in fourteenth-century Florence.

In the fifteenth century, there are signs that ready-made works were becoming more common. Some merchants, such as the Florentine Bartolommeo Serragli, now specialized in the sale of these commodities. Serragli searched Rome for antique marble statues for the Medici; he ordered fabrics in Florence for Alfonso of Aragon; he employed Donatello, fra Lippo Lippi and Desiderio da Settignano; he dealt in illuminated manuscripts and terracotta madonnas, chess sets and mirrors (Corti and Hartt, 1962). Again, Vespasiano da Bisticci, whose activities as a bookseller have already been discussed, was also a middleman who arranged for illuminators, such as Attavante degli Attavanti, to work for customers they did not know, such as Federigo duke of Urbino and Matthias king of Hungary.

The market in reproductions also increased in importance at this time. Woodcuts of devotional images began to be produced shortly before the invention of printing. In the later fifteenth century, they were joined by woodcuts of topical events, such as the meeting of the pope and the emperor in 1468. After the invention of printing, book illustrations became important. Aldo Manuzio produced famous illustrated editions of Dante, Petrarch, Boccaccio and so on. Around 1470, the Della Robbia workshop in Florence was turning out coloured sculptures in terracotta, such as the miniature replicas of the Madonna of Impruneta, which were cheap and standardized and so presumably uncommissioned. Another fifteenth-century development was the rise of majolica, in other words of the painted, tin-glazed pottery jars and plates produced in Bologna, Urbino, Faenza and elsewhere. They were cheap enough to be bought by modest artisans (Goldthwaite, 1980, p. 402).

In the sixteenth century, the art market became still more important. Isabella d'Este, for example, was prepared to buy paintings and

---

[17] See Origo (1957), p. 41f. A general survey is given in Lerner-Lehmkuhl (1936).

statues second-hand. When Giorgione died in 1510, she wrote to a Venetian merchant that

> we are informed that among the stuff and effects of the painter Zorzo of Castelfranco there exists a picture of a night [*una nocte*], very beautiful and singular; if so it might be, we desire to possess it and we therefore ask you, in company with Lorenzo da Pavia and any other who has judgement and understanding, to see whether it is a really fine thing and if you find it such, to go to work . . . to obtain this picture for me, settling the price and giving me notice of it.

However, the answer was that the two pictures of this kind to be found in Giorgione's studio had been painted on commission, and that the clients were not prepared to let them go. Here, as elsewhere, Isabella was a little in advance of her time.

A year later, in 1511, it was an artist who took the initiative in a sale of uncommissioned work to the Gonzagas. Vittore Carpaccio wrote to Isabella's husband Gianfrancesco II, marquis of Mantua, that he had a watercolour of Jerusalem for which an unknown person, perhaps from the court of Mantua, had made an offer. 'And so it has occurred to me to write this letter to Your Sublime Highness in order to draw attention both to my name and to my work.' The apologetic preamble suggests that selling pictures in this way was not yet quite proper (Chambers, 1970b, no. 63). However, in 1535 Gianfrancesco's son Federico bought 120 Flemish paintings second-hand.

Isabella's agents, whom she employed to arrange commissions as well as to make offers for ready-made paintings, were not full-time specialist art dealers. One of them was a maker of clavichords. In Florence, however, a patrician, Giovanni Battista della Palla, has been described as 'an art dealer in the fullest and truest sense, that is, a systematic purchaser of contemporary as well as antique art works' (Wackernagel, 1938, p. 283). He is most celebrated for his activities on behalf of Francis I, king of France, for whom he bought, among other things, a statue of Hercules by Michelangelo, a statue of Mercury by Bandinelli, a *St Sebastian* by Fra Bartolommeo and a *Raising of Lazarus* by Pontormo. It was in pursuit of further works by the last artist that – according to Vasari in his life of Pontormo – Palla went to the house of a certain Borgherini, but was driven out by Borgherini's wife, who called him 'a vile second-hand dealer, a fourpenny merchant [*vilissimo rigattiere, mercantatuzzo di quattro danari*]'. It was doubtless worth risking a scolding, since there were great profits to be made selling to the king of France. Vasari tells us that 'the merchants' received from Francis four times what they had paid Andrea del Sarto.

There are other cases of the sale of uncommissioned works in sixteenth-century Florence. Ottaviano de'Medici, a keen collector, bought two paintings by Andrea del Sarto which had been made for someone else. There are also references by Vasari to the exhibition of paintings in public, a form of advertising perhaps related to the rise of the market. Bandinelli, for example, painted a *Deposition of Christ* and 'exhibited it [*lo messe a mostra*]' in a goldsmith's shop (cf. Koch, 1967). In Venice too there is evidence of an art market. To return to Bellini's *Nativity*, at one point, when negotiations with Isabella d'Este seemed to be breaking down, the artist informed her that he had found someone who wanted to buy it. The first-known case of a Titian portrait being bought by someone other than the sitter goes back to a purchase by the duke of Urbino in 1536. A certain Zuan or Giovanni Ram, a Catalan resident in Venice, seems to have been active as an art dealer in the early sixteenth century. Paintings were exhibited at the Ascension Week fair in Venice – Lotto and the Bassanos were among the exhibitors – and also at St Anthony's fair at Padua (Francastel, 1960; Koch, 1967).

Woodcuts and engravings, made to be sold to an unknown public, became more common in the sixteenth century. Some artists were beginning to specialize in the new media: Giulio and Domenico Campagnola, for example, who concentrated on landscape, or Marcantonio Raimondi, who produced engraved versions of paintings by Leonardo and Raphael, thus making them much better known. The age of the mechanically reproduced work of art, lamented by critics such as Walter Benjamin (1936), goes back further than is generally realized (cf. Hind, 1930).

In the middle of the sixteenth century, the market system was still very far from having equalled, let alone displaced, the personalized patronage system. For examples of the dominance of the new system, we have to wait till the seventeenth century, to the commercial opera houses of Venice and the art market of the Dutch Republic.

It is impossible to give a direct answer to the question whether the arts flourished in Renaissance Italy because of the patrons, as Filarete suggests in the epigraph to this chapter, or in spite of them, as is implied by Michelangelo. What can be discussed, however, is the somewhat complicated relation between patronage and the unequal distribution of artistic achievement among different parts of Italy.

In the previous chapter, it was suggested that art flourished in Florence and Venice in particular because these cities produced many of their own artists. This is not the whole story. There were also cities which attracted artists and writers from elsewhere. Rome is the obvious example to take, and the patronage of the popes (notably Nicholas V and Leo X) and of the cardinals is the obvious explanation.[18] Urbino, Mantua and Ferrara are other famous examples of cities with few important native artists, which nevertheless became important cultural centres. In all three cases the stimulus came from the patron, from the ruler or his wife. In Urbino, it was Federico da Montefeltre who made the arts important by attracting Luciano Laurana from Dalmatia, Piero della Francesca from Borgo San Sepolcro, Justus from Ghent, Francesco di Giorgio from Siena. In Mantua, Isabella d'Este and her husband gave commissions, as we have seen, to Bellini, Carpaccio, Giorgione, Leonardo, Mantegna, Perugino, Titian and other non-Mantuans. Their only Mantuan painter was a minor master, Lorenzo Leombruno.

At these small courts, the patron seems to be calling art into existence where there was none before. However, two qualifications to this thesis need to be borne in mind. The first is that such patronage was parasitic on the art of major centres such as Florence and Venice in the sense that it would have been impossible without them. The second qualification is that the achievements of princely patrons rarely outlived them. Alfonso of Aragon, for example, was an effective patron in many fields. He took five humanists into his permanent service (Panormita, Fazio, Valla and the Decembrio brothers). He built up a chapel of 22 singers and paid his organist the unusually large sum of 120 ducats a year. He invited the painter Pisanello to his court in Naples and commissioned works from major sculptors such as Mino da Fiesole and Francesco Laurana. He bought Flemish tapestries and Venetian glass. When the king died, all this activity stopped. The artists and writers came from outside his kingdom and the Neapolitan nobles did not follow Alfonso's example and take an interest in patronage.

In contrast to Alfonso, Lorenzo de'Medici had everything in his favour as a patron. Living in Florence, he had instant access to major artists and did not to have to go to the trouble of attracting them from a distance. He was not a lone patron, but one of many, great and small. The importance of his patronage has been exaggerated in the past (Chastel, 1961; cf. Elam, 1978; Alsop, 1982, ch. 12). The issue here, however, is not its extent but its facility. Patronage was structured; easier in some parts of Italy, more difficult in others.

As for the rise of the market, it is likely to have given artists and

---

[18] Leo's patronage, often exaggerated, was cut down to size by Gnoli (1938).

writers more freedom at the price of more insecurity. It involved the rise of reproduction and even mass production, Yet it may well have encouraged the increasing differentiation of subject matter and individualism of style noted in the first chapter: the exploitation of the artist's unique qualities in order to catch the eye of a purchaser.

5

---ᔕᘜᘉᔕ---

THE USES OF WORKS OF ART

Chi volessi per diletto
Qualche gentil figuretta,
Per tenerla sopra letto
O in su qualche basetta?
Ogni camera s'asetta
Ben con le nostre figure.[1]

THE idea of a 'work of art' is a modern one, although art galleries and museums encourage us to project it into the past. Even the idea of 'literature' is a modern one. This chapter, however, is concerned with the different uses, for contemporary owners, viewers or listeners, of paintings, statues, poems, plays and so on.[2] They did not regard these objects in the same ways as we do. For one thing, paintings might be regarded as expendable. A Florentine patrician, Filippo Strozzi the younger, asked in his will of 1537 for a monument in the family chapel in Santa Maria Novella, which contained a fresco by Filippino Lippi. 'Do not worry about the painting which is there now, which it is necessary to destroy', Strozzi ordered, 'since of its nature it is not very durable [di sua natura non è molto durabile].'[3] If we want to understand what the art of the period meant to contemporaries, we have to look first at its uses.

RELIGION AND MAGIC

The most obvious use of paintings and statues in Renaissance Italy was religious. In a secular culture like ours, we may well have to remind ourselves that what we see as a 'work of art' was viewed by

---

[1] 'Who wants some elegant statuette for their delight? You can put it above your bed or on a stand. Our figures make any room look well.' Carnival song of the sculptors of Florence in Singleton (1936).

[2] In the first edition of this book the title of the chapter was 'functions'. However, conscious uses (including non-utilitarian ones), rather than unconscious functions was and is its real subject. Cf. the distinction between 'manifest' and 'latent' functions in Merton (1957), pp. 19–84.

[3] Quoted, but translated differently, in Goldthwaite (1968), p. 102n.

contemporaries primarily as a sacred image. The idea of a 'religious' use is not very precise, so it is probably helpful to distinguish magical, devotional and didactic functions, although these divisions blur into one another, while 'magic' does not have quite the same meaning for us as it did for a sixteenth-century theologian. It is more precise and so more useful to refer to the thaumaturgic and other miraculous powers attributed to particular images, as in the case of certain famous Byzantine icons. Some gonfalons or processional banners, for example those painted by Benedetto Bonfigli in Perugia, seem to have been considered a defence against plague. The Madonna is shown protecting her people with her mantle against the arrows of the plague, and the inscription on one gonfalon begs her 'to ask and help thy son to take the fury away' (Bombe, 1909). The popularity in the fifteenth and sixteenth centuries of images of St Sebastian, who was also associated with defence against plague (below p. 000), suggests that the thaumaturgic function was still an important one. When he was working in Italy in the 1420s and 1430s, the Netherlander Guillaume Dufay wrote two motets to St Sebastian as a defence against plague. Music was generally believed to have therapeutic power; stories were current about cures effected by playing to the patient.

A celebrated Italian example of another kind of miraculous power is the image of the Virgin Mary in the church of Impruneta, near Florence, which was carried in procession to produce rain in times of drought or to stop the rain when there was too much, as well as to solve the political problems of the Florentines. For example, the Florentine apothecary Luca Landucci records in his journal that in 1483 the image was brought to Florence 'for the sake of obtaining fine weather, as it had rained for more than a month. And it immediately became fine' (Casotti, 1714; Landucci, 1927; Trexler, 1972a).

Some Renaissance paintings appear to belong to a magical system outside the Christian framework. The frescos by Francesco del Cossa in the Palazzo Schifanoia at Ferrara are concerned with astrological themes, as Aby Warburg (1932, pp. 249–69; 1966, pp. 242–72) pointed out, and they may well have been painted to ensure the good fortune of the duke.[4] It has also been argued (following a suggestion of Warburg's); that Botticelli's famous *Primavera* may have been a talisman, in other words an image made in order to draw down favourable 'influences' from the planet Venus (Yates, 1964, p. 76f). We know that the philosopher Ficino made use of such images, just as

---

[4] On magic and astrology, see pp. 179ff below.

he played 'martial' music to attract influences from Mars: a Renaissance *Planets Suite* (Walker, 1958). When Leonardo (as Vasari tells us) painted the thousand-eyed Argus guarding the treasury of the duke of Milan, it is difficult to tell whether he simply intended to make an appropriate classical allusion or whether he was also attempting a piece of protective magic. It is similarly difficult to tell how serious Vasari is being when he works a variant of the Byzantine icon legends into his life of Raphael. He tells us that a painting of Raphael's was on the way to Palermo when a storm arose and the ship was wrecked. The painting, however, 'remained unharmed . . . because even the fury of the winds and the waves of the sea had respect for the beauty of such a work'. In a similar way, we need at least to entertain the possibility that the images of traitors and rebels painted on the walls of public buildings in Florence and elsewhere were a form of magical destruction of fugitives who were beyond the reach of conventional punishment; the equivalent of piercing wax images of one's enemies.

Other images were made and bought in order to stimulate devotion. The term 'devotional pictures' (*quadri di devotione*) was current in this period, when images and religious fervour seem to have been more closely associated than usual, whether the images were crucifixes (recommended by leading preachers such as Bernardino of Siena and Savonarola) or the new medium of the woodcut, or a new type of religious painting, small and intimate, suitable for a private house, not so much an icon as a narrative, which would act as a stimulus to meditation on the Bible or the lives of the saints (Wackernagel, 1938, p. 172f; Ringbom, 1965; Baxandall, 1972, 45f).

A vivid illustration of the devotional uses of the image comes from Rome, from the fraternity of St John Beheaded (*San Giovanni Decollato*), which comforted condemned criminals in their last moments by means of *tavolette*, in other words small pictures of the martyrdom of saints which were employed, in the words of their recent historian, 'as a kind of visual narcotic to numb the fear and pain of the condemned criminal during his terrible journey to the scaffold' (Edgerton, 1985, p. 172).

The increasing importance of devotional images seems to have been linked to the increasing lay initiatives in religious matters characteristic of the fourteenth and fifteenth centuries, from the foundation of religious fraternities to the singing of hymns or the reading of pious books at home. Surviving inventories of the houses of the wealthy reveal images of Our Lady in almost every room. In the castle of the Uzzano family, Florentine patricians, there were two paintings of the 'sudary' (Christ's face imprinted on Veronica's towel), and immediately before one of them a predella is listed, as if people commonly knelt before the sacred image (Bombe, 1928).

As the fifteenth-century friar Giovanni Dominici put it, parents should keep sacred images in the house because of their moral effect on the children. The infant Jesus with St John would be good for boys, and also pictures of the Massacre of the Innocents, 'in order to make them afraid of arms and armed men'. Girls, on the other hand, should fix their gaze on Saints Agnes, Cecilia, Elizabeth, Catherine, and Ursula (with her legendary 11,000 virgins) to give them 'a love of virginity, a desire for Christ, a hatred for sins, a contempt for vanities'.[5] In a similar way, Florentine girls, whether young nuns or young brides, would be given images, or more exactly dolls, of the Christ-child to encourage identification with his mother (Klapisch-Zuber, 1985, ch. 14).

An interesting example of the devotional use of certain images, and a material sign of spectator response, is what one might call pious vandalism, the defacing of the painted devils in a painting by Uccello, for instance, or the scratching out of the eyes of the executioner of St James in a fresco by Mantegna (Edgerton, 1985, p. 91). The equivalent, one might say, of the audience hissing the villain in a melodrama. In fact, the religious plays of the period had similar aims. These *rappresentazioni sacre*, as they were called, which were written and acted in the fourteenth, fifteenth and sixteenth centuries, were rather like the miracle and mystery plays of late medieval England (a reminder of the difficulty of distinguishing between 'Renaissance' and 'Middle Ages', particularly in the case of popular culture). They usually end with angels exhorting the audience to take to heart what they have just seen. At the end of a play about Abraham and Isaac, for example, the angel points out the importance of 'holy obedience' (*santa ubidienzia*) (D'Ancona, 1872).

Ex votos are a kind of devotional image which appear in Italy during the fifteenth century, recording a vow made to a saint in a time of danger, whether illness or accident. Those which have survived, in the sanctuary of the Madonna of the Mountain at Cesena, for example, which contains 246 examples earlier than 1600, are probably only a tiny proportion of those that once existed (Novelli and Massaccesi, 1961). It may well have been this kind of occasion that most often persuaded ordinary people to commission paintings. The artistic level of the majority of *ex votos* is not high, but the category does include a few well-known Renaissance paintings, notably Mantegna's

---

[5] Dominici, *Regola del governo di cura familiare*, p. 131f.

Madonna della Vittoria, commissioned by Gianfrancesco II, marquis of Mantua, after the battle of Fornovo, in which he had, at least in his own eyes, defeated the French army. It was the Jews of Mantua who actually paid for the painting, though not out of choice. Again, Carpaccio's *Martyrdom of 10,000 Christians* and Titian's *St Mark Enthroned* were both commissioned to fulfil vows in time of plague, while Raphael's *Madonna of Foligno* was painted for the historian Sigismondo de'Conti, apparently to express his gratitude for his escape when a meteor fell on his house.

Another use of religious paintings was didactic. As pope Gregory the Great had already pointed out in the sixth century, 'Paintings are placed in churches so that the illiterate can read on the walls what they cannot read in books.'[6] A good deal of Christian doctrine was illustrated in Italian church frescos of the fourteenth centuries: the life of Christ, the relation between the Old and New Testaments, the Last Judgement and its consequences and so on. The religious plays of the period consider many of the same themes, so that each medium reinforced the message of the others and made it more intelligible.[7]

A special case of the didactic is the presentation of controversial topics from a one-sided point of view, in other words, propaganda. Like rhetoric, painting was a means of persuasion. Paintings commissioned by Renaissance popes, for example, present arguments for the primacy of popes over general councils of the Church, sometimes by drawing historical parallels. For pope Innocent VIII, for example, Botticelli painted the *Punishment of Korah*, illustrating a scene from the Old Testament in which the earth opened and swallowed up Korah and his men after they had dared to challenge Moses and Aaron. An earlier fifteenth-century pope, Eugenius IV, had made reference to Korah when condemning the Council of Basel (Ettlinger, 1965; cf. Numbers, 16, 1– 34). In a similar manner, Raphael painted for pope Julius II, who was in conflict with the Bentivoglio family of Bologna, the story of Heliodorus, who tried to plunder the Temple of Jerusalem but was expelled by angels (Jones and Penny, 1983, ch. 5; cf. 2 Maccabees, 3, 7–40). Again, after the Reformation, paintings in Catholic churches in Italy and elsewhere tended to illustrate points of doctrine which the Protestants had challenged (Mâle, 1951).

Following the Reformation, the Catholic Church became much more concerned to control literature and, to a lesser degree, painting. An Index of Prohibited Books was drawn up (and made official at the Council of Trent in the 1560s), and Boccaccio's *Decameron*, among

---

[6] This sentence was much quoted in the Renaissance, for example by fra Michele da Carcano (in Baxandall, 1972, p. 41), and by Dolce, *Aretino* (1557), p. 112.

[7] It does not seem useful to argue like Kernodle (1944), which came first, art or theatre.

SANDRO BOTTICELLI, *THE PUNISHMENT OF KORAH, DATHAN AND ABIRON*
Sistine Chapel, Vatican. Photograph from The Mansell Collection.

other works of Italian literature, was first banned and then severely expurgated.[8] Michelangelo's *Last Judgement* was discussed at the Council of Trent, which ordered the naked bodies to be covered by figleaves (Blunt, 1940, ch. 9; De Maio, 1978). An Index of Prohibited Images was considered, and Veronese was on one occasion summoned before the Inquisition of Venice to explain why he had included in a painting of the *Last Supper* what the inquisitors called 'buffoons, drunkards, Germans, dwarfs and similar vulgarities' (Schaffran, 1960).

POLITICS

The visual defence of the Papacy has introduced the subject of political propaganda, at least in the vague sense of images and texts glorifying or justifying a particular regime, if not in the more precise sense of recommending a particular policy. There are so many examples of glorification from this period that it is difficult to know where to begin, whether to look at republics or principalities, at large-scale works such as frescos or small-scale ones such as medals. Like the coins of ancient Rome, the medals of Renaissance Italy often carried political messages. Alfonso of Aragon, for example, had his portrait medal by Pisanello (1449) inscribed 'Victorious and a Peacemaker [*Triumphator et Pacificus*]' (Hill, 1930, p. 12 and plate 9). On his triumphal arch there was a similar inscription, 'Pious, Merciful, Unvanquished [*Pius, Clemens, Invictus*]'. The king, who had recently won Naples by force of arms, seems to be telling his new subjects that if they submit they will come to no harm, but that in a conflict he is bound to win. In Florence, at the end of the regime of the elder Cosimo de'Medici, a medal was struck showing Florence, personified in the usual manner as a young woman, with the inscription 'Peace and Public Liberty [*Pax Libertasque Publica*]' (Hill, 1930, p. 236). Under Lorenzo the Magnificent, medals were struck to commemorate particular events, such as the defeat of the Pazzi conspiracy or Lorenzo's successful return from Naples in 1480. The sculptor Gian Cristoforo Romano commemorated the peace arranged between Ferdinand of Aragon and Louis XII with a medal giving the credit to pope Julius II and describing him as 'the restorer of justice peace and faith [*Iustitiae pacis fideique recuperator*]' (Hill, 1930, p. 56). Mechanically reproducible as they were, and relatively cheap,

---

[8] On Boccaccio, see Sorrentino (1935); on literary censorship in general, see Guidi in Rochon (1982).

School of Piero della Francesca, *Portrait of Alfonso of Aragon*
Musée Jacquemart-André, Paris. Photographie Bulloz.

medals were a good medium for spreading political messages and giving a regime a good image.

Statues displayed in public were another way of glorifying warriors, princes and republics. Donatello's great equestrian statue at Padua honours a *condottiere* in Venetian service, Erasmo da Narni, nicknamed 'Gattamelata', who died in 1443, and it was commissioned by the state. (By contrast, the monument to Bartolommeo Colleoni in Venice was effectively paid for by the *condottiere* himself.) A number of Florentine statues had a political meaning which is no longer immediately apparent. In their wars with greater powers (notably Milan), the Florentines came to identify with David defeating Goliath, with Judith cutting off the head of the Assyrian captain Holofernes, or with St George (leaving Milan the role of the dragon). Donatello's memorable renderings of all three figures are thus republican statements. When the Florentine Republic was restored in 1494, political symbols of this kind reappeared, notably Michelangelo's great *David*, which refers back to Donatello's *David* and so by extension to the dangers which the Republic had successfully survived in the early fifteenth century. The statue thus 'demands a knowledge of contemporary political events before one can understand it as a work of art' (Seymour, 1967, p. 56; cf. Hartt, 1964).

Paintings, too, carried political meanings. In Venice, the Republic was glorified by the commissioning and display of official portraits of its doges, and of scenes of Venetian victories in the Hall of the Great Council in the Doge's Palace. In Florence, when the Republic was restored in 1494, a Great Council was set up on the Venetian model, together with a hall in the Palazzo della Signoria as a meeting-place, complete with victory paintings on the walls, the battles of Anghiari and Cascina commissioned from Leonardo and Michelangelo. When the Medici returned in 1513, the paintings were destroyed. This destruction of works by major artists suggests that the political uses of art were taken extremely seriously by contemporaries (Wilde, 1944); so does the employment of Vasari, Bronzino and other painters by Cosimo de'Medici, grand duke of Tuscany, to redecorate the Palazzo Vecchio with frescos of the achievements of the regime and to paint official portraits of the grand-ducal family (Pope-Hennessy, 1966, pp. 180–5; Levey, 1971; Cox-Rearick, 1984). What is more difficult to decide, at this distance in time, is whether certain paintings carried more precise messages; whether, for example, they recommended certain policies. One example which has attracted considerable attention is Masaccio's great fresco of *The Tribute Money* in the Brancacci Chapel in Santa Maria del Carmine in Florence. The subject is an unusual one; it carries a clear moral,

DONATELLO, *JUDITH AND HOLOFERNES*
Piazza della Signoria, Florence. Photograph from The Mansell Collection.

BENEVENUTO CELLINI, *COSIMO I DE MEDICI*
Museo Nazionale, Florence. Photograph from The Mansell Collection.

MASACCIO, *THE TRIBUTE MONEY* (DETAIL).
Carmine Church, Florence. Photograph from The Mansell Collection.

'Render unto Caesar', and it was painted at a time, 1425, when proposals to introduce a new tax, the famous *catasto*, were under discussion. Is it a pictorial defence of the tax? Or is its message one about papal primacy, like Botticelli's *Punishment of Korah*? (Meiss, 1963; Molho, 1977).

In other cases, the political reference of a painting is clear, but its political purpose is rather more doubtful: for example, the images of traitors and rebels. In 1440, for instance, Andrea del Castagno is said to have painted images of rebels hung by their feet on the façade of the gaol in Florence. As a result he was nicknamed 'Andrew the Rope' (*Andrea degli impiccati*). In 1478, it was Botticelli's turn to paint the images of the Pazzi conspirators in the same place. In 1529–30, during the siege of Florence, it was Andrea del Sarto who painted on the same building the images of captains who had fled. One wonders why this was done. Was it, as suggested earlier, magical destruction? Or were the paintings made primarily to give information, like a 'wanted' poster? This would at least be a plausible explanation of the public display in Milan of the images of bankrupts. The most likely explanation of these paintings, however, given the importance of honour and shame in the value system of this society (below p. 194), is that they were executed to dishonour the victims and their families, to destroy them socially, to make them infamous.[9] Such an explanation is made more plausible by the existence of a literary equivalent. In Florence, the public herald had the duty of writing what were called *cartelli d'infamia*, in other words verses insulting the enemies of the Republic.

It is less necessary to dilate upon literature here, since its potential for political persuasion is obvious enough. Suffice it to say that the epics in Latin and Italian discussed in the last chapter were poems in praise of rulers through their ancestors, real and imaginary, and justifications of their rule, no less political than their model, Virgil's *Aeneid*, which was commissioned to give Augustus a good public image and – according to some classical scholars – even to defend certain of his policies. Historical works, the prose equivalents of epic according to Renaissance literary theory, were often used for similar purposes; that was why governments pensioned humanist historians such as Lorenzo Valla in Naples, Marcantonio Sabellico in Venice, or Benedetto Varchi in the Florence of the grand duke Cosimo de'Medici. They were supposed to be new Livys, just as the states they celebrated were new Romes. Some poems carried more precise and more topical messages, for example the 'laments' put into the mouths

---

[9] Shame is emphasized in both the recent monographs on the subject, Ortalli (1979) and Edgerton (1985), esp. p. 76.

of rulers at their fall (such as Cesare Borgia, who lost everything on
the death of his father, pope Alexander VI, or Giovanni Bentivoglio,
who was driven from Bologna by Julius II), or cities at times of crisis
(Venice in 1509, following a major defeat at Agnadello, or Rome in
1527, after it was sacked by imperial troops (Medin and Frati, 1890).
Luigi Pulci's famous epic the *Morgante* (1478) seems to be, among
other things, a plea for a crusade against the Turks, an aim which the
poet is known to have supported. Ariosto makes a similar point in his

Orlando Furioso (1516), urging Frenchmen and Spaniards to fight Muslims rather than their fellow Christians (in other words, they should desist from their wars in Italy).

The mobilization of the arts in an attempt to persuade was most elaborate in the cases where least is now left for posterity to view and judge, in other words in court and civic festivals, which often carried fairly precise and extremely topical political messages as well as contributing to the general task of celebrating or legitimating a particular regime. In the case of Venice, with its elaborate ducal processions and its annual Marriage of the Sea, a recent historian speaks, not without reason, of 'government by ritual', stressing the image of a harmonious hierarchical society projected by these quasi-dramatic forms (Muir, 1981, p. 185f). As for topical references, a good example comes from 1511, during the famous war of the League of Cambrai, in which the very existence of Venice (or at least of her empire) was at stake. The Scuola di San Rocco (above p. 90) exhibited an allegorical *tableau vivant,* including Venice (personified as a woman) and the king of France (the principal enemy of the Republic), flanked by the pope with a placard asking why France had denied the true faith (Muir, 1981, p. 238f). In Florence, the political uses of festivals are most obvious in the period following the Medici restoration of 1513. A notable example is that of the state entry into Florence of the Medici pope, Leo X, in 1515, through an elaborate sequence of triumphal arches in which the theme of the return of the golden age was emphasized (Shearman, 1975). In this field too the second Cosimo, that is, the grand duke of Tuscany, showed his awareness of the political value of the arts. Not only was his wedding to Eleonora of Toledo in 1539 the occasion for an elaborate display, but the annual celebrations marking Carnival and the feast of St John the Baptist (patron saint of Florence) were more or less taken over by Cosimo and his men and used with what a recent writer calls – with particular appropriateness in this context – a 'conscious Machiavellianism' (Plaisance, 1975).

One has the impression – it is difficult to be more precise – that the political uses of the media were greater and also more self-conscious in the sixteenth century than they had been in the fifteenth. Faced with the wider diffusion of unorthodox ideas made possible by the invention of printing, governments, like the Church, turned to censorship. When Guicciardini's great *History of Italy* was published, posthumously, in 1561, a number of anticlerical remarks had been expurgated. It was, however, not the Church but the grand duke of Tuscany who was responsible for the expurgations, so as to preserve good relations between the Grand Duchy and the Papacy. On the positive side, Cosimo de'Medici showed his awareness of the political uses of culture by founding first the Florentine Academy and then the Academy of Design. In other words, he tried to turn Tuscan 'cultural capital' (the primacy of its language, its literature, its art) into political capital for his regime (Plaisance, 1973; Bertelli, 1976).

The political messages discussed so far are those delivered on behalf of those in power. However, opponents of the various regimes were far from silent. They could, for example, make their views known by a kind of secular iconoclasm. After the defeat of the Venetian forces at Agnadello in 1509 the revolt of the subject cities, such as Bergamo and Cremona, was marked by the defacing of the sculpted lion of St Mark, placed in each city as a sign of Venetian domination. On the death of pope Julius II, his statue in Bologna, another sign of domination, also met its end. *Graffiti* already had their place in the politics of Italian city- states (and were sometimes recorded in chronicles or private letters). A literary development from these *graffiti* were the so-called 'pasquinades' (*pasquinate*), verses satirizing the popes and cardinals which came from the later fifteenth century onwards to be attached to the pedestal of a fragment of a classical statue. The verses, attributed to the statue, were written on occasion by distinguished writers, such as Pietro Aretino, whose pungent verses on the conclave following the death of Leo X did much to make his reputation (Larivaille, 1980, p. 47f).

There remain some uses of the arts which do not fit our categories of 'religion' and 'politics', at least in the strict sense. One could perhaps widen the latter category to include the use of portraits of marriageable daughters in negotiations between princes. Even the portraits of private persons can be seen as a kind of propaganda, with the artist collaborating with the sitter to present a favourable image of an individual, or of his or her family, to impress rival families, or perhaps posterity.[10] It is worth pausing to think how much of the material culture of Renaissance Italy was produced for the use or the glory not so much of individuals as of families, especially noble families, or families with noble pretensions. The most important and expensive item was of course the house or 'palace' as the Italians like to call it, a symbol of the family as well as a shelter for its members, designed to impress outsiders rather than to provide the inhabitants with comfortable surroundings. Comfort is a more recent ideal, dating from the eighteenth century or thereabouts. Older ideals were

---

[10] I argue this case in 'The presentation of self in the Renaissance portrait', forthcoming in my *Historical Anthropology of Early Modern Italy* (Cambridge, 1987).

modesty and defence. The fifteenth, sixteenth and seventeenth centuries, on the other hand, were the heyday in Italy of what is often called 'conspicious consumption', in which nobles built to sustain the honour of the house and to make their rivals envious.[11] The house (especially its façade), and its contents formed part of a family's 'front', the setting and the stage props for the long-playing drama in which their status was displayed.[12]

Other material objects were associated with important and highly ritualized moments of family history, notably births, marriages and deaths. The *desca di parto* or 'birth tray', on which refreshments were brought to the new mother, was often painted with appropriate themes such as the triumph of love. The cassone, a large chest with paintings on the outside – and sometimes inside the lid as well – was associated with marriage, for it contained the bride's trousseau.[13] Pictures were frequently given as wedding presents, and newly-weds not infrequently had their portraits painted, the bride wearing the new clothes given her by the husband's family and sometimes bearing their badge, thus marking her as theirs (Klapisch-Zuber, 1985, p. 225f). The open allusions to sexuality permitted at weddings seem to have affected the conventions of nuptial art, which includes such Renaissance masterpieces as Mantegna's *Camera degli Sposi* at Mantua, Raphael's *Galatea*, and Sodoma's *Marriage of Alexander and Roxanne*, the last two painted for the Sienese banker Agostino Chigi (Barolsky, 1978, pp. 28f, 89f, 93f). Poetry and plays might also be associated with the happy occasion; Poliziano wrote his pastoral drama *Orfeo* for a double betrothal at the court of Mantua. To commemorate deaths in the family, there were funeral monuments, some of them extremely grand affairs. Since our period includes Michelangelo's Medici Chapel and his tomb for pope Julius II, always concerned for the glory of the della Rovere family, no more need be said on that account. If states employed artists and writers to defame enemies, so, on occasion, did noble families. The painter Francesco Benaglio of Verona was once commissioned to go at night and paint obscene pictures by torchlight on the walls of the palace of a nobleman (the enemy of his client), presumably to put him to public shame (Simeoni, 1903).

---

[11] Goldthwaite (1987), p. 77f; cf. my 'Conspicuous consumption in early modern Italy', forthcoming in the volume cited in note 10.

[12] The analysis of 'front' offered by Goffman (1956) p. 22f seems particularly appropriate to the behaviour of nobles in Italy in the sixteenth and seventeenth centuries.

[13] See Callmann's (1974) discussion of a famous Florentine *cassone* workshop.

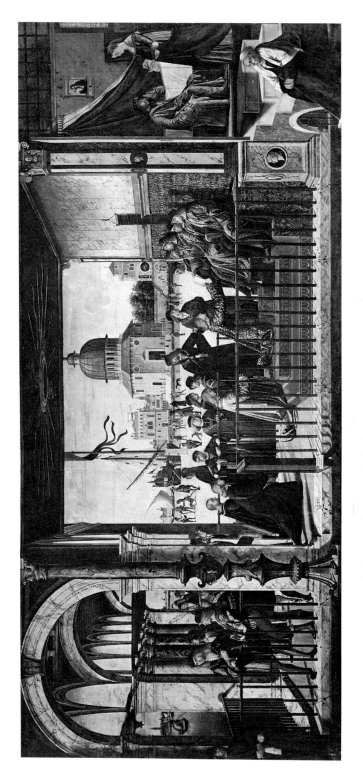

VITTORE CARPACCIO, *THE RECEPTION OF THE ENGLISH AMBASSADORS AND ST URSULA TALKING TO HER FATHER*
Accademia di Belle Arti, Venice. Photograph from The Mansell Collection.

ART FOR PLEASURE

We arrive at last at what now seems the natural 'use' of the arts: to give pleasure. The playful side of the arts must not be forgotten, although it has not often been studied.[14] The increasing importance of this function is one of the most significant changes in the period. By the mid-sixteenth century, the writer Lodovico Dolce went so far as to suggest that the purpose of painting was 'chiefly to give pleasure [*principalmente per dilettare*]'. The carnival song of the sculptors of Florence – quoted in the epigraph to this chapter – catches the new mood. It should be noticed, however, that as the song makes clear, pleasure (*diletto*) is taken in the statue as a contribution to interior decoration. We are still a long way from modern ideas of 'art for art's sake'. Even the Gonzagas, who cared a good deal about painting, seem to have thought of it primarily in this way. Isabella asked Giovanni Bellini for a picture 'to decorate a study of ours [*per ornamento d'uno nostro studio*]', while her son Federico wrote to Titian in 1537 telling him that the new rooms in the castle were finished, all that was lacking were the pictures 'made for these rooms [*fatte per tali lochi*]'. Sabba di Castiglione, a knight of the Order of Rhodes, gave some advice, which has become notorious, for the decoration of a nobleman's house with classical statues or, if these are not available, with works by Donatello or Michelangelo.[15]

In architecture, we see the increasing importance of the pleasure house, the country villa, where, as the greatest designer of such houses, Palladio, put it, a man 'tired of the bustle of cities, will restore and console himself'.[16] In literature too there was increasing emphasis (especially in prefaces) on pleasure – the author's, and more particularly the reader's – a shift which may well be related to the gradual commercialization of literature and art. But what gave pleasure to spectators, readers or listeners in the Renaissance? An attempt to answer this question will be made in the next chapter.

---

[14] Barolsky (1978) is one of the rare examples.
[15] Sabba di Castiglione, *Ricordi* (1549), no. 109; trans. in Klein and Zerner (1966), p. 23.
[16] Palladio, *I Quattro Libri dell'Architettura* (1570), book 2, ch. 12.

6

TASTE

Everyone has a certain natural taste . . . for beauty and ugliness [*un certo gusto . . . del bello e del brutto*].
Dolce, *Aretino* (1557) p. 102

NEITHER artists nor patrons were completely free to make aesthetic choices. Their liberty was limited, whether they realized this or not, by the need to take into account the standards of taste of their period. These standards need to be described in order that we may look at works of art and literature – if only momentarily – with the eyes of contemporaries.[1] To reconstruct the taste of the time, historians can use two main kinds of literary source. A number of treatises on art and beauty were produced in this period by famous humanists such as Alberti and Bembo, and also by a number of lesser figures. These treatises, which have often been studied, have the advantage of explicitness, but they are often rather abstract. They need to be supplemented by the analysis of the standards implied by a more practical criticism, the judgements on individual works of art, literature and so on to be found in contracts, in private letters, in poems, in biographies, in stories. It is interesting to find, for example, that whereas the term 'sublime' only became important in art theory in the eighteenth century, it was used in this period by the poet Veronica Gambara, in a letter to Beatrice d'Este (sister of Isabella), praising Correggio's painting of St Mary Magdalen for expressing *il sublime*. Another precious piece of evidence is the memorandum to Ludovico Sforza, cited in the previous chapter, in which the agent tries to find works to distinguish the styles of four leading painters to help the duke make a choice between them, contrasting the 'virile air' of Botticelli, the 'sweeter air' of Filippino Lippi, the 'angelic air' of Perugino and the 'good air' of Ghirlandaio.[2]

The sources are, of course, written in Latin as well as Italian. The Latin sources will not be ignored, but the emphasis here will fall on

---

[1] On 'the period eye', cf. Baxandall (1972), ch. 2.
[2] See Chambers (1970b), no. 95. On this letter and the concept of *aria*, see Baxandall (1972), pp. 26, 109f.

143

Italian texts because they are closer to the ordinary speech and thought of the time.

THE VISUAL ARTS

It would not be difficult to draw up a list of some 50 terms which came regularly to the lips and pens of Italians of the period when they were appraising paintings, sculptures and buildings. Some are general, almost vacuous, terms such as 'beauty' (*bellezza, pulchritudine*), but others are more precise and so more revealing. It may be useful to distinguish five clusters of terms centred around the concepts of nature, order, richness, expressiveness and skill.

Naturalism v Idealism

The 'return to nature', a favourite formula of modern historians of the Renaissance, does in fact correspond to a commonplace of the period. For example, the humanist Bartolommeo Fazio praised Jan van Eyck for a portrait 'which you would judge to lack only a voice' and for 'a ray of the sun which you would take to be real sunlight', while he described Donatello's achievement as 'to produce lively expressions [*vivos vultus ducere*]' (Baxandall, 1964). Another humanist, Cristoforo Landino, described Donatello's statues as having 'great vivacity [*grande vivacità*]', so that the figures all seemed to be in movement (Morisani, 1953). Another sought-after quality in painting was three-dimensionality or 'relief' (*rilievo*). The Florentine writer Giambattista Gelli, for example, made fun of Byzantine art as 'without any relief', so that the figures looked not like men but like clothes spread out on a wall or 'flayed skins'.[3] The great preacher Girolamo Savonarola seems to have been articulating the assumptions of his audience when he remarked that 'The closer they imitate nature, the more pleasure they give. And so people who praise any pictures say: look, these animals seem as if they were alive, and these flowers seem natural ones.'[4]

A similar concern with naturalism is to be found in Vasari's *Lives* (Blunt, 1940, ch. 8). The horses painted in a stable by Bramantino, for example, were so lifelike that a horse mistook the image for reality and kicked it. The importance here of Vasari's variation on the well-known Greek stories about illusionistic grapes and curtains is that the illusionism is described as a triumph. Again, what Vasari

---

[3] Gelli, 'Vite d'artisti', p. 37.
[4] Savonarola, *Prediche e Scritti*, pp. 2, 47.

finds remarkable in the *Mona Lisa* is that the lady's mouth 'appeared to be living flesh rather than paint', while her eyebrows 'were completely natural, growing thickly in one place and lightly in another and following the pores of the skin'. Similarly, what impresses him in Leonardo's *Last Supper* is that 'The texture of the tablecloth is imitated so skilfully that linen itself cannot look more real [*non mostra il vero meglio*].' His praise of these particular paintings for naturalism rather than other qualities may make Vasari seem somewhat naïf today, so it may be worth emphasizing that he was articulating a common assumption of the period, which was in fact shared by Leonardo, who once declared that the closer a painting was to the object it was imitating, the better.

The assumption was not shared by everyone, however. Some writers who now appear to share it in fact did not, the phrase 'to imitate nature' being more ambiguous than it may seem. There were two different ideas of nature in the Renaissance, the physical world (*natura naturata*, as philosophers called it) and the creative force (*natura naturans*). Naturalism in the modern sense involves the imitation of the first nature, but what some Renaissance writers advocate is the imitation of the second. As Alberti put it in his treatise on painting, nature rarely achieves perfection, and artists should aim at beauty, as nature does, rather than at 'realism' [*similitudine*]. Thus Alberti is saying in effect that artists should not paint what they see, but he is using the language of imitation to say so. Michelangelo expressed himself still more strongly. His objection to Flemish painting was that it was done merely 'to deceive the external eye'. Again, when he was designing the tombs of Lorenzo and Giuliano de'Medici, he did not represent them as 'nature had sculpted and created them [*come la natura gli avea effigiati e composti*]', but produced his own idealized versions.[5]

Order v Grace

A second cluster of evaluative terms refers to order or harmony. When Alberti tells the architect to imitate nature the creator, he explains that its aim is 'a certain rational harmony [*concinnitas*] of all the parts making up a whole so that nothing can be added or subtracted or changed for the better'.[6] Similarly, Ghiberti wrote that 'only proportion makes beauty [*la proportionalità solamente fa pulchritudine*]'. To say that they 'have proportion' is a favourite term

---

[5] On Michelangelo's views of art, see Clements (1963) and Summers (1981); ch. 20 discusses Michelangelo's idea of imitation.

[6] Alberti, *De re aedificatoria*, book 6, ch. 2.

of praise for works of art. Another term in this cluster is 'order' (*ordine*) (Summers, 1981, p. 197f). Another is 'symmetry', used not only of buildings, as might have been expected, but of paintings as well; Landino declared that symmetry had been revived by the thirteenth-century painter Cimabue. 'Measure' (*misura*) is another common term; yet another is 'rule' (*regola*). Analogies were commonly drawn between the proportions of buildings and those of the human body, and between visual and musical harmony. The basic attitude implied by the use of these terms and analogies was that beauty follows rules, rules which are not arbitrary but rational and indeed mathematical. Even gardens were supposed to be orderly: Alberti suggests that 'The trees ought to be planted in rows exactly even, and answering to one another exactly upon straight lines.'[7] The little that is known about Italian gardens in this period suggests that he was expressing the conventional view. Topiary, for example, was revived in fifteenth-century Italy.[8] The 'elegant ordination of vegetables', as Sir Thomas Browne calls it in his *Garden of Cyrus*, is a vivid illustration of Renaissance values at a point where they differ strongly from our own.

Yet order was not to everyone's taste, whether in nature or in art. In the 1480s, in his pastoral romance the *Arcadia* – which was one of Sidney's models – the Neapolitan Jacopo Sannazzaro expressed a preference for wild beauty:

> It is usual for high and spreading trees produced by nature in fearsome mountains to give greater pleasure to those who look at them than plants skilfully clipped and cultivated in elaborate gardens [*le coltivate piante, da dotte mani espurgate, negli adorni giardini*] . . . who doubts that a fountain that issues naturally out of the living rock surrounded by green plants is more pleasing to us than all the other fountains, works of art made from the whitest marble and resplendent with much gold?[9]

It is surely this attitude that underlies the rise of landscape painting in our period.

Around the 1520s, there was a more general rejection of symmetry and artistic rules. Michelangelo's theory and practice are the great examples of this reaction, though its violence should not be exaggerated. Two famous remarks attributed to Michelangelo sum up his attitude, the dismissal of Dürer's book on proportion with the remark that 'one cannot make fixed rules, making figures as regular as posts'

---

[7] Alberti, *De re aedificatoria*, book 9 , ch. 4.
[8] On Renaissance gardens, see Coffin (1972).
[9] Sannazzaro, *L'Arcadia* (1504), opening.

and the declaration that 'All the reasonings of geometry and arithmetic, and all the proofs of perspective, are of no use to a man without the eye.'[10] As for practice, Michelangelo's Medici Chapel was described by Vasari as a reversal of 'the work regulated by measure, order and rule [*misura, ordine e regola*] which other men did according to a common use'.

If these values were to be rejected, what was to be put in their place? A favourite sixteenth-century term for the beauty which cannot be reduced to formulas or rules is 'grace' (*grazia*). In his delightful dialogue on *The Beauties of Women*, the Florentine Agnolo Firenzuola suggested that this grace was not a matter of mere vital statistics but something more mysterious, 'born from a hidden proportion and from rules which are not in our books'.[11] Thus the language of rules is used to argue that rules do not exist. Another mid-sixteenth-century Florentine, Benedetto Varchi, contrasted grace with beauty. Beauty is physical, objective and based on proportions, while grace is spiritual, subjective and impossible to define.[12] But how does one represent the spiritual in art? As the term became more popular in the sixteenth century, 'grace' is used to mean something like 'sweetness', 'elegance' or 'loveliness' (*dolcezza, leggiadria, venustà*). It is associated with Raphael and Parmigianino in particular.[13] It would be uncharitable to conclude that the 'mystery' consisted in making girls with sweet expressions and ten heads high, but there can be little doubt that some artists, associated with the movement we now call 'Mannerism' believed they had found a formula even for grace (cf. Smyth, 1962; Shearman, 1967).

Richness v *Simplicity*

A third cluster of terms of appraisal centres on the notion of richness in a broad sense which encompasses 'variety' (*varietà*); 'abundance' (*copiosità*); 'splendour' (*splendore*) and 'grandeur' (*grandezza*). Recurrent adjectives, which it would be difficult – and perhaps useless – to distinguish, include *illustre, magnifico, pomposo* (without the pejorative overtones of the English 'pompous'), *sontuoso* and *superbo*. The humanist Leonardo Bruni, called in, as we have seen, to advise on the third pairs of doors for the Baptistery in Florence, considered that they should be what he called *illustri*, in other words that they should

---

[10] See Clements (1963), no. 21; Summers (1981), pp. 352f, 380 (with a warning not to assume that Michelangelo 'had no patience with theories of proportion at all').

[11] Firenzuola, *Prose* (1548), p. 108f.

[12] Varchi, *Due lezioni* (1549).

[13] On Giovio's association of Raphael with *venustas*, see Zimmermann (1976)m p. 416.

'feed the eye well with variety of design'. Ghiberti, who actually
designed the doors, tells us that he aimed at 'richness'. Again, Alberti
objected to what he called 'solitude' in a 'history' (*istoria*, in the sense
of a painting which tells a story), suggesting that pleasure comes
primarily 'from copiousness and variety of things . . . I say that
history is most copious in which in their places are mixed old, young,
maidens, women, youths, boys, fowls, small dogs, birds, horses,
sheep, buildings, landscapes and all similar things'.[14]

Judgements on buildings in particular make frequent use of this
cluster of terms. Filarete, for example, rather overworks the term
'imposing' (*dignissimo*). Vasari tends to describe houses as *onoratissimo*,
sontuosissimo or *superbissimo*, the superlatives adding to the effect of
richness. As for painting, Vasari identifies the 'grand style' (*maniera
grande*) as the characteristic of the work he admires most, such as
Michelangelo's.

However, the values associated with simplicity also had their
admirers. Alberti, for example, despite his praise of copiousness, was
hostile to ornament, a 'secondary' kind of beauty as he called it. He
attacked 'confusion' in architecture, which sounds like a defect
related to the qualities of richness and variety. He argued in favour of
whitewashed churches on the grounds that 'purity and simplicity of
colour, as of life, must be pleasing to the divine being'.[15] He also
suggested that a sculptor will prefer pure white marble, and that
painters should use white rather than gold. One of his terms of praise
for works of art was 'modesty' (*verecundia*).

Alberti's defence of simplicity suits the work of his friends
Brunelleschi and Masaccio very well. Brunelleschi banished frescos
from his interiors, such as the church of San Lorenzo or the Pazzi
Chapel in Santa Croce. Masaccio's paintings were praised by Landino
because they were 'pure without ornament [*puro senza ornato*]'
(Morisani, 1953, p. 267f).

Expressiveness

For the humanist Bartolommeo Fazio, this was one of the most
important gifts of a painter. Pisanello, he wrote, excelled 'in expressing feeling [*sensibus exprimendis*]'. A *St Jerome* of his, for example,
was remarkable for the saint's 'majesty of countenance'. Roger van
der Weyden's *Cruxifixion*, Fazio continued, was noteworthy for its
depiction of the grief of the bystanders, and his *Passion* for its 'variety

---

[14] Alberti, *On Painting*, p. 75.
[15] Alberti, *De re aedificatoria*, book 7, ch. 10; *On Painting*, pp. 84–5. Cf. Gombrich
(1963), p. 16f.

INTERIOR OF THE PAZZI CHAPEL IN FLORENCE
Photograph from The Mansell Collection.

of feelings and emotions' (Baxandall, 1963). Again, Alberti advised the painter to 'move the soul of the spectator', explaining that 'These movements of the soul are made known by the movements of the body' – motion is a sign of emotion – and implying that to represent an emotion was to induce it in the beholder, who would 'weep with the weeping, laugh with the laughing, and grieve with the grieving'.[16] Leonardo emphasized the need for the painter to represent emotions such as anger, fear and grief, and his own comments in his notebooks on the subject of his *Last Supper* describe not the tablecloth which seems to have impressed Vasari so much, but gestures and emotions, like the apostle who makes 'a mouth of astonishment'.[17] To be fair, Vasari also noticed the expressive qualities of the painting, and commented that 'Leonardo succeeded brilliantly in imagining and reproducing the tormented anxiety of the apostles to know who betrayed their master; so in their faces one can read the emotions of love, dismay and anger, or rather sorrow, at their failure to grasp the meaning of Christ.' He had similar praise for Michelangelo, whose figures 'reveal thoughts and emotions which only he has known how to express'.

Skill

The last of our clusters of terms centres on the notion of skill, and may be illustrated from Fazio's praise of van Eyck for that quality (*artificium*). Alberti praises artists for the 'effort' (*istudio, industria*) underlying their selection of elements from the visible world to create a work of beauty. A work may also be praised for its overcoming of difficulties. Vasari, for example, praised Raphael's *Betrothal of the Virgin* because 'it is marvellous to see the difficulties which he went out of his way to look for' in representing the temple in perspective. 'Of all the terms of praise used by authors of the Late Renaissance', it has been suggested, 'perhaps none is more frequent or more important than *difficultà*' (Summers, 1981, p. 1877 and ch. 11). The successful overcoming of difficulties is sometimes called 'facility'. The problem was that artists with facility might not seem to have this quality because the spectator might not realize that there was a problem to overcome. Hence the advice to young painters to 'introduce at least one figure who is completely affected, mysterious and difficult [*sforciata, misteriosa e difficile*], which will show those who understand art how skilled you are'.[18] That the advice was taken

---

[16] Alberti, *On Painting*, p. 77.
[17] Leonardo da Vinci, *Literary Works*, ed. J. P. Richter. Oxford, 1939, p. 341f.
[18] Pino, *Dialoghi di pittura* (1954), p. 45.

RAPHAEL, *MARRIAGE OF THE VIRGIN*
Galleria Brera, Milan.

seriously is suggested by the fact that the fashionable term *peregrino* could mean both 'strange' and 'elegant' (Weise, 1950). Again, 'bizarre' does not seem to have been a pejorative term. At any rate, Vasari could use it of his own work.[19]

The increasingly frequent references to 'facility' and 'difficulty' suggest that the public – and perhaps the artists as well – were becoming more conscious of style and more interested in it. Pejorative terms tell a similar story. Artists such as Vasari and laymen such as Gelli, who has already been quoted, make considerable use of such terms as 'gross', 'rough' or 'clumsy' (*grosso, rozzo, goffo*), when describing medieval art. A final example is the increasing use of the term 'style' itself (*maniera*) (Weise, 1950; Smyth, 1962).

In short, an analysis of the vocabulary used to appraise painting, sculpture and architecture in the fifteenth and sixteenth centuries suggests – like an inspection of the objects themselves – a change in taste from the natural to the fantastic, and from the simple and modest to the complex, difficult and splendid.

MUSIC

It was a Renaissance commonplace that there were parallels between music and other arts, architecture in particular. Audible and visible proportions were thought to be analogous. This is the point of Alberti's warning phrase to his assistant Matteo de'Pasti (above p. 66) that if he changes the proportions of the pilasters, 'all that music turns into discord [*si discorda tutta quella musica*]' (Wittkower, 1949, p. 117f). In his report of 1535, the Franciscan scholar Francesco Zorzi (or Giorgi) described the proportions of the church of San Francesco della Vigna in Venice in musical terms such as 'diapason' and 'diapente' (Wittkower, 1949, p. 90f; cf. Foscari and Tafuri, 1983).

These analogies were treated as more than metaphors. They had practical consequences, at least on occasion. For example, Franchino Gaffurio, musical director at the cathedral of Milan, was called in as an architectural consultant. Analogies between music and the other arts were less precise, but they were not infrequently drawn, as in the case, already quoted of the comparison between Michelangelo and Josquin des Près.

The musical taste of the period is harder to reconstruct than its visual or literary taste. There is no musical equivalent of Vasari's *Lives* and, in any case, then as now it was more difficult for people to

---

[19] Vasari, letter to Alessandro de'Medici (1533) in Vasari, *Literarische Nachlass*, p. 17f.

THE INTERIOR OF SAN FRANCESCO DELLA VIGNA, VENICE.
Conway Library, Courtauld Institute of Art, © D. Howard.

explain why they liked a particular musical composition than why they liked a particular poem or painting. Hence the following paragraphs rely heavily on three treatises of the period, written by Johannes de Tinctoris, Pietro Aron and Nicolò Vicentino.

The most overworked term of praise was 'sweet' (*soave*, *dolce*), but this tells us little more about taste in music than a term like 'beauty' does in the case of the visual arts. More helpful is a cluster of terms centred on 'harmony' and having much in common with the visual cluster centred on 'order'. Again, the basic idea is that success depends on following rules. Tinctoris, for example, frequently criticizes the composers of his day for what he calls their 'inexcusable errors'. He wrote a treatise on proportion in music. Pietro Aron uses similar terms of praise such as *ordinato*.

An acute problem for the writers on music of this period was that of the discord. The problem springs from a fundamental difference between music and the visual arts, a difference disguised by their use of a common vocabulary of order and harmony. The discords which occur in the music of the time can be compared either to decoration or to asymmetry in the visual arts. In the first case they are desirable, but in the second case they are to be shunned. Tinctoris found it difficult to make up his mind on this point. In one passage he compared musical discords to figures of speech, while in another he defined the discord as 'a mixture of two voices which naturally offends the ear'. His conclusion is a compromise; that discords may be permitted, provided that they are little ones (*discordantiae parvae*). Aron, nearly 50 years later, was prepared to go further towards accepting discords. For Tinctoris, a piece of music must both begin and conclude with a perfect concord; for Aron, it is only necessary for it to end that way.

Another group of terms centres on the idea of expressiveness. In this case the analogy with the visual arts will be obvious, but there seems to have been a time lag; it was only in 1500 or even later that the expressive became important, in theory and practice alike. Thus one of the characters in Castiglione's *Courtier* contrasts the effects on the listeners of two styles of singing practised by Bidon of Asti in Rome and Marchetto Cara in Mantua:

> Bidon's style of singing is so skilful, quick, vehement, rousing and varied in its melodies [*tanto artificiosa, pronta, veemente, concitata e di così varie melodie*] that everyone who hears it is moved and set on fire . . . our Marchetto Cara is no less emotional in his singing, but with a softer harmony; he makes the soul tender and penetrates it calmly and in a manner full of mournful sweetness [*flebile dolcezza*].[20]

---

[20] Castiglione, *Il cortegiano*, book 1, ch. 37.

Some music of the period was clearly composed to communicate emotion, for example to reinforce the feelings expressed in a text. Josquin's mournful setting of Dido's lament from Virgil's *Aeneid* is a famous example. The madrigals of the 1520s and 1540s by Costanzo Festa, Adriaan Willaert, Jacques Arcadelt and others furnish many more instances. For the theory behind these expressive songs, however, we have to wait until the 1550s. As Nicolò Vicentino (a pupil of Willaert's) put it, 'If the words speak of modesty, in the composition one will proceed modestly, and not wildly; if they speak of gaiety, one will not write sad music, and if of sadness, one will not write gay music; when they are bitter, one will not make them sweet . . .' He is echoed by Gioseffe Zarlino:

> Musicians are not supposed to combine harmony and text in an unsuitable manner. Therefore it would not be fitting to use a sad harmony and a slow rhythm with a gay text, or a gay harmony and quick and light-footed rhythms to a tragic matter full of tears . . . the composer should set each word to music in such a way that where it denotes harshness, hardness, cruelty, bitterness and other similar things the music will be similar to it, that is, somewhat hard and harsh, though without offending.[21]

There are further parallels between music and the sister arts. Tinctoris suggested, for example, that 'variety should be most diligently searched for in all counterpoint'. Music was even expected to imitate nature, notably hunting scenes and battles, such as Heinrich Isaak's *A la battaglia*.

LITERATURE

'A picture is nothing but a silent poem', wrote Bartolommeo Fazio. If the idea was not already a commonplace in the early fifteenth century, when he expressed it, it rapidly became one. The analogy, usually supported by a phrase from Horace, 'as is painting, so is poetry [*ut pictura poesis*]', was one of which contemporaries never seemed to tire (Lee, 1940). It also informed their practical criticism. When the humanist Poliziano described the medieval poet Cino da Pistoia as the first who 'began to abandon the old uncouthness [*l'antico rozzore*]', he was in effect describing Cino as a kind of Cimabue or Giotto. Five central concepts in the literary criticism of the period have their parallels in the visual arts in particular: decorum, grandeur, grace, variety and similitude.[22]

---

[21] Zarlino, *Institutioni harmoniche* (1558) book 4, ch. 32: the translation is Lowinsky's.
[22] For a general guide to this subject, see Weinberg (1961).

Decorum (*decoro, convenevolezza*) seems to have played a greater part in literary criticism than in art criticism. In the visual arts, it simply meant avoiding such obvious solecisms as placing an old head on an apparently youthful body or, more controversially, giving Christ on the cross the features of a peasant. In literature, however, decorum was invoked when discussing the central problem of the relationship between form (*forma*) and content (*materia*). The Venetian humanist Pietro Bembo, in his authoritative formulation of what was, or was becoming, the conventional wisdom, distinguished three styles (*maniere e stili*): high, medium and low: 'If the subject is a grand one, the words should be grave, stately, sonorous, spectacular, brilliant [*gravi, alte, sonanti, apparenti, luminose*]; if the subject is a low and vulgar one, they should be light, plain, humble, ordinary, calm [*lievi, piane, dimesse, popolare, chete*]; if a middle one, the words should be in between.' Bembo went on to argue that Dante had broken this rule in his *Divine Comedy* because he had picked a lofty subject, yet introduced 'the lowest and vilest things'.[23]

As this example suggests, what pleased the critics most, if not the reading public, was a grand subject treated in the grand style. A whole cluster of terms centres on this idea of grandeur: 'dignity', for example, 'gravity', 'height', 'majesty', 'magnificence' (*dignità, gravità, altezza, maestà, magnificenza*). The contexts in which it was used suggest that the term 'sublime' (*sublime*) had a similar meaning, without the association with terror which it acquired, or regained, in the eighteenth century. To write in the grand style involved the exclusion of many topics – most obviously, ordinary people – and many words, such as 'owl' and 'bat'. Indeed, some critics even recommended the replacement of the terms 'sea' and 'sun' by such circumlocutions as 'Neptune' or 'the planet which marks the passage of time'. These phrases, which now seem unnatural and cumbrous, appear to have struck many readers of the time as elegant and stylish.[24]

A central concept in literary criticism, corresponding more or less to 'richness' in the visual arts, was that of variety, whether it referred to content or form. Bembo gave Boccaccio a good mark for his skilful use of variation in the prologues to the hundred different tales in his *Decameron*. Ariosto was much praised for the variety of themes in his *Orlando Furioso*. Even the Bible was praised, by Savonarola, on these grounds, for its 'diversity of stories, multiplicity of meanings, variety of figures'.

Another cluster of terms centred on the idea of giving pleasure

---

[23] Bembo, *Prose della volgar lingua* (1525).
[24] Besides Bembo, see Vida, *De arte poetica* (1527) and Daniello, *Poetica* (1536).

(*piacevolezza*), distinguished into 'elegance' (*leggiadria*), 'loveliness' (*vaghezza*), 'sweetness' and, of course, 'grace'. Perhaps the most important remark to make about these terms is that they often referred to what we might call the 'second-class' beauties of the middle style, lyric rather than epic, or even to the low style, to Boccaccio's *Decameron*, for example. The fact that the same adjectives were used of many paintings makes one wonder whether the same second-class implications were intended.

As in paintings, so in discussions of literature, the critics spoke much of 'imitation'. Not so much the imitation of nature, as in art criticism and indeed in the literary criticism of later periods, but rather the imitation of other writers; how to vary or transform what was borrowed, and how far to go without being a mere 'ape' of Virgil, Horace or Cicero. The topic – central to the whole Renaissance enterprise of the revival of antiquity – was also a controversial one, involving, among others, Poliziano and Bembo. Bembo favoured the imitation of a particular author such as Cicero, not in the sense of copying details but in that of absorbing the essence, of taking that author's style as a model to emulate. Poliziano, on the other hand, condemned what he called 'apes', 'parrots' and 'magpies', and declared his belief that he expressed himself, not Cicero (*me tamen, ut opinor, exprimo*). His letter now looks rather like a manifesto for Renaissance 'individualism' as Burckhardt saw it, but it should be added that Poliziano was not rejecting all literary imitation, merely the concern 'with reproducing Cicero alone [*anxiam . . . effingendi tantummodo Ciceronem*]'.[25]

VARIETIES OF TASTE

So far the emphasis has fallen on general assumptions held in the period, on a common language of taste. It might be summed up, crudely, in the formula beauty = nature = reason = antiquity. These different values were not consistent with one another in the way that the formula implies, but they were very often treated as consistent by contemporaries. This is not to say that there were no aesthetic disagreements in the period; we have already noted, for example, not only the controversy over imitation but the different valuations of simplicity. What is being asserted is simply that disagreements took

---

[25] Among the best recent discussions of this topic are Fumaroli (1980), p. 91f, and Greene (1982), ch. 8. The Poliziano letter (to Paolo Cortese, c. 1490) is in Greene (text p. 319, translation p. 150). For Bembo's exchange with Gianfrancesco Pico, in 1512, see Santangelo (1954), esp. p. 45f.

place within a common framework of assumptions which was all the more powerful for being unconscious. These assumptions made it difficult to think beyond certain limits, which might be called 'invisible barriers'. Ideas which passed these barriers appeared self-evidently absurd to most contemporaries.

However, it is now time to say something more about the varieties of taste. There were differences in taste between individuals. There were differences between the arts. There were also changes in taste during the period, as we have seen, with an increasing concern with richness and a growing unease about rules. This section will concentrate on three major contrasts: those dividing the inhabitants of different regions, the members of different social groups and, finally, the participants *in* from the opponents *of* the movement we call the Renaissance.

First, differences between regions. We have already seen that different parts of Italy made extremely unequal contributions to different arts. It is also obvious that different regions had their own styles in painting and building, which presumably correspond to differences in taste. In most cases, literary evidence about these regional variations is lacking, but there is one famous exception. The contrast between Florentine and Venetian traditions of taste became the subject of a debate, with the Venetians stressing colour while the Florentines stressed draughtsmanship (*disegno*). On the Florentine side, Vasari, however great his interest in Titian, was never prepared to admit him to be the equal of Michelangelo, while on the other Paolo Pino, who dramatizes the debate in his *Dialogue on Painting*, and Lodovico Dolce, in his *Aretino* insist on Titian's supreme greatness.[26]

Secondly, differences between social groups. Was Frederick Antal, for example (above pp. 34–6), correct in contrasting aristocratic and bourgeois taste in early fifteenth-century Florence? Or if he was mistaken in this instance, can a similar contrast be sustained for Renaissance Italy as a whole?

In this period as in others the language of taste was closely related to the language used to appraise social behaviour. Decorum was a social ideal as well as an aesthetic one. 'Grace' was a term applied to deportment before it was employed to describe works of art, and even *maniera* was originally associated with good manners rather than with artistic style (Blunt, 1940, p. 92f; Weise, 1950; Baxandall, 1971). The use of these terms underlines the fact that what we tend to

---

[26] For the nuances in Vasari's attitude to Venice in general and Titian in particular, see Roskill's introduction to Dolce, *Aretino*, p. 45f, and Rosand (1982), pp. 20–1. On *disegno* in Michelangelo, see Summers (1981), p. 250f.

call the taste of 'the time' was the creation of particular social groups and that it sometimes expressed their social prejudices. It was, for example, considered a breach of decorum to use technical terms when writing in the high style because an author should not show too much knowledge of the techniques of people of low status such as crafts-men. It was a breach of decorum to use new words because 'new men' were not acceptable socially. The poet Vida makes the analogy explicit: 'But yet admit no words into the song, Unless they prove the stock from whence they sprung.' Bembo's discussions of literary vocabulary suggest that he was preoccupied with the question of what was known in Britain in the 1960s as 'U' and 'non-U'. His preoccupation was brilliantly parodied by Aretino (a writer who did not come from the upper classes), in his story of the courtesan who declared that a window should be called *balcone*, never *finestra*; a door, *porta*, rather than *uscio*; and a face, *viso*, not *faccia*.[27]

According to contemporary theorists, different styles of building or music were appropriate for different social groups. Filarete, for example, declared that he could design houses for 'each class of persons [*ciascheduno facultà di persone*]' which differed not only in size but in style. Nicolò Vicentino distinguished two kinds of ancient music, one public, for 'ordinary ears [*vulgari orecchie*]', the other private, for ears which were 'cultivated [*purgate*]'.[28] In literature, the hierarchy of styles – high, middle and low – was associated with different social groups. Aristotle had said in his *Poetics* that tragedy dealt with good men, comedy with ordinary ones, but in the Renaissance he was believed to be referring to noblemen and com-moners. Literature in the high style was literature for and about the elite.

It is difficult enough to assess the effect of social background on artistic and literary taste even in our own day, let alone the fifteenth and sixteenth centuries. It would be unwise to make any very general or unqualified assertions. We certainly have to take account of the fact that humanists and nobles participated in what we call 'popular' culture.[29] Poliziano declared his enjoyment of folksongs, Lorenzo de'Medici wrote songs for Carnival, while the Neapolitan humanist Giovanni Pontano stood in the piazza to listen to a singer of tales (*cantastorie*) (Cocchiara, 1966, p. 29f). Ariosto also took pleasure in the romances of chivalry sung by the *cantastorie*, and his *Orlando Furioso* draws on this popular tradition (Bronzini, 1966). Conversely,

---

[27] Aretino, *Sei Giornate* (1975), p. 82.
[28] Filarete, *Treatise on Architecture*, books 11–12; Vicentino is quoted in Einstein (1949), vol. 1, p. 228.
[29] For a general discussion, see Burke (1978b), p. 23f.

the *Orlando Furioso* made its way into Italian popular culture via chapbook versions of particular cantos.

All this has to be borne in mind, but it does not imply that literary tastes did not vary according to the social group of readers or listeners. Ariosto did not simply imitate the *cantastorie*; he adapted traditional romances to his own milieu, the court of Ferrara. He writes, for example, with an irony not to be found in the texts of his predecessors. He was aware of the classical epic, though he refused to take Bembo's advice and write in the Virgilian manner. Again, the chapbooks did not simply reproduce cantos of Ariosto; they made changes, most obviously in the direction of greater simplicity. It is reasonable to assume that all these singers, writers and publishers knew what their different audiences wanted. There is evidence from the inventories of libraries (like those of the brothers de Maiano, already discussed) that Boccaccio's *Decameron*, with its 'low' style, was popular among merchants and their wives, especially in Tuscany, while Dante, despite Bembo's criticisms, was also widely read in this milieu. Petrarch's love lyrics, on the other hand, were read all over Italy but by young men and young ladies of noble family (Graf, 1888; Bec, 1967).

The last division of opinion to discuss here is the most central to this study, because it concerns the Renaissance itself. It is obvious enough that the Renaissance was a minority movement because the majority of the Italian population of the period comprised peasants who would have had little opportunity to learn about these cultural innovations, even if they had wanted to. However, the minority with the leisure and the skills necessary for involvement in the movement was not all of one mind about it. To revive a useful term from the Oxford of the sixteenth century, there were 'Trojans' as well as 'Greeks' in Renaissance Italy. More exactly, there was distaste for – or rather, strong disapproval of – aspects of the innovations of the period on two grounds in particular.

The more common argument put forward in this period against much art and literature was that they were temptations to immorality. San Bernardino of Siena was one of those who denounced the *Decameron*, long before it was ordered to be expurgated. Pope Eugenius IV condemned Panormita's poem *The Hermaphrodite*, which was burned in public in Bologna, Ferrara and Milan in 1431. Savonarola denounced painters who 'show the Virgin Mary dressed as a whore'. According to Vasari, the painter Baccio della Porta, better known as fra Bartolommeo, was persuaded by Savonarola's sermons that 'it was not good to keep paintings of male and female nudes in the house, where there were children' and put them on the bonfire during the famous 'burning of vanities' in Florence in 1497 (Steinberg, 1977). The figleaves painted onto the figures in Michelangelo's *Last Judgement* have been mentioned already. The Trojans must not be forgotten; but the number of surviving Renaissance nudes suggests that – till about 1550 at least – they were fighting a losing battle. The history of reactions to literature is a similar one. The year 1559 marked a turning point, with pope Paul IV's condemnation, on moral grounds, of a number of famous books, such as the jests of Poggio Bracciolini, the stories of Masuccio Salernitano, the poems of Luigi Pulci and Francesco Berni, and the complete works of Aretino.

The second objection to the arts was that they were idolatrous because they so often dealt with the pagan gods. When pope Adrian VI, a Netherlander of severe tastes, was shown the famous classical statue of Laocoön, installed in the Vatican by one of his predecessors, he is said to have remarked drily, 'Those are the idols of the ancients.' However, the number of paintings and poems from this period concerned with pagan mythology do not authorize the conclusion (drawn by some northerners, Erasmus no less than Adrian VI) that Italians were pagan. The myths were widely believed to have an allegorical meaning.[30] What kind of meaning, and what kind of people believed it, are topics for discussion in the next chapter.

---

[30] A famous defence of mythology on these grounds is the humanist Coluccio Salutati's treatise *The Labours of Hercules* (c. 1391).

7

ICONOGRAPHY

Invenzione means devising poems and histories by oneself, a virtue
practised by few modern painters, and it is something I regard as extremely
ingenious and praiseworthy.
Pino, *Dialoghi di pittura*, p. 44

ICONOGRAPHY is the study of the meaning of images, of the content
of what some Renaissance Italians called 'inventions' or 'stories'
(*invenzioni, istorie*). The iconographical – or iconological –
method involves the attempt to 'read' images as if they were texts
(often by juxtaposing them to texts), and to distinguish different
levels of meaning. Developed in the early twentieth century by Emile
Mâle, Aby Warburg, Erwin Panofsky and others in reaction against a
purely formal approach to the history of art, iconography has in turn
provoked criticism, or iconoclasm, on the grounds that it privileges
what has been called the 'discursive' aspect of the image, in other
words those features which show the influence of language, at the
expense of the 'figurative' aspects, which do not. Even if its importance is a matter for debate, this approach to the art of the Renaissance
remains a necessary one.[1]

For a social history of art, the question of the relative popularity of
different images is an important one, but it is less easy to answer than
it may look. There is not, for instance, any complete catalogue of the
Italian paintings of the Renaissance, so it is necessary to study a
sample instead. What does exist is a catalogue of dated paintings,
including 2,229 examples from Italy for the 120 years 1420–1539. In
2,033 cases, the subject is described. Of these 1,796 (about 87 per
cent) may be described as religious, and 237 (about 13 per cent) as
secular. Of the secular works, about 67 per cent are portraits. Of the
religious paintings, about half represent the Virgin Mary and about a
quarter show Christ, while nearly 23 per cent are concerned with the

---

[1] Panofsky (1955), ch. 1, explains and defends iconography (and distinguishes it from
'iconology', concerned with deeper levels of meaning); Bryson (1981) ch. 1, raises some
awkward questions about it. The problems in this approach to the study of Renaissance art
are discussed by Gilbert (1952); Gombrich (1972), pp. 1–25; and Hope (1981).

saints (leaving a few paintings of God the Father, the Trinity, or scenes from the Old Testament) (Errera, 1920).

Is this sample a reliable one? There are two problems here. Surviving pictures and dated pictures may not be representative of the whole group. Since works commissioned by the Church, which never dies, have a better chance of preservation than those commissioned for individual collections, it may well be that the figure of 13 per cent for secular paintings is something of an underestimate. It should be taken as a minimum. Dated pictures may also be a biased sample, more especially because the number of dated paintings increased steadily from a mere 31 in the 1420s to 441 in the decade 1510–19. Here, as elsewhere, there is a danger of making generalizations about the Renaissance as a whole on the basis of evidence from the later part of the period. If one is conscious of the danger, however, the statistics have their uses. It remains to try to draw out their significance.

It may surprise a modern reader to learn that in a Christian culture, pictures of Christ were only half as frequent as those of his mother, and scarcely more frequent than images of the saints. It should be added that he had been much less important in the thirteenth century, in France at least, and also that he was represented more frequently in the second half of the period than in the first. From this point of view at least the Reformation, Catholic and Protestant, was more of a culmination of late medieval trends than a reaction against them.[2] Pictures of Christ generally represent his birth or his passion, death and resurrection, but rarely anything in between. The obvious explanation for this pattern is a liturgical one: Christmas and Easter were and are the major events of the ecclesiastical year. Again, the Adoration of the Kings is a separate scene from the Nativity because it has its own feast, that of the Epiphany.

A bewildering variety of saints occurs in Italian paintings of this period. What modern art historians (or for that matter what Renaissance clerics) could confidently identify the attributes of (say) saints Eusuperio, Euplo, Quirico or Secondiano? Yet each of these saints had a church dedicated to him in Pavia. Which saints were the most popular? Exactly a hundred saints occur in our sample. St John the Baptist (who occurs 51 times) tops the list. Then comes St Sebastian

---

[2] The evidence may be summarized in the follow table (the figures are percentages):

	Mary	Christ	Saints
1420–79	52	18	30
1480–1539	53	26	20

On thirteenth-century France, see Mâle (1925).

(34); St Francis (30); St Catherine of Alexandria (22); St Jerome (22); St Anthony of Padua (21); St Roche (19); St Peter (18); St Bernardino of Siena (17). St Bernard and St Michael (with 15 paintings each) tie for tenth place.

The exact numbers should not be taken too seriously, but the relative position of the saints tells us something important about Italian culture. It may be worth juxtaposing this list of preferences with those revealed by the choice of children's names. In the group of 600 selected for special attention in this study, the most popular christian names were Giovanni, Antonio, Francesco, Andrea, Bartolommeo, Bernardo and Girolamo. To account for the pattern it would be necessary to write a monograph, or a whole shelf of monographs; here it is only possible to hazard a few hypotheses. The low position of St Peter, compared to his place in the formal church hierarchy, deserves comment. One explanation might be the relative unimportance of Rome, and the weakness of the papacy, until the later fifteenth century. All the same, the split revealed here between official and unofficial religion is a remarkable one.

At the top, the position of St John the Baptist is only to be expected, given the two facts of his importance in the official hierarchy, as the precursor of Christ, and as the patron of the city of Florence, and in particular of the great *Calimala* guild. St Sebastian, in the second place, and St Roche (San Rocco) in the seventh, owe their position to their role as protectors against the plague. Rocco was a fourteenth-century Frenchman who went to Italy and ministered to plague victims. He was particularly popular in the Veneto, especially after the translation of his relics to Venice in 1485. Yet he was never formally canonized. In the late sixteenth century, pope Sixtus V intended either to canonize him or delete him, but died before the ambiguity was resolved. His cult was essentially unofficial (Burke, 1984a). As for Sebastian, it seems to be the story of his martyrdom at the hands of archers which explains the belief in his protection against the 'arrows' of plague, as represented by Benozzo Gozzoli, for example, in a fresco in a church at San Gimignano, commemorating the plague of 1464.

The popularity of St Francis poses no problems: he was an Italian saint and he had the support of the religious order he had founded. His cult was strongest in his native Umbria and in Tuscany, but many important towns in other parts of Italy had churches dedicated to him. St Anthony of Padua might be regarded as a St Francis for the Veneto; he too was a Franciscan, who came from Portugal but preached in Padua, where he died in 1231. St Bernardino was another preacher, and another Franciscan. (It is worth noting that the rival order of friars, the Dominicans, produced no saint to rival the popularity of these three Franciscans.) St Jerome, like St Anthony, was particularly popular in the Veneto, in which he was born (near Aquileia). He was represented in two different ways, which suggests that he had two different 'images' and appealed to two kinds of people. Either he was a penitent in the desert, knocking his breast with a stone, the patron of hermits, or he was a scholar sitting in his study, making his translation of the Bible, an appropriate patron for humanists.

The cult of St Catherine of Alexandria, who far outshone St Catherine of Siena, is to be explained by her patronage of young girls. Her 'mystic marriage' to Christ made her an appropriate subject for paintings given as wedding presents. If one female saint out of eleven seems surprisingly little, the reason may well be that the others were eclipsed by the Virgin Mary, in her many forms, such as the Mother of Mercy (with supplicants sheltering under her cloak), the Virgin of the Rosary or the Virgin of Loreto (the Italian town to which the 'holy house' from Bethlehem was said to have been miraculously transported).

Since so much has been written about secular values in Renaissance Italy, the fact that the overwhelming majority of dated paintings are religious deserves emphasis. These images of the Virgin, Christ and the saints, doubtless commissioned for pious reasons, give us a glimpse of the culture of the silent majority. All the same, there is evidence of increasing interest in secular paintings in this period, and particularly in circles involved with the Renaissance as a movement.[3] Federico Gonzaga, commissioning a work from Sebastiano del Piombo, wrote in 1524 that he did not want 'saints stuff [*cose di sancti*]', but 'some pictures which are attractive and beautiful to look at'. He seems to have been part of a trend.

As we have seen, most secular paintings were portraits. Before the middle of the fifteenth century, they were relatively rare; only saints had their images painted. This is what gives its point to the opening lines of a poem by the Venetian patrician Leonardo Giustinian. The speaker tells his beloved that he has made a painting of her on a little sheet of paper as if she were one of the saints: (*io t' ho dipinta in su una carticella Come se fussi una santa di Dio*). Then it became customary to paint famous men, ancient or modern (the moderns including poets, soldiers and lawyers). The next stage, logically if not chronologically (one cannot be certain of the dates) was the painting of rulers in their own lifetime. Then came the portraits of patricians

---

[3] According to the sample in Errera (1920), the proportion of secular paintings rose from 5 per cent in the 1480s to 22 per cent in the 1530s.

and their wives and daughters, and finally those of merchants and craftsmen. At the end of the period, Aretino, a craftsman's son who was painted by Titian, denounced the democratization of the portrait in his own day, writing that 'it is the disgrace of our age that it tolerates the painted portraits even of tailors and butchers.' To distinguish themselves from others, nobles had to surround them-selves with objects symbolizing their status, from velvet curtains and classical columns to servants and hunting dogs.[4]

It is, however, with the iconography of narrative pictures that art historians have been most concerned, whether these *istorie* represent scenes from classical mythology, episodes from history, ancient or modern, or something more difficult to pin down. The scenes from classical mythology include some of the best-known paintings of the Renaissance. They frequently keep close to that favourite classical – and Renaissance – compendium of mythology, Ovid's *Metamorphoses*. Titian's famous *Bacchus and Ariadne,* for example, illustrates Ovid book 8, while the painting of the enchantress Circe by Dosso Dossi of Ferrara illustrates Ovid book 14. Others follow the descriptions of lost mythological paintings by the classical writer Philostratus of Lemnos. A number of paintings by Piero di Cosimo representing Bacchus, Vulcan and other mythological figures illustrate not only Ovid but also the account of the early history of mankind in the poem *On the Nature of Things* by the Roman poet Lucretius (Panofsky, 1939, pp. 33–67).

How important the exact subject matter was to contemporary viewers is very difficult to say. Was a St Sebastian or a Venus chosen primarily for its own sake, or as a pretext for representing a beautiful naked figure? How can a modern historian possibly answer such a question? It would certainly be a mistake to answer with confidence, but to avoid anachronistic interpretations we can at least investigate the ways in which paintings were described at the time. It is, for example, interesting to know that Titian called his mythological scenes 'poems' (*poesie*), even if we do not know exactly what he meant by the term; whether he was referring to the fact that he drew on Ovid's poem the *Metamorphoses* or whether he intended to imply that he was following his own imagination rather than a text.

Some of the most intriguing literary evidence concerns what we call 'landscape' because it suggests an increasing awareness of the back-grounds of paintings, and even a shift towards considering these features the true subject. Giovanni Tornabuoni asked Ghirlandaio in

---

[4] Bottari (1822–5), vol. 3, p. 1360. Cf. Castelnuovo (1973), and 'The presentation of self in the Renaissance portrait', forthcoming in my *Historical Anthropology of Early Modern Italy* (Cambridge, 1987).

the 1480s, as we have seen, for 'cities, mountains, hills, plains, rocks' in a commission to paint stories from the life of the Virgin Mary. In the correspondence of Isabella d'Este and her husband Gianfrancesco Gonzaga, there are references to 'views' (*vedute*), and in one case to 'a night' (*una nocte*). The latter may have been a *Nativity*, but to describe a religious painting in this way would itself be significant. In 1521 an anonymous Venetian observer (often identified with the patrician Marcantonio Michiel) recorded the existence of 'many little landscapes [*molte tavolette de paesi*]' in the collection of cardinal Grimani (Williamson, 1903). Again, the humanist bishop Paolo Giovio described some of Dosso Dossi's paintings, in the 1520s, as 'oddments [*parerga*]', consisting of 'sharp crags, thick groves, dark shores or rivers, flourishing rural affairs, the busy and happy activities of farmers, the broadest expanses of the land and sea as well, fleets, markets, hunts and all that sort of spectacle' (quoted in Gilbert, 1952, p. 204). In other words, what we call 'the rise of landscape' in this period seems to correspond to changes in the way in which contemporaries looked at pictures.[5]

What has been discussed so far is the more or less manifest content of Renaissance paintings. However, it is clear that some of them at least, like literary works, were intended to contain hidden meanings. How often this was the case, what the meanings were and how many contemporaries understood them are questions which require discussion, but they are rather more obscure.

It is advisable to begin this discussion with literature, where the hidden is sometimes at least made explicit in commentaries. Contemporaries were used to looking for hidden meanings in literature, if only because they were told from the pulpit that the Bible had four different interpretations, not only the literal but also the allegorical, the moral and the anagogical (Caplan, 1929; Auerbach, 1939). Some humanists looked for hidden meanings in worldly literature as well, even if they did not always distinguish the allegorical, the moral and so on as carefully as theologians did. In the fourteenth century, Petrarch, Boccaccio and Coluccio Salutati all interpreted classical myths as a 'poetic theology' (Trinkaus, 1970, pp. 689–721). In the fifteenth century, Cristoforo Landino wrote that when poetry 'most appears to be narrating something most humble and ignoble or to be singing a little fable to delight idle ears, at that very time it is writing in a rather secret way the most excellent things of all, which are drawn forth from the fountain of the gods'.[6] Commentaries expound-

---

[5] On the rise of landscape, see Gombrich (1966), pp. 107–21; and Turner (1966).

[6] Quoted in Weinberg (1961), p. 80, from Landino's commentary on Horace's *Art of Poetry*.

ed the hidden meanings (usually religious or philosophical) underlying the apparently secular or even frivolous surface of classical
writers such as Virgil and Ovid or modern ones like Petrarch and
Ariosto.

Ovid is a useful example to discuss at this point, because his
Metamorphoses inspired artists as well as poets of the Renaissance.
From the twelfth century onwards, it became customary to 'moralize'
him, in other words to give the poem an allegorical interpretation.
The allegorizations of Ovid by Giovanni da Bonsignore in the
fourteenth century were printed in some Renaissance editions of the
Metamorphoses, so that the reader could learn, for instance, that
Daphne (who, fleeing from Apollo, turned into a laurel tree) stands
for prudence while the laurel stands for virginity. The question how
commonly these myths were given this kind of interpretation in the
period remains problematic.

Ariosto was treated in a similar way by the all-purpose writer
Lodovico Dolce, who produced an edition of *Orlando Furioso* in
1542 in which the flight of Angelica in the first canto is interpreted in
terms of 'the ingratitude of women', while Ruggiero's combat with
Bradamante in the 45th canto reveals 'the qualities of a perfect
knight'. These interpretations are described as 'allegories', but in
modern terms they might be better described as symbols. Whereas
Bonsignore treated Ovid's characters as personifications of abstract
qualities, Dolce simply generalizes about human nature from the
actions of Angelica and Ruggiero.

One is left with the impression of a whole spectrum of hidden
meanings, whether intended by authors or read into them by commentators, meanings which seem to have had considerable appeal to
readers of the period. (Dolce, for example, would not have written
anything if he had not thought it would sell.) This impression is worth
bearing in mind when we turn to painting. Paintings of scenes from
the Old Testament are likely to have been read by some people at least
as the text was read, with an eye on what was to come; in other
words, characters from the Old Testament were seen as 'types' or
'figures' of the New. Eve and Judith were both taken to prefigure the
Virgin Mary. (Judith liberated Israel by cutting off the head of the
Assyrian captain Holofernes; Mary liberated mankind by giving birth
to Christ.)

New Testament scenes, by contrast, were painted for their own
sake, but they may have been given a more subtle theological meaning
on occasion, at least as an extra. At all events, it is interesting to find a
friar, Pietro da Novellara, writing to Isabella d'Este about a sketch by
Leonardo, offering the following theological interpretation, at least
hypothetically (note the 'may be'):

LEONARDO DA VINCI, *THE VIRGIN, CHILD AND SAINT ANNE*
Musée du Louvre, Cliché des Musées Nationaux, Paris.

A cartoon of a child Christ, about a year old, almost jumping out of his mother's arms to seize hold of a lamb. The mother is in the act of rising from St Anne's lap, and holds back the child from the lamb, an innocent creature which is a symbol of the Passion [*significa la passione*], while St Anne, partly rising from her seat, seems anxious to restrain her daughter, which may be a type of the Church [*forsi vole figurare la Chiesa*], who would not hinder the Passion of Christ (Cartwright, 1903, vol. 1, p. 319; cf. Chambers, 1970b, no. 86).

At this point it may finally be more or less safe to turn to the vexed question of the secular paintings of the Renaissance and their possible moral or allegorical meanings. At the end of the period, the evidence is sometimes extremely rich and precise; in the case of Vasari, for example, who explained his intentions in considerable detail. His portrait of the late Lorenzo de'Medici, he wrote, would show in the background a vase, a lamp and other objects, 'showing that the magnificent Lorenzo, by his remarkable method of government . . . enlightened his descendants, and this magnificent city'.[7] The programmes devised by humanists such as Giovio, Borghini and Caro (above pp. 109–10) are similarly detailed. Paintings of the fifteenth century pose more of a problem, notably Botticelli's, which have long been a subject of scholarly debate. His so-called *Primavera*, for example, illustrates a scene from another poem of Ovid's, the *Fasti*, dealing with the nymph Flora and the month of May, but there is a good deal in the painting which the text does not explain. Humanists sometimes interpret the classical gods, as we have seen, as symbols of moral or physical qualities. Marsilio Ficino wrote on one occasion that 'Mars stands for speed, Saturn for tardiness, Sol for God, Jupiter for the law, Mercury for reason, and Venus for humanity [*humanitas*].' As he was writing to the youth who commissioned the *Primavera*, it has been suggested that 'humanity' is what Venus represents in the picture (Gombrich, 1972, pp. 31–81; cf. Dempsey, 1968). Again, Botticelli's *Pallas and the Centaur* may be given a moral interpretation, with Pallas Athene (or, as the Romans called her, Minerva) standing for wisdom and the tamed centaur for the passions (Ettlinger and Ettlinger, 1976, p. 130f). In most cases we can do no more than conjecture what the hidden moral meaning may have been. Contemporaries (apart from the artist, the client and their intimates) will have had a similar problem. The important point is to remember that many contemporaries approached paintings with expectations of meanings of this kind.

Hidden political meanings also figured on the contemporary 'horizon of expectations', though they are even more difficult to decode,

---

[7] Vasari, *Literarische Nachlass*, p. 17f.

GIORGIO VASARI, *PORTRAIT OF LORENZO DE MEDICI*
Galleria Uffizi, Florence. Photograph from The Mansell Collection.

since topicality stales so rapidly. Could Botticelli's Pallas, for example, whose gown is adorned with the Medici device of interlaced diamond rings, stand for Lorenzo the Magnificent, and the Centaur for his enemies?[8]

To be sure not to project on to paintings and statues meanings which the artists and their clients did not have in mind, it is prudent to start with literature, and with explicit discussions of implicit political meanings. The preface to the 1542 edition of Ariosto's *Orlando Furioso*, suggests that the poem has a political message, contrasting 'the prudence and justice of an excellent prince' with 'the rashness and the negligence of an unwise king'.[9] Did contemporaries really read this poem as if it were putting forward a political theory, as if Ariosto were another Machiavelli? It is interesting to find that Machiavelli on occasion – in the seventeenth chapter of *The Prince* – quoted Virgil as an authority on politics, using Dido's apology to Aeneas for her intitial suspicions as evidence that a new prince has to be harsher than one who is well established.

When reading the literature of this period it is always worth entertaining the possibility – as contemporaries seem to have done – that the events narrated, whether real or imaginary, recent or remote, refer to or stand for incidents of the writer's own day. Take for instance one of the Florentine religious plays of the period, *Santi Giovanni e Paolo*. Its particular interest in this context is that it was written by a ruler, Lorenzo the Magnificent. It is in fact much concerned with the political problems of the emperor Constantine. The rebellion of Dacia and its suppression by order of the emperor is reminiscent of the rebellion of the city of Volterra against Lorenzo and the suppression of that revolt by Federico da Montefeltre. In the play, Constantine is made to emphasize the fact that he did everything for the common good. It looks as if Lorenzo was writing propaganda for himself (D'Ancona, 1872, esp. p. 257).

Paintings and statues may also carry political meanings. The figures represented may be allegories in the sense that the apparent subject stands for someone else. Decoding these allegories is necessarily speculative and interpretations are bound to be controversial, but the attempt at interpretation is not anachronistic. In this period, as in the Middle Ages, it was not uncommon to refer to living individuals as a 'new' or 'second' Caesar, Augustus, Charlemagne and so on. For instance, the great preacher fra Girolamo Savonarola called Charles VII of France the 'new Cyrus' after the famous king of Persia, and also the 'new Charlemagne' (Weinstein, 1970, p. 145). The comparisons

---

[8] On Medici symbolism in art, see Cox-Rearick (1984). A cautionary note was sounded in some reviews of this monograph.

are a kind of secular parallel to the Old Testament prefigurations of the New, discussed earlier in this chapter. It is therefore not implausible to suggest, for example, that certain statues of David stand for Florence, or that Piero della Francesca's paintings of the emperor Constantine refer to the Byzantine emperor, John VII Palaeologus, who had visited Italy to enlist help in the defence of his capital, Constantinople (a city which had been founded by Constantine), against the Turks (Ginzburg, 1981, ch. 2).

A particular elaborate political allegory can be seen in Raphael's fresco in the Vatican for Julius II and Leo X. The *Expulsion of Heliodorus* has already been discussed. Another fresco deals with the *Repulse of Attila*. Italians of the period, including Julius himself, often called the foreigners who invaded Italy after 1494 the 'barbarians'; this fresco elaborates the parallel between the two waves of barbarian invaders. Raphael went on to paint frescos of pope Leo III crowning Charlemagne as emperor in St Peter's and Leo IV thanking God for a Christian victory over the Saracens. To reinforce the parallel with his own day, Raphael has given the two popes the features of their namesake Leo X.[10] It would be a mistake to reduce these frescos to a commentary on current events; even the political point they were making, like Botticelli's *Punishment of Korah* (above p. 128), was essentially a more general one; a pictorial legitimation of papal authority. All the same, the topical references are worth bearing in mind and, still more important, the habit of using topical references and historical parallels to legitimate political claims. The relation between art and power, between systems of meaning and systems of domination, is at its most transparent in instances such as these.

If the political messages and the historical parallel inscribed in these frescos do not strike us with enough force today, one reason is that most of us are not sufficiently familiar with early medieval papal history, with Maccabees, or even with Numbers. Were contemporaries much better off? Who in this period was able to decode the iconography and read the message of the works we have been considering?

We know all too little about contemporary readings and responses, but the range of variation between them is clear enough. Raphael could afford to be allusive; the Vatican was not open to the public, and his paintings were for the eyes of members of the papal court. It is no coincidence that some of the paintings which have given art historians most trouble since they began to try to unravel their meanings, from Botticelli's *Primavera* to Giorgione's *Tempestà*, were

---

[9] The preface was written by the publisher, Gabriel Giolito.

[10] For a recent discussion with references, see Jones and Penny (1983), pp. 117f, 150f.

made to hang in private houses and to be enjoyed by the patrons and their friends.[11] Posterity looks at them through the keyhole. Even well-informed contemporaries might fail to read them. Vasari complained in his life of Giorgione that he could not understand some of his pictures, 'nor have I, by asking around as I have done, ever found anyone who does'.

Most secular paintings were probably intelligible to a larger minority. Scene from Greek and Roman history would not have been difficult to identify for anyone who had been to a grammar school. Ovid was also studied at grammar schools, and would have provided a key to most scenes from classical mythology. It is likely that the number of people able to understand these paintings rose in the fifteenth and sixteenth centuries, as humanist education spread.

Despite the difficulties they may cause viewers today, when the legends of the saints are no longer part of the culture, it is likely that religious paintings were not difficult to decode for anyone who heard sermons regularly, or watched performances of religious plays; in other words the majority of the urban population.

The attempt to discover which works of art and literature would have been intelligible to which groups, and the habits of mind with which they were interpreted, leads on to a wider question, that of the worldviews of Renaissance Italians. It will be investigated in the next chapter.

---

[11] On Giorgione's iconography and patrons, see Settis (1978).

PART III

THE WIDER SOCIETY

8

WORLDVIEWS: SOME DOMINANT TRAITS

A social group, large or small, tends to share certain attitudes – views of God and the cosmos, of nature and human nature, of life and death, space and time, the good and the beautiful. These attitudes may be conscious or unconscious. In a period of controversy people may be extremely conscious of their attitudes to religion or the state, while remaining virtually unaware that they hold a particular conception of space or time, reason or necessity.

It is not easy to write the history of these attitudes. Historians have stalked their quarry from different directions. One group, the Marxists, have concerned themselves with 'ideologies'. Aware of the need to explain as well as to describe ideas, they have sometimes ended by reducing them to weapons in the class struggle.[1] Another group, the French historians of 'collective mentalities', study assumptions and feelings as well as conscious thoughts, but find it difficult to decide where one mentality ends and another begins.[2] In this chapter I shall employ the somewhat more neutral term of 'worldview', while attempting to include what Raymond Williams calls 'structures of feeling', and to avoid the risk inherent in this third approach of providing description without analysis, or remaining at the level of consciously formulated opinions.[3]

In this chapter an attempt is made to move from the immediate environment of the art and literature of the Renaissance to the study of the surrounding society. The assumption behind it is that the relation between art and society is not direct but mediated through worldviews. More precisely, there are two assumptions behind the chapter, two hypotheses which need to be tested. In the first place, that worldviews exist, in other words that particular attitudes are associated with particular times, places and social groups, so that it is

---

[1] Famous examples include Borkenau (1934) and Mannheim (1952).

[2] For an extended discussion of the strengths and weaknesses of this approach, see Burke (1986). Gilbert (1957) offers a study of 'Florentine political assumptions' in more or less the French style.

[3] The models for this chapter are Tillyard (1943) and Lewis (1964), modified so as to allow analysis of the kind practised by historians of mentalities and ideologies.

not misleading to refer to 'Renaissance attitudes', for example, 'Florentine attitudes' or 'clerical attitudes'. In the second place, that these worldviews find their most elaborate expression in art and literature.

These hypotheses are not easy to verify. The sources, which are predominantly literary, are richer for the sixteenth century than for the fifteenth, much richer for Tuscany than for other regions, and in the overwhelming majority of cases the views they express are those of men of what we would call the upper or upper-middle class (the social structure of the period will be discussed below). As in the case of the study of aesthetic taste, it pays to look not only at relatively formal literary works, but also at documents produced in the course of daily life, such as official reports and private letters. To uncover unconscious attitudes the historian has to attempt to read between the lines, using changes in the frequency of certain keywords as evidence of a shift in values.[4]

This account will begin with a summary of some typical views of the cosmos, society, and human nature (needless to say, it will be extremely selective). It will end with an attempt to examine general features of the belief system, and signs of change. The quotations will usually come from well-known writers of the period, but the passages have been chosen to illustrate attitudes they shared with their contemporaries.

VIEWS OF THE COSMOS

Views of time and space are particularly revealing of the dominant attitudes of a particular culture, precisely because they are rarely conscious and because they are expressed in practice more often than in texts. In his famous study of the religion of Rabelais, the French historian Lucien Febvre emphasized the vague, task-orientated conceptions of time and space in sixteenth-century France, such as the habit of counting in 'Aves', in other words the amount of time it takes to say a 'Hail Mary' (Febvre, 1942, part 2, book 2, ch. 3). Febvre made the French appear, in these respects at least, almost as exotic as the Nuer of the Sudan, who were described at much the same time in an equally classic work by the British anthropologist E. E. Evans-Pritchard (1940, ch. 3).[5] Whatever may have been the assumptions of

---

[4] A pioneer in the study of what he called 'fashion-words' (*Modewörte*) was Weise (1950, 1961).

[5] The studies were independent, but both men owed a considerable debt to the ideas of Emile Durkheim.

the Italian peasants of this period, the evidence from the towns suggests that much more precise attitudes to time were widespread, like the mechanical clocks which both expressed these new attitudes and encouraged them. From the late fourteenth century, mechanical clocks came into use; a famous one was constructed at Padua to the design of Giovanni Dondi, a physician–astonomer who was a friend of Petrarch, and completed in 1364. About 1450, a clock was made for the town hall at Bologna; in 1478, another for the Castello Sforzesco in Milan; in 1499, another for Piazzo San Marco in Venice, and so on. By the late fifteenth century, portable clocks were coming in. In Filarete's utopia, the schools for boys and girls had an alarm clock (*svegliatoio*) in each dormitory. This idea at least was not purely utopian, for in Milan in 1463 the astrologer Giacomo da Piacenza had an alarm clock by his bed (Cipolla, 1967; Wendorff, 1980, p. 151f; Landes, 1983, p. 53f).

There is an obvious parallel between the new conception of time and the new conception of space; both came to be seen as precisely measurable. Mechanical clocks and pictorial perspective were developed in the same culture, and Brunelleschi was interested in both. The paintings of Uccello and Piero della Francesca (who wrote a treatise on mathematics) are the work of men interested in precise measurement working for a public with similar interests. Fifteenth-century narrative paintings are located in a more precise space and time than their medieval analogues.[6]

Changing views of time and space seem to have coexisted with a traditional view of the cosmos. This view, memorably expressed in Dante's *Divine Comedy*, was shared in essentials by his sixteenth-century commentators, who drew on the same classical tradition, especially the writings of two Greeks, the astronomer–geographer Ptolemy and the philosopher Aristotle. According to this tradition, the fundamental distinction was that between Heaven and Earth.

'Heaven' should really be in the plural. In the centre of the universe was the earth, surrounded by seven 'spheres' or 'heavens', in each of which moved a planet: Moon, Mercury, Venus, Sun, Mars, Jupiter and Saturn. The planets were each moved by an 'intelligence', a celestial driver often equated with the appropriate classical god or goddess. This fusion of planets and deities had permitted the survival of the pagan gods into the Middle Ages (Seznec, 1940).

The importance of the planets resided in their 'influences'. As they sang in a Carnival song by Lorenzo de'Medici, 'from us come all good and evil things'. Different professions, psychological types, parts of

---

[6] On Piero and the gauging of barrels, see Baxandall (1972), p. 86f. On space–time in narrative painting, see Francastel (1965).

the body and even days of the week were influenced by different planets (Sunday by the Sun, Monday by the Moon, and so on). Vasari offered an astrological explanation of artistic creativity in his life of Leonardo, remarking that 'The greatest gifts may be seen raining on human bodies from celestial influences.' To explain the past or discover what the future has in store, it was normal to consult specialists who calculated the configuration of the heavens at a particular time. The humanist physician Girolamo Fracastoro gave an account of the outbreak of syphilis in Europe in terms of a conjunction of the planets Saturn, Jupiter and Mars in the sign of Cancer. The philosopher Marsilio Ficino believed that the 'spirit' of each planet could be captured by means of appropriate music or voices ('martial' voices for Mars and so on), and by making an appropriate 'talisman' (an image engraved on a precious stone under a favourable constellation) (Walker, 1958, p. 17).

These beliefs had considerable 'influence' on the arts. Aby Warburg's iconographical analysis of frescos in the Palazzo Schifanoia in Ferrara showed that they represented the signs of the zodiac and their divisions into 36 'decans' (Warburg, 1932, 1966). The Florentine patrician Filippo Strozzi consulted 'a man learned in astrology' to ensure a good constellation before having the foundations of the Palazzo Strozzi laid on 6 August 1489, just as the treatises of Alberti and Filarete recommended (Goldthwaite, 1980, pp. 84–5). When a Florentine committee was discussing where to place Michelangelo's *David*, one speaker suggested that it should replace Donatello's *Judith*, which was 'erected under an evil star' (Gaye, 1839–40, vol. 2, p. 456) Klein and Zerner, 1966, p. 41). Raphael's patron, the papal banker Agostino Chigi, was interested in astrology and some of the paintings he commissioned refer to his horoscope (Saxl, 1934).

Astrology was permitted by the Church; it was not considered incompatible with Christianity. As Lorenzo de'Medici put it, 'Jupiter is a planet which moves only its own sphere, but there is a higher power which moves Jupiter' (D'Ancona, 1872, p. 264). The twelve signs of the zodiac were associated with the twelve apostles. A number of popes took an interest in the stars. Paul III, for example, summoned to Rome the astrologer who had predicted his election (Luca Gaurico, whose brother Pomponio's treatise on sculpture has already been quoted), and gave him a bishopric. Yet there was a sense in which theology and astrology formed two systems which in practice competed with each other. The saints presided over certain days; so did the planets. People might take their problems to a priest or to an astrologer. It was largely on religious grounds that some leading figures of the period rejected astrology, notably Pico della

Mirandola (who declared that 'astrology offers no help in discovering what a man should do and what avoid'), and fra Girolamo Savonarola.[7]

Above the seven heavens and beyond the sphere of the 'fixed stars', God was to be found. In the writing of the period, God was indeed almost everywhere. Even commercial documents might begin with the monogram YHS, standing for 'Jesus the Saviour of Mankind' (*Jesus Hominum Salvator*). When disaster struck, it was commonly interpreted as a sign of God's anger. 'It pleased God to chastise us' is how the Florentine apothecary Luca Landucci comments on the plague. When the French invasion of 1494 left Florence virtually unharmed, Landucci wrote that 'God never removed His hand from off our head.'[8] The name of God constantly recurs in private letters, like those of the Florentine lady Alessandra Macinghi negli Strozzi: 'Please God free everything from this plague . . . it is necessary to accept with patience whatever God wants . . . God give them a safe journey', and so on. Even Machiavelli ends a letter to his family 'Christ keep you all.'[9]

Of all the ways in which Christians have imagined God, two seem particularly characteristic of the priod. The emphasis of the sweetness of God and the 'pathetic tenderness' of attitudes to Christ, which the great Dutch historian Johan Huizinga (1919, ch. 14) noted in France and The Netherlands in the fifteenth century, can be found in Italy as well. Savonarola, for example, addresses Christ with endearments such as 'my dear Lord [*signor mio caro*]', or even 'sweet spouse [*dolce sposo*]'. Christocentric devotion seems to have been spread by the friars, not only the Dominican Savonarola but the Franciscans Bernardino da Siena, who encouraged the cult of the name of Jesus, and Bernardino da Feltre, who was responsible for the foundation of a number of fraternities dedicated to Corpus Christi, the body of Christ. The *Meditations on the Passion* attributed to the Franciscan saint Bonaventura were something of a best-seller in fifteenth-century Italy, and so was the *Imitation of Christ*, a devotional text from the fourteenth-century Netherlands.[10]

This image of a sweet and human saviour coexisted with a more detached view of God as the creator of the universe, its 'most beautiful architect [*bellissimo architetto*]' as Lorenzo de'Medici once called him, or the head of the firm (D'Ancona, 1872, p. 267).

---

[7] A good discussion of astrology can be found in Garin (1976).
[8] Landucci, *A Florentine Diary*.
[9] Strozzi, *Lettere* (1877); Machiavelli, letter of 11 April 1527.
[10] Bonaventura went through at least 26 editions, and the *Imitation* 9, see Schutte (1980), pp. 18–19.

Leonardo da Vinci addressed God as you who 'sell us every good thing for the price of labour'. Giannozzo Manetti, a Florentine merchant and scholar, liked to compare God to 'the master of a business who gives money to his treasurer and requires him to render an account as to how it may have been spent'.[11] He has transposed the Gospel parable of the talents from its original setting, that of a landlord and his steward, to a more commercial environment. Thus Renaissance Italians projected their own concerns on to the supernatural world.

The lower, 'sublunary' world on which man lived was believed to be composed of four elements – earth, water, air and fire – as illustrated in Vasari's *Room of the Elements* in the Palazzo Vecchio in Florence. The elements were themselves composed of the four 'contraries' – hot, cold, moist and dry.

There were also four levels of earthly existence – human, animal, vegetable and mineral. This is what has been called the 'great chain of being' (Lovejoy, 1936). The 'ladder' of being might be a better term because it makes the underlying hierarchy more evident. Stones were at the bottom of the ladder because they lacked souls. Then came plants, which had what Aristotle called 'vegetative souls', animals, which had 'sensitive souls' (that is, the capacity to receive sensations), and at the top humans, with 'intellectual souls' (in other words, the power of understanding). Animals, vegetables and minerals were arranged in hierarchies; the precious stones were higher than the semi-precious ones, the lion was regarded as the king of beasts, and so on.

More difficult to place on the ladder are the nymphs who wander or flee through the poems of the period; or the wood spirits who lived in lonely places and would eat boys (as the grandmother of the poet Poliziano used to tell him when he was small); or the 'demons' who lived midway between the earth and the moon and could be contacted by magical means (Ficino was one of those who tried). The philosopher Pietro Pomponazzi doubted whether demons existed at all.[12] It seems, however, that he was expressing a minority view. When reading the poems of the period or looking at Botticelli's *Primavera*, it is worth bearing in mind that the supernatural figures represented in them were viewed as part of the population of the universe and not mere figments of the artist's imagination.

The status of another earthly power is even more doubtful. Two common images of Fortune associated it, or rather her, with the winds and with a wheel. The wind image seems to be distinctively

---

[11] Vespasiano da Bisticci, *Vite di huomini illustri*, p. 375.
[12] On demons, see Walker (1958), p. 45f.

Italian. The phrase 'fortune of the sea' (*fortuna di mare*) meant a tempest, a vivid example of a change in affairs which is both sudden and uncontrollable. The Rucellai family, Florentine patricians, used the device of a sail, still to be seen on the façade of their church of Santa Maria Novella in Florence; here the wind represents fortune and the sail, the power of the individual to adapt to circumstances and to manage them (Warburg, 1966, pp. 213–46; Gilbert, 1949). The second image of fortune was the well-known classical one of the goddess with a forelock which must be seized quickly, because she is bald behind. In the 25th chapter of his *Prince*, Machiavelli recommended impetuosity on the grounds that fortune is a woman, 'and to keep her under it is necessary to strike her and beat her' [*è necessario, volendola tenere sotto, batterla e urtarla*]', while his friend the historian Francesco Guicciardini suggested that it is dangerous to try to make conspiracies foolproof because 'Fortune, who plays such a large part in all matters, becomes angry with those who try to limit her dominion.' It is hard for a modern reader to tell in these instances whether the goddess has been introduced simply to make more memorable conclusions arrived at by other means, or whether she has taken over the argument; whether she is a literary device, or a serious (or at any rate a half-serious) way of describing whatever lies outside human control.[13]

To understand and manipulate the world of earth, several techniques were available, including alchemy, magic and witchcraft. Their intellectual presuppositions need to be discussed.

Alchemy depended on the idea that there is a hierarchy of metals, with gold as the noblest, and also that the 'social mobility' of metals is possible. It was related to astrology because each of the seven metals was associated with one of the planets: gold with the Sun, silver with the Moon, mercury with Mercury, iron with Mars, lead with Saturn, tin with Jupiter and copper with Venus. It was also related to medicine because the 'philosopher's stone' which the alchemists were looking for was also the cure for all illnesses, the 'universal panacea'.

Jacob Burckhardt (1944, p. 334) believed that alchemy 'played only a very subordinate part' in Italy in the fifteenth and sixteenth centuries. It is dangerous to make general assertions about the popularity of such a deliberately esoteric subject as alchemy, but the odds are that he was wrong. The Venetian Council of Ten took it more seriously when they issued a decree against it in 1488. Several Italian treatises on the subject from the later part of our period have survived. The most famous is a Latin poem, published in 1515 and

---

[13] Guicciardini, *Ricordi*, no. 20; and see Doren (1922).

dedicated to Leo X, Giovanni Augurello's *Chrysopoeia*; there is a
story that the pope rewarded the poet with an empty purse. A certain
'J. A. Pantheus', priest of Venice, also dedicated an alchemical work
to Leo before inventing a new subject, 'cabala of metals', which he
carefully distinguished from alchemy, perhaps because the Council of
Ten were still hostile. On the other hand, some people treated the
claims of the alchemists with scepticism. St Antonino, the fifteenth-
century archbishop of Florence, held that the transmutation of metals
was beyond human power, while the Sienese metallurgist Vannoccio
Biringuccio suggested that it was 'a vain wish and fanciful dream' and
that the adepts of alchemy, 'more inflamed than the very coals in their
furnaces' with the desire to create gold, ought to go mining instead as
he did.[14]

There are only a few tantalizing indications of the possible relation
between alchemy and art and literature. Alchemy had its own
symbolic system, possibly adopted as a kind of code, in which, for
example, a fountain stood for the purification of metals, Christ for the
philosopher's stone, marriage for the union of sulphur and mercury, a
dragon for fire. To complicate matters, some writers used alchemical
imagery as symbols of something else (religious truths, for example).
The *Dream of Polyphilus*, an anonymous esoteric romance published
in Venice in 1499, makes use of a number of these symbols, and it is
possible that this love story has an alchemical level of meaning. Vasari
tells us that Parmigianino gave up painting for the study of alchemy,
and it has been suggested that his paintings make use of alchemical
symbolism (Fagioli Dell'Arco, 1970). Unfortunately, the fact that
alchemists used a number of common symbols (while giving them
uncommon interpretations) makes the suggestion impossible to
verify.

Magic was discussed more openly than alchemy, at least in its white
form; for, as Pico della Mirandola put it:

> Magic has two forms, one of which depends entirely on the work and
> authority of demons, a thing to be abhorred, so help me the god of
> truth, and a monstrous thing. The other, when it is rightly pursued, is
> nothing else than the utter perfection of natural philosophy . . . as the
> former makes man the bound slave of wicked powers, so does the latter
> make him their ruler and lord. (Cassirer et al., 1948, p. 246f).

It should be noted that Pico believed in the efficacy of the black magic
he condemns.

From a comparative point of view it might be useful to define

---

[14] See Thorndike (1934), vol. 4; Biringuccio, *Pirotechnia* (1540), p. 35f.

magic, cross-culturally, as the attempt to produce material changes in the world as the result of performing certain rituals and writing or uttering certain verbal formulas ('spells', 'charms' or 'incantations') requesting or demanding that these changes take place. It would follow from this definition that the most influential group of magicians in Renaissance Italy were the Catholic clergy, since they claimed in this period that their rituals, images and prayers could cure the sick, avert storms and so on.[15]

From the point of view of contemporaries, however, the distinction between religion and magic was an important one. The Church – or, to be more sociologically exact, the more highly educated clergy – generally regarded magic with suspicion. Books of spells were burned in public by San Bernardino of Siena and also by Savonarola. It would be too cynical to explain this opposition to magic (and in some cases, as we have seen, to astrology) merely in terms of rivalry and competition. There were other grounds for clerical suspicion. Magic could be black for two reasons. First, it could be destructive as well as productive or protective.

Secondly, the magician might employ the services of evil spirits. Thus Giovanni Fontana, a fifteenth-century Venetian who made a number of mechanical devices to produce spectacular effects, gained the reputation of a necromancer who received assistance from spirits from hell, just as John Dee gained a sinister reputation in sixteenth-century Cambridge as a result of the too successful 'effects' he contrived for a performance of Aristophanes. No doubt many of their contemporaries viewed Brunelleschi and Leonardo in a similar light. At a more learned level, the philosopher Agostino Nifo argued that the marvels of magic showed that – contrary to Aristotle's belief – demons really existed.

The literature of the period is steeped in magic. Romances of chivalry, for example, are full of sorcerers and of objects with magical powers. In Ariosto's *Orlando Furioso*, the magician Merlino and the enchantress Alcina play an important part. Angelica has a magic ring; Astolfo is turned into a tree; Atlante's castle is the home of enchantment, and so on. We should imagine the book's first readers as people who, if they did not always take magic too seriously, did not take it too lightly either. They believed in its possibility. In the same milieu as Ariosto, at the court of Ferrara, Dosso Dossi painted a picture of Circe, the enchantress of the *Odyssey*, who attracted much interest in Renaissance Italy.

One reason for this interest in Circe is that she was taken to be a

---

[15] This argument is developed in Thomas (1971), ch. 1. On the use of images, see above p. 125.

witch, notably by Gianfrancesco Pico della Mirandola (the nephew of the universal man), who published a dialogue on witchcraft in 1523 in which he made considerable use of the testimony of ancient writers such as Homer and Virgil.[16] Witchcraft was the poor man's magic, or rather the poor woman's; that is, a considerable proportion of the elite of educated men distinguished magic from witchcraft and associated the latter with poor women who were supposed to have made a pact with the devil, to have been given the power to do harm by supernatural means but without study, to fly through the air and to attend nocturnal orgies called 'sabbaths'.[17] Particularly vulnerable to these accusations were those villagers, male and female, who were called in by their neighbours to find lost objects by supernatural means or to heal sick people and animals. 'Who know how to cure illness knows how to cause it [*Qui scit sanare scit destruere*]' went a proverb current at the time.[18] It is more difficult to say whether the neighbours thought that these powers were or were not diabolical, and hardest of all to reconstruct what the accused thought she or he was doing. In Rome in 1427, two women confessed that they turned into cats, murdered children and sucked their blood; but the record does not tell us, in this case as in the majority of trials, what pressure had been brought to bear on the accused beforehand.

An illuminating exception is the case of a certain Chiara Signorini, a peasant woman from the Modena area, accused of witchcraft in 1520. She and her husband had been expelled from their holding, whereupon the lady who owned the land had fallen ill. Chiara offered to cure her on condition that the couple were allowed to return. A witness claimed to have seen Chiara place at the door of the victim's house 'fragments of an olive-tree in the form of a cross . . . a fragment of the bone of a dead man . . . and an alb of silk, believed to have been dipped in chrism'. When Chiara was interrogated, she described visions of the Blessed Virgin, which her interrogator attempted to interpret as a diabolical figure. After torture, Chiara agreed that the devil had appeared to her, but she would not admit to having attended a 'sabbath'. The use of the cross and the holy oil, like the vision of the Blessed Virgin, may well be significant. Some of the 'spells' which inquisitors confiscated took the form of prayers. What one group views as witchcraft, another may take to be religion. In this

---

[16] On Pico and the intellectual and social context of his dialogue, see Burke (1977).

[17] Fifteenth-century Italian treatises on witchcraft are conveniently collected in Hansen (1901), p. 17f. Bonomo (1959), although outdated in some respects, remains a useful survey of witch-hunting in Italy.

[18] So said a woman at a trial at Modena in 1499, quoted in Ginzburg (1966b), ch. 3. The Latin is, of course, that of the court, not the speaker.

DOSSO DOSSI, *CIRCE*
Galleria della Villa Borghese, Rome. Photograph from The Mansell Collection.

conflict of interpretations, it was the interrogator, backed by his instruments of torture, who had the last word (Ginzburg, 1961).

Nevertheless, a few writers did express scepticism about the efficacy of magic and witchcraft. The humanist lawyer Andrea Alciato, for example, suggested (as Montaigne was to do) that so-called witches suffered from hallucinations of night flight and so on and deserved medicine rather than punishment (Hansen, 1901, p. 310f). The physician Girolamo Cardano pointed out that the accused confessed to whatever the interrogators suggested to them, simply in order to bring their tortures to an end.[19] Pietro Pomponazzi, who taught the philosophy of Aristotle at the university of Padua, argued in his book *On Incantations* that the common people simply attributed to demons actions which they did not understand. He offered naturalistic explanations of apparently supernatural phenomena such as the extraction of arrows by means of incantations and the cure of the skin disease called 'the king's evil' by virtue of the royal touch. Pomponazzi held similar views about some of the miracles recorded in the Bible and about cures by means of relics, arguing that the cures may have been due to the faith of the patients, and that dogs' bones would have done just as well as the bones of the saints. It is not surprising to find that this book, which undermined the Church's distinction between religion and magic, was not published in the philosopher's lifetime.[20]

VIEWS OF SOCIETY

The first thing to say about 'society' in Renaissance Italy is that the concept did not yet exist. It was not until the later seventeenth century that a general term began to be used (in Italian as in English, French and German) to describe the whole social system. A good deal was said and written, however, about various forms of government and social groups, and about the differences between the present and the past.[21]

In Italy as in other parts of Europe, a recurrent image, which goes back to Plato and Aristotle, was that of the 'body politic' (*corpo politico*). It was more than a metaphor. The analogy between the human body and the political body was taken seriously by many people and it underlay many more specific arguments. Thus a character in Castiglione's *Courtier* could defend monarchy as a 'more natural form of government' because 'in our body, all the members obey the rule of the heart'.[22] The ruler was often described as the 'physician' of this body politic, a commonplace which sometimes makes its appearance even in a writer as original and as deliberately shocking as Machiavelli, who wrote in the third chapter of the *Prince* that political disorders begin by being difficult to diagnose but easy to cure, and end up easy to diagnose and difficult to cure.

---

[19] Cardano, *De rerum varietate*, (1557), p. 567.

[20] Pomponazzi, *De incantationibus* (written c. 1520; posthumously published 1556).

[21] Since this book was first published, two major studies of Renaissance political thought have appeared: Pocock (1975) and Skinner (1978).

[22] Castiglione, *Il Cortegiano*, (1528), book 4, ch. 19. On the body politic in general, see Archambault (1967).

However, in Italy this 'natural' or 'organic' language of politics was less dominant than elsewhere. A rival concept to the 'body politic', that of 'the state' (*lo stato*) was developing, with a range of reference which included public welfare, the constitution and the power structure. One character in Alberti's dialogue on the family declares that 'I do not want to consider the state as if it were my own property, to think of it as my shop [*ascrivermi lo stato quasi per mia ricchezza, riputarlo mia bottega*].'[13] 'If I let a mere subject marry my daughter', says the emperor Constantine in a play written by Lorenzo de'Medici, *Saints John and Paul*, 'I will put the state into great danger [*in gran pericolo metto/Lo stato*].' Machiavelli uses the term 115 times in his *Prince* (and only in five cases in the traditional sense of the 'state of affairs') (D'Ancona, 1872, p. 244; Hexter, 1973, ch. 3; Rubinstein, 1971).

The existence within the peninsula of both republics and principalities made people unusually aware that the political system (*governo, reggimento*) was not god-given but man-made and that it could be changed. In a famous passage of his *History of Italy*, Francesco Guicciardini reports the discussions which took place in Florence after the flight of the Medici in 1494 about the relative merits of oligarchy (*governo ristretto*), democracy (*governo universale*) or a compromise between the two.[24] This awareness of the malleability of institutions is central to the contemporary literature on the ideal city-state. The treatises on architecture by Alberti and Filarete sketch social as well as architectural utopias. Leonardo's designs for an imaginary city express the same awareness that it is possible for social life to be planned (Garin, 1963; Bauer, 1965). Machiavelli offers a quite explicit discussion of political innovation (*innovazione*). In Florence between 1494 and 1530 the many reports and discussions of political problems which have survived show that the new language of politics, and the awareness of alternatives it implied, was not confined to Machiavelli and Guicciardini but was much more widespread. It was this awareness which Jacob Burckhardt emphasized and discussed in his *Civilization of the Renaissance in Italy* in his chapter on 'The State as a Work of Art [*Der Staat als Kunstwerk*]'.[25]

Awareness of differences in social status seems also to have been unusually acute in Italy; at least, the vocabulary for describing these differences was unusually elaborate. The medieval view of society as consisting of three groups – those who pray, those who fight and

---

[23] Alberti, *I libri della famiglia*, book 3, p. 221.
[24] Guicciardini, *Ricordi*, book 1.
[25] This point emerges clearly from the major –and somewhat neglected – study by von Albertini (1955).

those who work the soil – was not one which appealed to the inhabitants of Italian cities, most of whom performed none of these functions (Duby, 1980; Niccoli, 1979). Their model of society was differentiated not by functions but by grades (*generazioni*) and it probably developed out of the classification of citizens for tax purposes into rich, middling and poor. The phrases 'fat people' (*popolo grasso*) and 'little people' (*popolo minuto*) were commonly used, especially in Florence, and it is not difficult to find instances of a term like 'middle class' (*mediocri*).[26] However, contemporaries did not think exclusively in terms of income groups. They differentiated families and individuals according to whether they were or were not noble (*nobili, gentilhuomini*); whether or not they were citizens (*cittadini*), in possession of political rights; and whether they were members of the greater or lesser guilds. One of the most important but also one of the most elusive items in their social vocabulary was *popolare*, because it varied in significance according to the speaker. If he came from the upper levels of society, he was likely to use it as a pejorative term to denote all ordinary people. At the middle level, on the other hand, a greater effort was made to distinguish the *popolo*, who enjoyed political rights, from the *plebe*, which did not. The point of view of this 'plebs' has gone unrecorded (Gilbert, 1965, p. 19f; cf. Cohn, 1980, ch. 3).

Awareness of the structure of society and of potentially different structures is also revealed in discussions of the definition of nobility, whether based on birth or individual worth, which are relatively frequent in the period, from the treatise of the Florentine jurist Lapo da Castiglionchio (written before 1381) and Poggio Bracciolini's dialogue *On True Nobility* to the debate in Castiglione's *Courtier*. This discussion needs to be placed in the context of political and social conflict in Florence and elsewhere, but it is also related to contemporary concern with the value of the individual (below, p. 193).

Renaissance Italy was also remarkable for a view of the past taken by some artists and humanists, a view which was possibly more widespread. With the idea of the malleability of institutions, already discussed, went an awareness of change over time, a sense of anachronism. The term 'anachronism' is literally speaking an anachronism because the word did not yet exist, but in his famous critique of the authenticity of the document known as the *Donation of Constantine*, the humanist Lorenzo Valla did point out that the text contained expressions from a later period. He was well aware that 'modes of speech' (*stilus loquendi*) were subject to change, that

---

[26] Difficulties in the interpretation of the term *popolo minuto* and its synonyms are discussed by Cohn (1980), p. 69n.

language had a history.[27] Another fifteenth- century humanist, Flavio Biondo, argued that Italian and other romance languages had developed out of Latin. Biondo also wrote a book called *Rome Restored*, in which he tried to reconstruct classical Rome on the basis of literary evidence as well as the surviving remains. In another book he discussed the private life of the Romans, the clothes they wore and the way in which they brought up their children (Weiss, 1969).

By the later fifteenth century, this antiquarian sensibility had become fashionable and had begun to affect the arts. In the *Dream of Polyphilus*, the Venetian romance already mentioned, the lover searches for his beloved in a landscape of temples, tombs and obelisks and even the language is a consciously archaic Latinate Italian (Mitchell, 1960). Among the artists whose work illustrates the growing interest in antiquarianism are Mantegna and Giulio Romano. Like his master and father-in-law Jacopo Bellini, Mantegna was extremely interested in copying ancient coins and inscriptions. He was a friend of humanists such as Felice Feliciano of Verona. His reconstructions of ancient Rome in the *Triumphs of Caesar* or the painting of Scipio introducing the cult of the Cybele are the pictorial equivalents of Biondo's patient work of historical reconstruction (Saxl, 1957, pp. 150–60). As for Giulio Romano, his painting of Constantine in battle draws heavily on the evidence of Trajan's Column, as Vasari pointed out in his life of the artist, 'for the costumes of the soldiers, the armour, ensigns, bastions, stockades, battering rams and all the other instruments of war'.

Vasari himself shared this sense of the past. His *Lives* are organized around the idea of development in time, from Cimabue to Michelangelo. He believed in progress in the arts, at least up to a point, but he also believed that individual artists ought to be judged by the standards of their own day, and he explained that 'my intention has always been to praise not absolutely but, as the saying goes, relatively [*non semplicemente ma, come s'usa dire, secondo ché*], having regard to place, time, and other similar circumstances' (Panofsky, 1955, pp. 169–225).

Another material sign of the awareness of the past is the fake antique, which seems to have been a fifteenth-century innovation. The young Michelangelo made a faun, a Cupid and a Bacchus in the classical style. He was essentially competing with antiquity, but by the early sixteenth century the faking of classical sculptures and Roman coins was a flourishing industry in Venice and Padua. This response to two new trends, the fashion for ancient Rome and the rise

---

[27] For a general survey see Burke (1969) and Weiss (1969). On Valla, Kelley (1970), ch. 1.

of the art market, depended – like the detecting of the fakes – on a sense of period style (Kurz, 1967).

This new sense of the past is one of the most distinctive but also one of the most paradoxical features of the period. Classical antiquity was studied in order to imitate it more faithfully, but the closer it was studied, the less imitation seemed either possible or desirable. 'How mistaken are those', wrote Francesco Guicciardini, 'who quote the Romans at every step. One would have to have a city with exactly the same conditions as theirs and then act according to their example. That model is as unsuitable for those lacking the right qualities as it would be useless to expect an ass to run like a horse.'[28] However, many people did quote the Romans at every step; Guicciardini's friend Machiavelli was one of them.

Another paradox was that at a time when Italian culture was strongly marked by the propensity to innovate, innovation was generally considered a bad thing. In political debates in Florence, it was taken for granted that 'new ways' (*modi nuovi*) were undesirable, and that 'every change takes reputation from the city' (Gilbert, 1957). In Guicciardini's *History of Italy*, the term 'change' (*mutazione*) seems to be used in a pejorative sense, and when a man is described, like pope Julius II, as 'desirous of new things [*desideroso di cose nuove*]' the overtones of disapproval are distinctly audible. Innovation in the arts was doubtless less dangerous, but it was rarely admitted to be innovation. It was generally perceived as a return to the past. When Filarete praises Renaissance architecture and condemns the Gothic, it is the latter which he calls 'modern [*moderno*]'. It is only at the end of the period that one can find someone (Vasari, for example), cheerfully admitting to being *moderno* himself (above p. 17).

VIEWS OF MAN

Classical views of the physical constitution of man, and the distinction between four personality types (choleric, sanguine, phlegmatic and melancholy), were taken seriously by writers in this period, and they are not without relevance to the arts. Ficino, for example, joined the suggestion (which comes from a text attributed to Aristotle) that all great men are melancholics to Plato's concept of inspiration as divine frenzy, and argued that creative people (*ingeniosi*) were melancholic and even 'frantic' (*furiosi*). He was thinking of poets in

---

[28] Guicciardini, *Ricordi*, no. 110.

particular, but Vasari applied his doctrine to artists and so helped create the modern myth of the bohemian (Klibansky, 1964; cf. p. 83 above).

However, the major theme of this section is inevitably one which contemporaries did not discuss in treatises but was discovered (or, as some critics would say, invented) by Jacob Burckhardt: Renaissance individualism. 'In the Middle Ages' wrote Burckhardt (1944, p. 81), in one of the most frequently quoted passages of his essay, '. . . Man was conscious of himself only as a member of a race, people, party, family or corporation, only through some general category. In Italy this veil first melted into air . . . man became a spiritual *individual*, and recognized himself as such.' He went on to discuss the passion for fame and its corrective, the new sense of ridicule, all under the general rubric of 'the development of the individual'. For the use of this 'blanket term', he has been severely criticized (Nelson, 1933). As it happens, Burckhardt came to be rather sceptical about the interpretation he had launched, and towards the end of his life he confessed to an acquaintance that 'You know, so far as individualism is concerned, I hardly believe in it any more, but I don't say so; it gives people so much pleasure.'[29]

The objections are difficult to gainsay, and yet we need the idea of individualism, or something like it. The idea of the self, as the anthropologist Marcel Mauss pointed out half a century ago, is not natural. It is a social construct, and it has a social history.[30] Indeed, the concept of person current (indeed, taken for granted) in a particular culture needs to be understood if we are to comprehend that culture, and as another anthropologist, Clifford Geertz (1983, pp. 59–70), suggested, it is a good way into that culture for an outsider.

If we ask about the concept of person current – among elites, at least – in Renaissance Italy, we may find it useful to distinguish the self-consciousness with which Burckhardt was particularly concerned from self-assertiveness, and both from the idea of the unique individual.[31]

The idea of the uniqueness of the individual goes with that of a personal style in painting or writing, an idea which has been discussed already (p. 25). At the court of Urbino, the poet Bernardo Accolti went by the nickname *L'unico Aretino*. The poet Vittoria Colonna

---

[29] Burckhardt's Swiss German, not often recorded, is worth repeating. 'Ach wisse Si, mit dem Individualismus, i glaub ganz nimmi dra, aber i sag nit; si han gar a Fraid' (from Werner Kaegi's introduction to Walser (1932), xxxvii).

[30] His lecture of 1938 is reprinted with a valuable commentary in Carrithers et al. (1985), ch. 1–2.

[31] Nelson (1933) distinguishes five elements in individualism.

described Michelangelo as *unico*. An anonymous Milanese poem declares that just as there is only one God in Heaven, so there is only one 'Moro' (Lodovico Sforza) on earth. In his biographies, the bookseller Vespasiano da Bisticci often refers to men as 'singular' (*singolare*).

There is rather more to say about self-assertion. Burckhardt (1944, p. 87f) argued that the craving for fame was a new phenomenon in the Renaissance. The Dutch historian Huizinga (1919, ch. 4) retorted that on the contrary, it was 'essentially the same as the chivalrous ambition of earlier times'. The romances of chivalry do indeed suggest that the desire for fame was one of the leading motives of medieval knights, so what Burckhardt noticed may have been no more than the demilitarization of glory. However, it is remarkable quite how often self-assertion words occur in the Italian literature of this period. Among them we find 'competition' (*concertazione, concorrenza*); 'emulation' (*emulazione*); 'glory' (*gloria*); 'envy' (*invidia*); 'honour' (*onore*); 'shame' (*vergogna*); 'valour' (*valore*); and, hardest of all to translate, a concept of great importance in the period referring to personal worth, which we have already met when discussing its complementary opposite, fortune: *virtù* (see Gilbert, 1951). Psychologists would say that if words of this kind occur with unusual frequency in a particular text, as they do, for example, in the dialogue on the family by the humanist Leon Battista Alberti, then its author is likely to have had an above-average achievement drive, which in Alberti's case his career does nothing to refute. That the Florentines in general were unusually concerned with achievement is suggested by the *novelle* of the period, which often deal with the humiliation of a rival (see Rotunda, 1942); by the institutionalization of competitions between artists; by the sharp tongues and the envy in the artistic community, as recorded by Vasari, notably in his life of Castagno; and, not least, by the remarkable creative record of that city.

At any rate self-assertion was an important part of the Tuscan image of man. The humanists Bruni and Alberti both described life as a race. Bruni wrote that some 'do not run in the race, or when they start, become tired and give up half way'; Alberti, that life was a regatta in which there were only a few prizes: 'Thus in the race and competition for honour and glory in the life of man it seems to me very useful to provide oneself with a good ship and to give an opportunity to one's powers and ability [*alle forze e ingegno tuo*], and with this to sweat to be the first.'[32] Leonardo da Vinci recommended

---

[32] Bruni, *Epistolae*, vol. 1, p. 137; Alberti, *I libri della famiglia*, p. 139.

artists to draw in company because 'a sound envy' would act as a stimulus to do better.[33] For a hostile account of the same kind of struggle, we may turn to the Sienese pope Pius II (who was not exactly backward in the race to the top), and his complaint that 'In the courts of princes the greatest effort is devoted to pushing others down and climbing up oneself.'[34]

It is not unreasonable to suggest that competition encourages self-consciousness, and interesting to discover that the Tuscan evidence for this kind of individualism is once again richer than anything to be found elsewhere. The classic phrase of the Delphic oracle, 'know thyself', quoted by Marsilio Ficino among others, was taken seriously in the period, although it was sometimes given a more worldly interpretation than was originally intended.

The most direct evidence of self-awareness is that of autobiographies, or more exactly (since the modern term 'autobiography' encourages an anachronistic view of the genre) of diaries and journals written in the first person, of which there are about a hundred surviving from Florence alone (Bec, 1967; Brucker, 1967; Guglielminetti, 1977; Anselmi et al., 1980). The local name for this kind of literature was *ricordanze*, which might be translated 'memoranda', a suitably vague word for a genre which had something of the account book in it, and something of the city chronicle, and was focused on the family, but none the less reveals something about the individual who wrote it: the apothecary Luca Landucci, for example, who has been quoted more than once in these pages, or Machiavelli's father Bernardo, or the Florentine patrician Giovanni Rucellai, who left a notebook dealing with a variety of subjects, a 'mixed salad' as he called it.[35] Even if these memoranda were not intended to express self-awareness, they may have helped to create it. Rather more personal in style are the autobiographies of pope Pius II (written, like Caesar's, in the third person, but none the less self-assertive for that), of Guicciardini (a brief but revealing memoir), of the physician Girolamo Cardano (a Lombard, for once, not a Florentine) and of the goldsmith Benvenuto Cellini.

Autobiographies are not the only evidence for the self-consciousness of Renaissance Italians. There are also paintings. Portraits were often hung in family groups and commissioned for family reasons, but self- portraits are another matter. Most of them are not pictures in their own right but representations of the artist in the corner of a painting devoted to something else, like the figure of

---

[33] Leonardo da Vinci, *Literary Works*, ed. J. P. Richter. Oxford, 1939, p. 307.
[34] Pius II, *De curialium miseriis epistola*, p. 32.
[35] Rucellai, *Il Zibaldone*.

Benozzo Gozzoli in his fresco of the procession of the Magi, Pinturicchio in the background to his *Annunciation*, or Raphael in his *School of Athens*. In the course of the sixteenth century, however, we find self-portraits in the strict sense by Parmigianino, for example, and Vasari, and more than one by Titian. They remind us of the importance of the mirrors manufactured in this period, in Venice in particular. Mirrors may well have encouraged self-awareness. As the Florentine writer Giambattista Gelli put it in a Carnival song he wrote for the mirror-makers of Florence, 'A mirror allows one to see one's own defects, which are not as easy to see as those of others' (Singleton, 1936, p. 357f).

Evidence of self-awareness is also provided by the conduct books, of which the most famous are Castiglione's *Courtier* (1528), Giovanni Della Casa's *Galateo* (1558) and the *Civil Conversation* of Stefano Guazzo (1574). All three are manuals for the 'presentation of self in everyday life' as the sociologist Erving Goffman (1959) puts it – instructions in the art of playing one's social role gracefully in public. They inculcate conformity to a code of good manners rather than the expression of a personal style of behaviour, but they are nothing if not self-conscious themselves and they encourage self-consciousness in the reader. Castiglione recommends a certain 'negligence [*sprezzatura*]', to show that 'whatever is said or done has been done without pains and virtually without thought', but he admits that this kind of spontaneity has to be rehearsed. It is the art which conceals art, and he goes on to compare the courtier to a painter. The 'grace' (*grazia*) with which he was so much concerned was, as we have seen, a central concept in the art criticism of his time. It is hard to decide whether to call Castiglione a painter among courtiers or his friend Raphael a courtier among painters, but the connections between their two domains are clear enough. The parallel was clear to Giovanni Pico della Mirandola in his famous *Oration on the Dignity of Man*, in which he has God say to man that 'as though the maker or moulder of thyself, thou mayest fashion thyself in whatever shape thou shalt prefer' (Cassirer et al., 1948, p. 225).

The dignity of man was a favourite topic for writers on the 'human condition' (the phrase is theirs, *humana conditio*). It is tempting to take Pico's treatise on the dignity of man to symbolize the Renaissance, and to contrast it with pope Innocent III's treatise on the misery of man as a symbol of the Middle Ages. However, both the dignity and the misery of man were recognized by writers in both Middle Ages and Renaissance. Many of the arguments for the dignity of man (the beauty of the human body, its upright posture and so on) are commonplaces of the medieval as well as the classical and Renaissance

PINTURICCHIO, SELF PORTRAIT (DETAIL FROM THE *ANNUNCIATION*)
Chiesa di S. Maria Maggiore, Spello.

traditions. The themes of dignity and misery were considered as complementary rather than contradictory (Trinkaus, 1970; Craven, 1981).

All the same, there does appear to have been a change of emphasis revealing an increasing confidence in man in intellectual circles in the period. Lorenzo Valla, with characteristic boldness, called the soul the 'man–God [*homo deus*]', and wrote of the soul's ascent to heaven in the language of a Roman triumph. Pietro Pomponazzi declared that those (few) men who had managed to achieve almost complete rationality deserved to be numbered among the gods. Adjectives such as 'divine' and 'heroic' were increasingly used to describe painters, princes and other mortals. Alberti had called the ancients 'divine' and Poliziano had coupled Lorenzo de'Medici with Giovanni Pico as 'heroes rather than men', but it is only in the sixteenth century that this heroic language became commonplace. Vasari, for example, described Raphael as a 'mortal god' and wrote of the 'heroes' of the house of Medici. Matteo Bandello referred to the 'heroic house of Gonzaga' and to the 'glorious heroine' Isabella d'Este. Aretino, typically, called himself 'divine'. The famous references to the 'divine Michelangelo' were in danger of devaluation by this inflation of the language of praise (Weise, 1961, pp. 79–119).

These ideas of the dignity (indeed divinity) of man had their effect on the arts. Where pope Innocent III, for example, found the human body disgusting, Renaissance writers admired it, and the humanist Agostino Nifo went so far as to defend the proposition that 'nothing ought to be called beautiful except man'. By 'man' he meant woman, and in particular Jeanne of Aragon. One might have expected paintings of the idealized human body in a society where such views were expressed. The derivation of archiectural proportions from the human body (again, idealized) also depended on the assumption of human dignity. Again, at the same time that the term 'heroic' was being overworked in literature, we find the so-called 'grand manner' dominant in art. If we wish to explain changes in artistic taste, we need to look at wider changes in worldviews.

Another image of man, common in the literature of the time, is that of a rational, calculating, prudent animal. 'Reason' (*ragione*) and 'reasonable' (*ragionevole*) are terms which recur, usually with overtones of approval. They are terms with a wide variety of meanings, but the idea of rationality is central. The verb *ragionare* meant 'to talk', but then speech was a sign of rationality which showed man's superiority to animals. One meaning of *ragione* is 'accounts': merchants called their account books *libri della ragione*. Another meaning is 'justice': the *Palazzo della Ragione* in Padua was not so much

the 'Palace of Reason' as the court of law. Justice involved calculation, as the classical and Renaissance image of the scales should
remind us. *Ragione* also meant 'proportion' or 'ratio'. A famous early
definition of perspective, in the life of Brunelleschi atrributed to
Manetti, called it the science which sets down the differences of size in
objects near and far *con ragione*, a phrase which can be (and has
been) translated either as 'rationally' or 'in proportion'.

The habit of calculation was central to Italian urban life. Numeracy
was relatively widespread, taught at special 'abacus schools' in
Florence and elsewhere. A fascination with precise figures is revealed
in some thirteenth-century texts, notably the chronicle of fra Salim-
bene of Parma and Bonvesino della Riva's treatise on 'The Big Things
of Milan', which lists the city's fountains, shops and shrines and
calculates the number of tons of corn the inhabitants of Milan
demolished every day.[36] The evidence for this numerate mentality is
even richer in the fourteenth century, as the statistics in Giovanni
Villani's chronicle of Florence bear eloquent witness, and richer still
in the fifteenth and sixteenth century. In Florence and Venice in
particular, an interest was taken in statistics of imports and exports,
population and prices. Double-entry book-keeping was widespread.
The great *catasto* of 1427, a household-to-household survey of a
quarter of a million Tuscans who were then living under Florentine
rule, both expressed and encouraged the rise of the numerate
mentality (Herlihy and Klapisch-Zuber, 1985). Time was seen as
something 'precious', which must be 'spent' carefully and not
'wasted'; all these terms come from the third book of Alberti's
dialogue on the family. In similar fashion, Giovanni Rucellai advised
his family to 'be thrifty with time, for it is the most precious thing we
have'.[37] Time could be the object of rational planning. The humanist
school master Vittorino da Feltre drew up a timetable for the
students. The sculptor Pomponio Gaurico boasted that since he was a
boy he had planned his life so as not to waste it in idleness.

With this emphasis on reason, thrift (*masserizia*) and calculation
went the regular use of such words as 'prudent' (*prudente*), 'carefully'
(*pensatamente*) and 'to foresee' (*antevedere*). The reasonable is often
identified with the useful, and a utilitarian approach is characteristic
of a number of writers in this period. In Valla's dialogue *On pleasure*,
for example, one of the speakers, the humanist Panormita, defends an
ethic of utility (*utilitas*). All action – writes this fifteenth-century
Jeremy Bentham – is based on calculations of pain and pleasure.
Panormita may not represent the author's point of view. What is

---

[36] See Murray (1978), p. 182f, which discusses the 'arithmetical mentality'.
[37] Rucellai, *Il Zibaldone*, p. 8.

relevant here is what was thinkable in the period, rather than who exactly thought it. This emphasis on the useful can be found again and again in texts of the period, from Alberti's book on the family to Machiavelli's *Prince*, with its references to the 'utility of the subjects [*utilità de'sudditi*]', and the need to make 'good use' of liberality, compassion and even cruelty. Again, Filarete created in his ideal city of Sforzinda a utilitarian utopia which Bentham would have appreciated, in which the death penalty has been abolished because criminals are more useful to the community if they do hard labour for life, in conditions exactly harsh enough for this punishment to act as an adequate deterrent.[38]

Calculation affected human relationships. The account-book view of man is particularly clear in the reflections of Guicciardini. He advised his family:

> Be careful not to do anyone the sort of favour that cannot be done without at the same time displeasing others. For injured men do not forget offences; in fact, they exaggerate them. Whereas the favoured party will either forget or will deem the favour smaller than it was. Therefore, other things being equal, you lose a great deal more than you gain.[39]

Italians (adult males of the upper classes, at any rate) admitted a concern (unusual for other parts of Europe in the period, whatever may be true of the 'age of capitalism') with controlling themselves and manipulating others. In Alberti's dialogue on the family, the humanist Lionardo suggests that it is good 'to rule and control the passions of the soul', while Guicciardini declared that there is greater pleasure in controlling one's desires (*tenersi le voglie oneste*) than in satisfying them. If self-control is civilization, as the sociologist Norbert Elias suggests in his famous book on *The Civilizing Process*, then even without their art and literature, the Italians of the Renaissance would still have a good claim to be described as the most civilized people in Europe.[40]

TOWARDS THE MECHANIZATION OF THE WORLD PICTURE

It is time to end this necessarily incomplete catalogue of the beliefs of Renaissance Italians, and to try to see their worldview as a whole.

---

[38] Filarete, *Treatise on Architecture*, book 20, p. 282f.
[39] Guicciardini, *Ricordi*, no. 25.
[40] See Elias (1939), a book which does not place enough emphasis on the role of the Italians in the process of change he describes and analyses so well.

One striking feature of this view is the coexistence of many traditional attitudes with others which would seem to be incompatible with them.

Generally speaking, Renaissance Italians, including the elites who dominate this book, lived in a mental universe which was, like that of their medieval ancestors, animate rather than mechanical, moralized rather than neutral and organized in terms of correspondences rather than causes.

A common phrase of the period was that the world is 'an animal'. Leonardo developed this idea in a traditional way when he wrote that 'We can say that the earth has a vegetative soul, and that its flesh is the land, its bones are the structure of the rocks . . . its blood is the pools of water . . . its breathing and its pulses are the ebb and flow of the sea.'[41] The operations of the universe were personified. Dante's phrase about 'the love that moves the sun and the other stars' was still taken literally. Magnetism was described in similar terms. In the *Dialogues on Love* (1535) of the Jewish physician Leone Ebreo, a work in the neoplatonic tradition of Ficino, one speaker explains that 'the magnet is loved so greatly by the iron, that notwithstanding the size and weight of the iron, it moves and goes to find it'.[42] The discussions of the 'body politic' (above p. 188) fit into this general picture. 'Every republic is like a natural body' as the Florentine theorist Donato Giannotti put it. Writers on architecture draw similar analogies between buildings and animate beings, analogies which are now generally misread as metaphors. Alberti wrote that a building is 'like an animal', and Filarete that 'A building . . . wants to be nourished and looked after, and through lack of this it sickens and dies like a man.' Michelangelo went so far as to say that whoever 'is not a good master of the figure and likewise of anatomy' cannot understand anything of architecture because the different parts of a building 'derive from human members'.[43] Not even Frank Lloyd Wright in our own century could match this organic theory of architecture.

The universe was 'moralized' in the sense that its different characteristics were not treated as neutral in the manner of modern scientists. Warmth, for example, was considered to be better in itself than cold, because the warm is 'active and productive'. It was better to be unchangeable (like the heavens) than mutable (like the earth); better to be at rest than to move; better to be a tree than a stone.

---

[41] Leonardo da Vinci, Literary Works, ed. J. P. Richter. Oxford, 1939, no. 1000.

[42] Leone Ebreo, *Dialoghi d'Amore*, second dialogue, part 1.

[43] Filarete, *Treatise on Architecture*, book 1, p. 8f; Letter of Michelangelo quoted in Ackerman (1970), p. 37.

Another way of making some of these points is to say that the universe was seen to be organized in a hierarchical manner, thus resembling (and also justifying or 'legitimating') the social structure. Filarete compared three social groups – the nobles, the citizens and the peasants – to three kinds of stone – precious, semi-precious and common. In this hierarchical universe it is hardly surprising to find that genres of writing and painting were also graded, with epics and 'histories' at the top and comedies and landscapes towards the bottom. However, more than hierarchy was involved on occasion. 'Prodigies' or 'monsters', in other words extraordinary phenomena, from the birth of deformed children to the appearance of comets in the sky, were interpreted as 'portents', as signs of coming disaster.[44]

The different parts of the universe were related to one another not so much causally, as in the modern world picture, as symbolically, according to what were called 'correspondences'. The most famous of these correspondences was between the 'macrocosm', the universe in general, and the 'microcosm', the little world of man. Astrological medicine depended on these correspondences, between the right eye and the sun, the left eye and the moon, and so on. Numerology played a great part here. The fact that there were seven planets, seven metals and seven days of the week was taken to prove correspondences between them. This elaborate system of correspondences had great advantages for artists and writers. It meant that images and symbols were not 'mere' images and symbols but expressions of the language of the universe and of God its creator. Historical events or individuals might also correspond to one another, since the historical process was often believed to move in cycles rather than to 'progress' steadily in one direction. Charles VIII of France was viewed by Savonarola as a 'Second Charlemagne' and as a 'New Cyrus'; more than the equivalent, almost the reincarnation of the great ruler of Persia (Weinstein, 1970, pp. 145, 166–7). The emperor Charles V was also hailed as the 'Second Charlemagne'. The Florentine poets who wrote of the return of the golden age under Medici rule may well have been doing something more than turn a decoratively flattering or flatteringly decorative phrase. The idea of the Renaissance itself depends on the assumption that history moves in cycles and employs the organic language of 'birth'.

This 'organic mentality' as we may call it, so pervasive was it, met a direct challenge only in the seventeenth century from Descartes, Galileo, Newton and other 'natural philosophers'. The organic model of the cosmos remained dominant in the fifteenth and sixteenth

---

[44] The discussion of 'the prose of the world' in Foucault (1966), ch. 2, has become a classic. For a more thorough analysis, see Céard (1977).

centuries. All the same, a few individuals, at least on occasion, did make use of an alternative model, the mechanical one, which is hardly surprising in a culture which produced engineers such as Mariano Taccola, Francesco di Giorgio Martini and, of course, Leonardo (Gille, 1964). Giovanni Fontana, who wrote on water-clocks among other subjects, once referred to the universe as this 'noble clock', an image which was to become commonplace in the seventeenth and eighteenth centuries. Leonardo da Vinci, whose comparison of the microscosm and the macrocosm has already been quoted, makes regular use of the mechanical model. He described the tendons of the human body as 'mechanical instruments' and the heart too as a 'marvellous instrument'. He also wrote that 'the bird is an instrument operating by mathematical law', a principle underlying his attempts to construct flying-machines.[45] Machiavelli and Guicciardini saw politics in terms of the balance of power. In the twentieth chapter of the *Prince*, Machiavelli refers to the time when Italy was 'in a way in equilibrium [*in un certo modo bilanciata*]', while Guicciardini makes the same point at the beginning of his *History of Italy*, observing that at the death of Lorenzo de'Medici, 'Italian affairs were in a sort of equilibrium [*le cose d'Italia in modo bilanciate si mantenessino*]'. The widespread concern with the precise measurement of time and space, discussed earlier in this chapter, fits in better with this mechanical worldview than with the traditional organic one. The mechanization of the world picture was really the work of the seventeenth century, but in Italy at least, the process had begun.[46]

There would seem to be a case for talking about the pluralism of worldviews in Renaissance Italy, a pluralism which may well have been a stimulus to intellectual innovation. Such a coexistence of competing views naturally raises the question of their association with different social groups. The mechanical world picture has sometimes been described as 'bourgeois' (Borkenau, 1934). Was it in fact associated with the bourgeoisie? It will be easier to answer this question after discussing what the bourgeoisie were, and the general shape of the social structure in Renaissance Italy. This is the task of the following chapter.

---

[45] On the coexistence of organic and mechanical modes of thought in Leonardo, see Dijksterhuis (1961), pp. 253–64.

[46] Cf. Delumeau (1967), who stresses progress in the capacity for abstraction.

9

THE SOCIAL FRAMEWORK

THIS chapter continues the process of moving outward from the art and literature of the Renaissance, the milieux in which they were produced, and the worldviews they expressed. It is essentially concerned with organizations, formal and informal, and their relationship to Renaissance culture. It deals in the first place with an institution which existed to propagate a worldview, the Church; next with political institutions; then with the social structure; and finally, at the very base of society, with the economy.

RELIGIOUS ORGANIZATION

If modern Christians could visit Renaissance Italy, they would probably be very much surprised, not to say shocked, by what they would find going on in church, and even an Italian Catholic might raise an eyebrow.[1] The Venetian cardinal Gasparo Contarini described men walking through a church 'talking among themselves about trade, about wars, and very often even about love'. Walking through churches, especially during Mass, was frequently forbidden (at Modena in 1463, for example, and at Milan in 1530), frequently enough for us to conclude that it must have happened all the time. One might expect to find beggars in church, or horses, or gamblers, or a school master giving lessons, or a political meeting in progress. The parishioners ate, drank and danced in the church to celebrate major festivals like that of the patron saint.

Churches might be used as storehouses for grain or wood. A visitation of the diocese of Mantua in 1535 reported on a church in which 'the chaplain has a kitchen, beds and other things which are not very appropriate for a holy place; but ... he may be excused because his dwelling is very small' (Tacchi-Venturi, 1910, p. 179f; Putelli, 1935, p. 16). Valuables might be kept in the sacristy; there were, after all, few other safe places.

---

[1] Since this book was first published, a general survey of the Italian Church has appeared in Hay (1977).

The Dutch historian Johan Huizinga's (1919, ch. 12) remark that in the Middle Ages, people were inclined 'to treat the sacred with a familiarity which did not exclude respect' remains true for the Renaissance, with the proviso that their familiarity did not necessarily include respect either. The distinction between the sacred and profane was not drawn in quite the same place and it was not drawn as sharply as it would be in the later sixteenth century after the Council of Trent. Nor was it drawn by everyone. As late as 1580, Montaigne, who was visiting Verona, was surprised to see men standing and talking during mass, their hats on their heads and their backs to the altar.[2]

There was a similar lack of sharp distinction between clergy and laity. The Roman census of 1526 records a friar working as a mason (*il frate muratore*). The clergy lacked a special kind of education until seminaries were set up after the Council of Trent. 'How many' asked a participant in the Lateran Council of 1514, 'do not wear clothes laid down by the sacred canons, keep concubines, are simoniacal and ambitious? How many carry weapons like soldiers . . .? How many go to the altar with their own children around them? How many hunt and shoot with crossbows and guns? (Tacchi-Venturi, 1910, p. 36) It does not seem possible to answer his rhetorical questions, or even to say how many clergy there were, a question complicated by the existence of marginal cases, men in minor orders, including such famous names as Poliziano and Ariosto. All that the evidence allows is an estimate of their number in particular cities in particular years. In Florence in 1427, for example, a city of some 38,000 people, there were about 300 secular priests, but over 1,100 monks, friars and nuns (Herlihy and Klapisch-Zuber, 1978, table 10). By 1550 the total population had risen to nearly 60,000, but the proportion of clergy had climbed still more steeply to just over 5,000 or nearly 9 per cent (Battara, 1935, pp. 79–80). In Venice in 1581, a city of about 135,000 people had nearly 600 secular priests but the friars and nuns brought the clerical total to more than 4,000 (Beltrami, 1954, p. 79).

The clergy were very far from being a homogeneous body, either culturally or socially. It is necessary to distinguish at least three groups: the bishops, the rank-and file secular clergy and the members of religious orders.

Bishops were generally nobles. Some sees were virtually hereditary in particular families, the dynasty being perpetuated by the practice of uncles resigning in favour of their nephews. The other main avenue to a bishopric was the patron–client system. A young doctor of canon

---

[2] Montaigne, *Journal de voyage en Italie*, p. 68.

law would enter the household of a cardinal, serve him as secretary or in some other capacity, and obtain a bishopric through his influence. In Italy as elsewhere in Europe, bishops generally knew their law; better, in fact, than their theology.[3]

Parish priests also depended on patronage, since the right to appoint to a particular benefice often belonged to a particular family. Some rectors or holders of benefices did not do the work themselves but hired a deputy or 'vicar' to do it for them, often for a small proportion of the income. In the early sixteenth century, some chaplains in the diocese of Milan had an income of only 40 lire a year, less than that of an unskilled labourer. Some priests were active as horse or cattle dealers as a way of making ends meet. Whether rectors or vicars, parish priests had little formal training. They learned what they had to do by what has been called 'apprenticeship', in other words by helping and watching (Hay, 1977, p. 52). Stories of their ignorance were common and may well have been exaggerated for effect, but diocesan visitations regularly revealed priests who lacked breviaries, or could be described in laconic but devastating terms such as 'he knows nothing' or 'he is illiterate' (Hay, 1977 , pp. 49–57).

Finally, there were the religious orders. There were monks, notably the Benedictines, including the poet Teofilo Folengo, and the particularly strict Order of Camaldoli, one of whose members was the fifteenth-century humanist Ambrogio Traversari, a friend of Niccolò de Niccoli and Cosimo de'Medici and translator of some of the Greek Fathers of the Church.[4] There were five mendicant orders. The Servites, devoted to the Blessed Virgin, had been founded at Florence. The Augustinians included Luigi Marsigli, a friend of Niccoli and the humanist Coluccio Salutati. Among the Carmelites, devoted to Our Lady of Mount Carmel, were Fra Lippo Lippi and the Latin poet Giovanni Battista Spagnolo, better known as 'the Mantuan'. The Dominicans included the painter fra Angelico and the preacher fra Girolamo Savonarola. The Franciscans had several leading preachers, among them San Bernardino of Siena (Hay, 1977, pp. 58–61; Zarri, 1984). If they did not produce a major artist, they certainly had an influence on the arts (Francastel, 1965, pp. 305–15).

It was the friars who made sermons important in Italian religious life, in the towns at least, at a time when many of the parish clergy seem to have been 'dumb dogs that will not bark', as reformers liked to describe their English equivalents. San Bernardino even told his congregation that if they had a choice between Mass and a sermon,

---

[3] The most useful single monograph on bishops is Alberigo (1959), Cf. Hay (1977), pp. 18–20.

[4] On the Benedictines in fifteenth-century Italy, see Collett (1985), ch. 1.

they should choose the sermon. Enthusiasts took his sermons down in shorthand, and legal proceedings were sometimes postponed so that everyone could go and listen (Origo, 1963; Bronzini, 1978). Some preachers had little to learn from actors. One is said to have read to his congregation a letter from Christ, while another, fra Roberto da Lecce, entered the pulpit to preach a crusade wearing a full suit of armour. If sermons receive no more than a brief mention in this study, it is not because they were unimportant in the cultural life of the time, but because they belong to late medieval tradition rather than to Renaissance innovation, and because the printed collections which survive are a highly abbreviated and incomplete record and no firm basis for the reconstruction of actual performances.[5]

Religious festivals were another kind of performance which it is hard to reconstruct but which meant a great deal to Italians in the fifteenth and sixteenth centuries. The feast of Corpus Christi, for example, was growing in importance in the fifteenth century. It was celebrated with special magnificence at Viterbo in 1462 by Pius II and his cardinals, as the pope records in his memoirs; the decorations included a fountain which ran with water and wine and 'a youth impersonating the Saviour, who sweated blood, and filled a cup with a healing stream from a wound in his side'.[6] A famous painting by Gentile Bellini represents the Corpus Christi procession in Venice as it went through Piazzo San Marco. In the sixteenth century, *tableaux vivants* became an important element of Venetian Corpus Christi processions (Muir, 1981, pp. 223–30). Religious plays were another important element in these festivals – performances within the performance. Corpus Christi was one great occasion for plays; another, in Florence at least, was the feast of the Epiphany, when the plays represented the three wise men, or kings, Jasper, Baltasar and Melchior, bringing their gifts to the infant Christ. In Rome, a Passion Play was performed every year at the Colosseum. As a fifteenth-century German visitor recorded, 'This was acted by living people, even the scourging, the crucifixion, and how Judas hanged himself. They were all the children of wealthy people, and it was therefore done orderly and richly.'[7]

Among the most important festivals were those of the patron saints of cities: St Ambrose in Milan, St Mark in Venice, St John the Baptist in Florence and so on. Such feasts were events on which civic prestige depended and on which communal values were solemnly reaffirmed. In Florence, for example, the feast of St John was celebrated with

---

[5] On Italian preaching, see Rusconi (1981) and Nigro (1983).
[6] Pius, *Commentarii*, book 8.
[7] von Harff, *Pilgrimage* (1496), p. 40.

races, jousts and bull-fights. The subject towns of the Florentine empire sent deputations to the capital, there was a banquet for the Signoria (the town council), and there were the usual floats, races, cavalcades, hunts, jugglers, tight-rope walkers and giants (impersonated by men on stilts).[8]

Central to the organization of these plays and festivals were religious fraternities (*compagnie, scuole*). These voluntary associations of the laity were widespread in the fourteenth and fifteenth centuries, when at least 420 of them were found in north and central Italy alone. Their main role may be described as the imitation of Christ: this underlay their frequent practice of flagellation, their banquets (a ritual of solidarity modelled on the Last Supper), their washing of the feet of the poor on special occasions, and their concern with what were known as the seven works of temporal mercy: visiting the sick, feeding the hungry, giving drink to the thirsty, clothing the naked, helping prisoners, burying the dead and giving lodging to pilgrims. Some specialized in a particular function. The fraternity of St Martin (*Buonomini di San Martino*) was founded in Florence in 1442 to aid the poor, especially the genteel poor, and named after the saint who had divided his cloak with a beggar. Others comforted condemned criminals, like the Roman fraternity of St John Beheaded (*San Giovanni Decollato*) of which Michelangelo was a member.[9]

The importance of the fraternities as the patrons of art has already been discussed (above p. 90). They played an important part in religious festivals, walking in procession and performing in pageants and plays. It was, for example, the Fraternity of the Magi in Florence which performed the pageant of the three kings; the Fraternity of St John, also in Florence, which performed Lorenzo de'Medici's play *Saints John and Paul*; and the Fraternity of the Gonfalon in Rome which put on the regular Good Friday Passion play at the Colosseum (the painter Antoniazzo Romano was a member and he painted the scenery).[10] Fraternities often sang hymns in praise of the Virgin and the saints, in their processions and in church, and these hymns (*laude*) were sometimes distinguished examples of religious poetry and might be set to music by leading composers such as Guillaume Dufay.[11] Fraternities also listened to special sermons, which might be delivered by laymen. It is curious to think of Machiavelli in the pulpit, but it is

---

[8] See Guasti (1884). Important observations on the politics of the feast are to be found in Trexler (1980), pp. 240f, 326f, 406f, 450f etc.

[9] On St Martin, see Trexler (1973); on St John, see Edgerton (1985), ch. 5. An important study of the rituals and social relationships of Florentine fraternities is Weissman (1982).

[10] On the Fraternity of the Magi, see Hatfield (1970).

[11] Some fifteenth-century texts are in Monti (1920).

still possible to read the 'exhortation to penitence' he delivered to the Florentine Fraternity of Piety. It has been argued that the Platonic Academy of Florence owes as much to these fraternities as to Plato's original Academy (Kristeller, 1956).

POLITICAL ORGANIZATION

A distinctive feature of the political organization of Renaissance Italy was the importance of city-states and in particular of republics. Around the year 1200, 'some two or three hundred units existed which deserve to be described as city-states' (Waley, 1969, p. 11). By the fifteenth century, most of them had lost their independence, but not the Renaissance cities *par excellence*, Florence and Venice. Their constitutions make a study in contrasts.

If ever there were a state apparently well suited to the functional analysis which dominated sociology and social anthropology in the first half of the twentieth century, it is surely Venice. The Venetian constitution was celebrated for its stability and balance, thanks to the mixture of elements from the three main types of government, with the doge representing monarchy, the Senate aristocracy, and the Great Council democracy. In practice the monarchical element was a weak one. Despite the outward honours paid to the doge, whose head appeared on coins, he had little real power. The Venetians had already developed the distinction, best known from Walter Bagehot's famous description of the British constitution in the nineteenth century, between the 'dignified' and the 'efficient' parts of the political system. The Great Council, by contrast, did participate in decision-making, but this council of nobles was not exactly democratic. As for conflicts, they were not absent but hidden behind the fiction of consensus.

Like the idea of the mixed constitution, Venetian stability or 'harmony' was not a neutral descriptive term. It was part of an ideology, part of the 'myth of Venice' as historians call it today; in other words, the idealized view of Venice held by Venetians from the ruling class, such as cardinal Gasparo Contarini, whose *Commonwealth and Government of Venice* (1543) did much to propagate it.[12] Relatively speaking, however, there was a kernel of truth in the idea of Venetian stability. The political system did not change very much during the period. If Venice was ruled by the few, the few were unusually numerous. All adult patricians were members of the Great

---

[12] On the 'myth of Venice', see Logan (1972), ch. 1, and Finlay (1980), ch. 1.

Council (*Maggior Consiglio*), over 2,500 of them in the early sixteenth century. Hence the size of the Hall of the Great Council and the need for large paintings to fill it. (Davis, 1962, ch. 3; cf. Chambers, 1970a, ch. 3; Finlay, 1980, ch. 2; on the paintings for the Hall, see p. 132 above).

Florence, by contrast, had an unstable political system, compared by Dante in his *Divine Comedy* – which exile gave him the leisure to write – to a sick woman twisting and turning in bed, uncomfortable in every position.[13] As a sixteenth-century Venetian observer put it, 'They have never been content with their constitution, they are never quiet, and it seems that this city always desires a change of constitution, so that no particular form of government has ever lasted more than fifteen years.' He commented, rather smugly, that this was God's punishment for the sins of the Florentines (Segarizzi, 1916, p. 39). It may have rather more to do with the fact that Florentines enjoyed political rights at the age of 14, while Venetians were not considered politically adult till they were 25, and had to be old men before their ideas were taken seriously. The average age of a doge of Venice on his election was 72 (Finlay, 1978).

For whatever reason, change was the norm in Florence. In 1434, Cosimo de'Medici returned from exile and took over the state. In 1458 a Council of Two Hundred was set up. In 1480 it was replaced by a Council of Seventy. In 1494 the Medici were driven out, and a Great Council set up on the Venetian model. In 1502 a kind of doge was created, the 'gonfaloniere for life'. In 1512 the Medici returned in the baggage of a foreign army. In 1527 they were driven out again, and in 1530 returned again. It may not be too fanciful to suggest that there is some link, however difficult it may be to specify it, between the political culture and the artistic culture of the Florentines, and the propensity to innovate in these two spheres. By contrast, the less unstable Venetians were slower to welcome the Renaissance.

Apart from this tendency to structural change, Florence differed from Venice in that offices rotated more rapidly; the chief magistrates, or *Signoria*, were in office for only two months at a time. The minority of Florentines involved in politics was much larger than in Venice, with more than 6,000 citizens (craftsmen and shopkeepers as well as patricians), eligible for the chief magistracies alone.[14]

The other three major powers in Italy were effectively monarchies, two hereditary (Milan and Naples) and one elective (the Papal States).

---

[13] *Purgatorio*, Canto 6: 'Vedrai te simigliante a quella inferma, Che non può trovar posa in su le piume, Ma con dar volta suo dolore scherma.'

[14] Studies of the Florentine political system include Molho (1968); Kent (1975, 1978); Rubinstein (1976); Brucker (1977); Stephens (1983); and Butters (1985) ch. 1.

Here, as in smaller states like Ferrara, Mantua and Urbino, the key institution was the court. So many major works of Renaissance art and literature, from Mantegna's *Camera degli sposi* to Ariosto's *Orlando Furioso*, were produced in this milieu that it is important to understand what kind of place it was. This task has become easier thanks to recent specialized studies produced in the wake of Norbert Elias's pioneering sociology (or anthropology) of court society.[15]

Courts numbered hundreds of people: in 1527 the papal court, for example, was about 700 strong. From this point of view, the small circle surrounding Lorenzo de'Medici, the first citizen of a republic, does not qualify for the title of 'court' at all (contrast Pottinger, 1978). This court population was extremely heterogeneous, and ran from great nobles holding offices such as constable, chamberlain, steward or master of the horse, through lesser courtiers such as gentlemen of the bedchamber, secretaries and pages, down to servants such as trumpeters, falconers, cooks, barbers and stable boys. Harder to place in the hierarchy (indeed, professional outsiders), but commonly in attendance to entertain the prince, were his fools and midgets. The position of his poets and musicians may not have been so very different.

A crucial feature of the court was that it served two functions which were becoming more and more divergent: the private and the public; the household of the prince and the administration of the state. The prince generally ate with his courtiers. When he moved, most of the court moved with him, despite the logistic problems of transporting, feeding and accommodating a group equivalent to the population of a small town. When Duke Lodovico Sforza decided to go from Milan to his favourite country residence, Vigevano, or to his other castles and hunting lodges, it took 500 horses and mules to transport the court and its belongings (Malaguzzi-Valeri, 1913, vol. 1 ch. 3). Alfonso of Aragon, king of Naples, was similarly mobile much of the time, visiting different parts of an empire which included Catalonia, Sicily and Sardinia. His officials were forced to follow his example, indeed to follow him in a quite literal sense. In December 1451, for instance, Alfonso summoned his council to Capua, where he happened to be hunting, in order to decide his dispute with the city of Barcelona (Ryder, 1976a).

The cultural importance of the court as an institution was that it brought together a number of gentlemen – and ladies – of leisure. It was crucial to what Elias calls 'the civilizing process'. Like elegant manners, an interest in art and literature helped show the difference

---

[15] After Elias (1969), see Quondam (1978); Ossola (1980); and Prosperi (1980).

between the nobility and ordinary people. As in the salons of seventeenth-century Paris, the presence of ladies stimulated conversation, music and poetry. We must, of course, beware of idealizing the Renaissance court. Castiglione's famous *Courtier* must not be taken too literally. It was planned as a courtly equivalent of Plato's treatise on the ideal republic, and it should also be regarded (as the history of the revisions to the text demonstrates), as an exercise in public relations, from the defence of the threatened duchy of Urbino in the first draft to the censorship of anticlerical remarks in the final version when the author was launching himself on a second, ecclesiastical career (Guidi in Rochon, 1982, pp. 97–115). It is likely that courtiers often found time hanging heavily on their hands. Even in the pages of Castiglione we find them turning to practical jokes as well as to parlour games in order to alleviate boredom. One of the speakers in the dialogue describes courts where the nobles throw food at one another or make bets about eating the most revolting things: so much for 'civilization'.

A good corrective to the all too beautiful picture painted by Castiglione is the little book produced by the humanist Enea Silvio Piccolomini in 1444, 14 years before he became pope as Pius II. The *Miseries of Courtiers*, as it is called, is doubtless something of a caricature and it draws on a tradition of literary and moral commonplaces, but it adds a few sharp personal observations. If a man seeks pleasure at court, writes Enea, he will be disappointed. There is music at court it is true, but it is when the prince wants it, not when you want it, and perhaps just when you had been hoping to sleep. In any case you cannot sleep comfortably because the bedclothes are dirty, there are several other people in the same bed (which was normal in the fifteenth century), your neighbour coughs all night and pulls the bedclothes off you, or perhaps you have to sleep in the stables. The servants never bring the food on time, and they whisk the plates away before you have finished. You never know when the court is going to move; you make ready to leave, only to find that the prince has changed his mind. Solitude and quiet are impossible. Whether the prince stands or sits, the courtier always has to be on his feet.[16] These do not sound like the conditions most likely to stimulate creativity, but they are the conditions in which poets such as Ariosto, to take only the most famous example, must have worked.

Courts existed all over Europe, and there were city-states, in practice if not always in strict political theory, in The Netherlands, in Switzerland and in Germany. It is worth asking whether Italian forms

---

[16] Pius II, *De curialium miseriis epistola*.

of political organization were distinctive in this period, and if so, whether this distinctiveness encouraged the cultural movement we call the Renaissance. As the Italian historian Federico Chabod (1964) asked, 'Was there a Renaissance state?'

Chabod's answer is a qualified 'yes', not so much on the grounds of the political consciousness of which Jacob Burckhardt made so much, as of the rise of bureaucracy. 'Bureaucracy' is a term with many meanings. It will make for clarity if we follow the precise definitions of the German sociologist Max Weber, and distinguish two political systems, the patrimonial and the bureaucratic, on six criteria in particular.

Patrimonial government is essentially personal, but bureaucratic government is impersonal (the public sphere is separated from the private, and it is the holder of the office rather than the individual whom one obeys). Patrimonial government is carried out by amateurs, bureaucratic government by professionals, trained for the job, with appointment by merit rather than favour, a fixed salary, and an ethos of their own. Patrimonial government is informal, while bureaucrats put everything on record in writing. Patrimonial government is unspecialized, but in the bureaucratic system the officials practise an elaborate division of labour and are careful to define the frontiers of their political territories. Patrimonial government appeals to tradition, bureaucratic government to reason and to the law (Weber, 1968, part 2, chs 10–14).

There is certainly a case for arguing that some at least of the states of Renaissance Italy were precociously bureaucratic, thanks to Italian urbanization and the consequent spread of literacy and numeracy, discussed above; thanks to the existence of republics, where loyalty was focused not on the ruler but the impersonal state; and thanks to the existence in Italy of the capital of a huge international organization, the Catholic Church. The distinction between public and private was certainly drawn quite explicitly by some contemporaries, like the speaker in Alberti's dialogue on the family who rejected the idea of treating the former in any way as if it were the latter (ch'io in modo alcuno facessi del publico privato).[17] There was an institutional means of preventing officials confusing public and private to their own advantage: the sindacato. When an official's term of office expired in Florence, Milan and Naples, he had to remain behind until his activities had been investigated by special commissioners or 'syndics'.[18] The pope's dual role as head of the Church and ruler of

---

[17] Alberti, I libri della famiglia, p. 221.
[18] On Milan, see Santoro (1948) and Chabod (1958); on Naples, see Coniglio (1951) and Ryder (1976a).

the Papal States also encouraged awareness of the distinction between an individual and his office (Prodi, 1982, p. 50f).

Again, full-time officials were relatively numerous, especially in Rome, and a doctorate in law was something of a professional training for them.[19] Some had tenure and developed a corporate ethos. Fixed money salaries were not uncommon and some of them were relatively high. In Venice at the beginning of the sixteenth century, secretaries in the chancery averaged 125 ducats a year, about the salary of branch managers of the Medici bank. Attempts were made to ensure appointment by merit rather than by purchase, favour or neighbourhood. In Rome, too, the role of secretaries increased in importance in the period (see Kraus, 1960, a Weberian analysis).

In the greater Italian states, there was considerable demarcation of function between oficials. In Milan under Lodovico Sforza, for example, there was a secretary for ecclesiastical affairs, a secretary for justice and a secretary for foreign affairs, who was in turn served by subordinates who specialized in the affairs of different states (Santoro, 1948). In Florence and Venice specialist committees were set up, concerned with trade, naval affairs, defence and so on. In Rome in the later sixteenth century, pope Sixtus V set up 'congregations' or standing committees of cardinals with specialized functions ranging from ritual to the navy. It was in Renaissance Italy that diplomacy first became specialized and professionalized (Mattingly, 1955). The importance of written records in administration was increasing. The most striking examples of the collection of information come from the censuses, notably the Florentine *catasto* of 1427, dealing with every individual under the rule of the Florentine *Signoria*.[20] It was, of course, less difficult to undertake a census of a small state like Florence than of a large one like France. As for the filing and retrieval of information, some sixteenth-century rulers such as Cosimo d'Medici, grand duke of Tuscany, and popes Sixtus V and Gregory XIII, took a particular interest in the setting up of archives (Prodi, 1982, p. 117). There was also increasing awareness, in Rome in particular, of the need for budgeting, in other words for calculating income and expenditure in advance (Partner, 1980).

One is left with an impression of Italian self-consciousness and innovation in the political field as in that of the arts. In so far as a bureaucratic mode of domination had developed, it is useful to speak of a 'Renaissance state'. All the same, the extent and speed of change must not be exaggerated. Italy had no lack of courts, and at court, as

---

[19] A good brief account of the Roman bureaucracy is in D'Amico (1983), p. 19f.

[20] See Herlihy and Klapisch-Zuber (1978). In the sixteenth century there were censuses of the state of Milan and the cities of Rome, Venice and Naples, not to mention lesser cities.

we have seen, public administration was not separated from the private household of the ruler; loyalty was focused on a man, not an institution; and the ruler by-passed the system whenever he wished to grant a favour to a suitor. In appointments and promotions, the prime necessity was the prince's favour As Pius II remarked in his complaint of the miseries of courtiers, 'at the courts of princes, what matters are not services but personalities [*non enim servitia in curiis principum sed personae ponderantur*]'.[21]

At the court of Rome, official positions were regularly sold, especially in the reign of Leo X, and the department of the Datary grew up to deal with this business (Partner, 1976, p. 60f; D'Amico, 1983, p. 27f). Offices were also sold in the states of Milan and Naples. The buyer of the office might not exercise it in person but 'farm' it, in other words pay a substitute to perform the duties for the fraction of the proceeds, like the 'vicar' in a parish. Offices were seen as investments, and were expected to bring in an income. However, official salaries were often inadequate. In Milan in the middle of the fifteenth century, the chancellor of the duke's council was paid little more than an unskilled labourer. Administrators relied on presents, fees and other perquisites, such as the right to a proportion of confiscated goods.

Even the administration of republics was in many ways far removed from Max Weber's model of an impersonally efficient bureaucracy. Indeed, in some respects, such as the corporate ethos of officials, Florence seems to have been less bureaucratic than Milan (Witt, 1983, p. 112f). The official system may have stressed equality and merit, but one also has to take into account what Italians today call the *sottogoverno*, the underbelly of the administration. In Venice, for example, some offices were bought, sold and given as dowries. In any Italian state of this period it is difficult to underestimate the importance of family connections and also of what was known euphemistically as 'friendship' (*amicizia*), in other words the links between powerful patrons and their dependents or 'clients'. The many surviving letters addressed to members of the Medici family in the years immediately before Cosimo came to power in 1434 give a vivid impression of the importance of *amicizia* to both parties.[22] These letters give substance to the contemporary complaint by Giovanni Cavalcanti that the Florentine commune 'was governed at dinners and in private studies [*alle cene e negli scrittoi*] rather than in the Palace'.[23]

---

[21] Pius II, *De curialium miseriis epistola*, p. 35.
[22] These letters form the documentary basis of Kent (1978); on *amicizia*, see p. 83f.
[23] Cavalcanti, *Istorie fiorentine*, book 2, ch. 1.

Many of the political conflicts of the time were struggles between rival 'factions', in other words between groups of patrons and clients. Perugia, where the Oddi fought the Baglioni, and Pistoia, where the Panciatichi fought the Cancellieri, were notorious for their factionalism. As Machiavelli put it in the twentieth chapter of his *Prince*, it was necessry 'to control Pistoia by means of factions [*tenere Pistoia con le parte*]'. Local rivalries continued to give some substance to the venerable party terms 'Guelf' (originally a supporter of the pope) and 'Ghibelline' (a supporter of the emperor) as late as the sixteenth century. The importance of patronage in political and social life gave its force to the Italian proverb, 'you can't get to heaven without saints [*senza santi non si va in Paradiso*]', picturing the next world in the image of this one. The patronage of artists and writers formed part of this wider system.

At this point we may return to the links between politics and culture. Which was the better form of government for the arts, the republic or the principality? Contemporaries discussed the question, but their opinions were divided. Leonardo Bruni argued, as we have seen (p. 28), that Roman culture flourished and died with the republic, and Pius II suggested that 'The study of letters flourished most of all at Athens, while it was a free city, and at Rome, while the consuls ruled the commonwealth.'[24] On the other hand, the fifteenth-century humanist, Giovanni Conversino da Ravenna complained bitterly that 'Where the multitude rules, there is no respect for any accomplishment that does not yield a profit . . . everybody has as much contempt for the poets as he is ignorant of them, and will rather keep dogs than maintain scholars or teachers' (quoted in Baron, 1955, p. 139).

The fact that the two great republics, Florence and Venice, were the cities where most artists and writers originated is an obvious point in favour of the Bruni thesis. However, it is not enough to record a correlation; we have to try to explain it. Although it is impossible to measure the achievement drive, it is reasonable to expect it to be greater in republics because they are organized on the principle of competition, so that parents are more likely to bring up their children to try to excel others. One might also expect this drive to be stronger in Florence, where the system was more open, than in Venice, where the major public offices were virtually monopolized by the nobility. So it was better for an artist or writer to be born in a republic; he had a better chance of developing his talents.

When they were developed, however, he needed patronage; and

---

[24] Pius II, *De curialium miseriis epistola*, p. 39.

here it is less easy to say which political system benefited artists and writers most. In republics there was civic patronage, at its most vigorous in Florence in the early fifteenth century, when artisans still participated in the government, and Brunelleschi was elected to one of the highest offices, that of 'prior', in 1425. It was helped by *campanilismo*, a sense of local patriotism fuelled by rivalry with the neighbouring commune, and expressed architecturally in the magnificent town halls of the period (the Sienese deliberately built their tower higher than that of Florence). Civic patronage was weaker in the later fifteenth century and weaker in Venice than in Florence, despite the official and quasi-official positions of Bembo, Titian and others. It is not surprising to find artists who had been born and trained in republics attracted to courts; Leonardo to Milan, Michelangelo to Rome, and so on. An enterprising prince who was willing to spend the money could make his court an artistic centre fairly quickly, by buying up artists who were already in practice. What he could not do was to produce artists. Whether young men chose to follow the career of artist or not depended, as we have seen, on the social structure.

THE SOCIAL STRUCTURE

One reason for the trend towards bureaucratic government not going further was that impersonal administration was impossible in what was still essentially a face-to-face society. Only two cities, Naples and Venice, had populations over 100,000, the size of Cambridge in the 1980s. Loyalty to one's quarter of town, or ward, or *rione* (as in Rome), or *sestiere* (as in Venice) was strong, a loyalty which has survived – whatever the reason – among the *contrade* of Siena today, and is symbolized in the famous *palio* (Dundes and Falassi, 1975). Within the quarter, the neighbourhood (*vicinanza*) was a meaningful unit, a stage for local social dramas of solidarity and enmity. In Florence, the neighbourhood, or more exactly the *gonfalone* (a quarter within the quarter, or a sixteenth of the city) was a focus for political activity, as is shown by a recent study of one of them. 'Red Lion' (*Lion Rosso*) (Kent and Kent, 1982; cf. Kent, 1978, p. 61f). The parish was often a community, and so was the street, which was frequently dominated by a particular trade, such as the goldsmiths in Via del Pellegrino in Rome. Cities were small enough for the sound of a particular bell, such as the *marangone* in Venice, or the bell in the Torre del Mangia in Siena, to announce the opening of the gates, or the beginning of the working day, or to call the citizens to arms or to a council (Hook, 1979, p. 96f). Official impersonality was hindered by the fact that citizens might know officials in their private roles.

Renaissance Florence seems in some ways more like a village than a city, in the sense that so many of the artists and writers with whom we are concerned knew one another, often intimately. A vivid illustration of relationships in this face-to-face society is the meeting of experts called by the *Opera del Duomo* of Florence in 1503 to decide where to display Michelangelo's *David*. Present were 30 men, mainly artists, including Leonardo, Botticelli, Perugino, Piero di Cosimo, Cosimo Rosselli, the Sangallos and Andrea Sansovino, all recorded in the minutes as discussing one another's suggestions. 'Cosimo has said exactly where I think it should go', says Botticelli, and so on (Gaye, 1839–40, vol. 2, pp. 454–63; Klein and Zerner, 1966, pp. 39–44).

However, Italian society was certainly complicated enough to need an elaborate system of classification. A simple way of illustrating this complexity is to quote a few examples of annual income, in lire, in order to show the range in variation, which works out at 3,500 to one.[25]

L140,000	the richest Venetian cardinal c. 1500
L77,000	great merchant, Venice c. 1500
L21,000	Doge of Venice c. 1500
L12,500	ambassador, Venice, c. 1500
L3,750	captain of infantry, Milan c. 1520
L900	secretary in the Chancery, Venice c. 1500
L900	master shipwright, Venice c. 1500
L600	branch manager, Medici Bank, Florence c. 1450
L400	silkweaver, Florence c. 1450
L250	soldier, Milan c. 1520
L250	court trumpeter, Milan c. 1470
L200	young bank clerk, Florence c. 1450
L150	soldier, Venice c. 1500
L120	mason or carpenter, Milan c. 1450
L70	shop-boy, Florence c. 1450
L60	labourer, Milan c. 1450
L50	servant, Venice c. 1500

---

[25] I have converted different currencies (florins, ducats etc.) into lire because this was the standard 'money of account' of the period. The annual figures are sometimes conversions of daily rates, in which case I have multiplied by 250 not 365. I have made no allowance for changes in prices because Italy was struck by serious inflation only in the mid-sixteenth century. The sources used are Fossati (1928); Lane (1934); Barbieri (1938); Sardella (1948); Chabod (1961); de Roover (1963). On workers' wages, cf. Goldthwaite (1980), appendix 3.

in Renaissance Italy. The evidence is too fragmentary and the different systems of taxation and so on in different states make precise comparison virtually impossible.[26] This is particularly unfortunate in a field where the historian who does not make a statement about quantities says virtually nothing, for there is no society without some measure of social mobility, and no society where mobility is 'perfect', in other words where the status of individuals has a purely random relation to that of their parents. All societies are somewhere in between these two extremes; what matters is the precise position.

All the same there are good reasons for asserting that social mobility was relatively high in the cities of fifteenth-century Italy, and above all in early fifteenth-century Florence, with 'new men' (*gente nuova*) coming in from the countryside and becoming citizens and holding office, in number sufficient to alarm patricians such as Rinaldo degli Albizzi who, according to a contemporary chronicle, launched a violent attack on these new men in a meeting held in 1426.[27] The competitiveness, the envy and the stress on achievement of the Florentines (discussed above p. 194) look very much like characteristics of a mobile society.

By the later fifteenth century, however, the ranks had closed. In Padua, Verona, Bergamo and Brescia, the change came earlier, perhaps as a result of their incorporation into the Venetian empire (Ventura, 1964, ch. 2). In Venice itself there was little opportunity for new men to enter the patriciate throughout the period, whatever mobility there may have been at lower levels (Lane, 1973, pp. 111f, 151f, 252f).

The second question which this section attempts to answer is whether Italian society of this period may reasonably be described as 'bourgeois'. That it was bourgeois has been the assumption of many historians of the Renaissance, as we have seen, but this bold statement needs to be hedged about with at least a few qualifications and distinctions (Jones, 1978).

In the fifteenth and sixteenth centuries, Italy was one of the most highly urban societies in Europe. In 1550, about 40 Italian towns had a population of 10,000 or more. Of these, about 20 had a population of 25,000 or more, as follows (Beloch, 1961, p. 327f) (figures have been rounded to the nearest 5,000):

[26] Two good general discussions of the problem, however, are in Delumeau (1973) and Herlihy (1973).
[27] Cavalcanti, *Istorie fiorentine*, book 3, ch. 2. Recent discussions are in Kent (1975) and Brucker (1977), pp. 256f, 472f.

210,000	Naples
160,000	Venice
70,000	Milan, Palermo
60,000	Bologna (1570), Florence, Genoa (1530)
50,000	Verona
45,000	Rome (55,000 in 1526)
40,000	Mantua, Brescia
35,000	Lecce, Cremona
30,000	Padua, Vicenza
25,000	Lucca, Messina (1505), Piacenza, Siena
20,000	Perugia, Bergamo, Parma, Taranto, Trapani

In the rest of Europe, from Lisbon to Moscow, there were probably no more than another 20 towns of this size. About a quarter of the population of Tuscany and the Veneto was urban; in all the regions of Europe, only Flanders is likely to have had a higher proportion of townsmen.

It must not be assumed that all these townsmen were bourgeois. Renaissance Florence and other cities rested on the backs of what contemporaries called the *popolo minuto*, the 'labouring classes' (Cohn, 1980). All the same, the relative importance of Italian towns is obviously linked with the relative importance of merchants, professional men, craftsmen and shop-keepers. All these groups are sometimes called 'bourgeois'; none of them fits the traditional model of a society divided into clergy, nobles and peasants. However, we do need to distinguish between them. Rich merchants are sometimes important as patrons. The craftsmen sire the artists, and the professional men sire the writers and humanists, whether they are lawyers (Machiavelli's father), physicians (Ficino's father), notaries (Brunelleschi's father) or professors (Pomponazzi's father).

To go beyond these relatively precise points requires speculation. Was there an affinity between Renaissance values, notably the concern with abstraction, measurement and the individual, and the values of one or more groups within the bourgeoisie? The analogies are obvious enough, but the point must not be made too crudely. Machiavelli is a master of political calculation, but he expressed contempt for Florence as a city governed by shop-keepers (*uomini nutricati nella mercanzia*) and he described himself as 'unable to talk about gains and losses, about the silk-guild or the wool-guild'.[28]

There are other links between the social structure of Renaissance Italy and its art and literature. The importance of the lineage and the

---

[28] Letter to Vettori, 9 April 1513. This statement makes it likely that the Niccolò Machiavelli who worked in a bank was a different man, despite Maffei (1973).

spices came to Venice every year from Alexandria, and 300,000 ducats, besides merchandise, went back in return. The spices were resold to the merchants of Augsburg, Nuremberg and Bruges.[32]

Secondly, there was the craft–industrial town such as Milan or Florence. Florence was the industrial town *par excellence*, and cloth-making the chief industry; a late fifteenth-century description of the city lists 270 cloth-making workshops, compared to 84 for wood-carving and inlay, 83 for silk, 74 for goldsmiths and 54 for stone-dressers. Through cloth-making the Florentines became involved in trade. Their *Calimala* guild (discussed earlier as a patron of the arts) imported cloth from France and Flanders, arranged for it to be 'finished' (sheared, dyed and so on), and re-exported it (Doren, 1901). Cloth-making was also important in Milan, but the city was best known for its armourers and other metal-workers (Barbieri, 1938). Genoese silks had an international reputation, while Venice was famous for its glass, its ship-building and, from the 1490s or thereabouts, for its printing industry; Aldo Manuzio was the most scholarly and the most famous but far from the only Venetian printer of the sixteenth century (Lane, 1973).

Thirdly, there was the service city. One of the most profitable services to offer was financial. From the fourteenth century to the sixteenth, the Italians dominated European banking. The leading firms included the Bardi and the Peruzzi of Florence (till Edward III and other rulers bankrupted them), the Medici and, at the end of the period, the Pallavicini and the Spinola of Genoa, who lent vast sums to King Philip of Spain. Capital cities offered other kinds of service: Naples and Rome, for example, which were cities of officials and centres of power. In the case of Naples, the hinterland for the 'services' provided by judges, advocates, tax collectors and so on was the Kingdom of Naples or, in the reign of Alfonso of Aragon, his entire Mediterranean empire. In the case of Rome, the hinterland was sometimes the Papal States, but for some functions it was the whole Catholic world. Rome was, as a contemporary critic remarked, 'a shop for religion [*una bottega delle cose di Cristo*]'. Its invisible exports included indulgences and dispensations. This huge business required management, and an important role was played by the pope's bankers, from the Medici to Agostino Chigi of Siena, best known for his patronage of Raphael (de Roover, 1963; Gilbert, 1980, ch. 4).

Despite the growing importance of grain imports, this elaborate urban structure rested on the foundation of Italian agriculture (Sereni, 1961, 1973; Jones, 1965, 1966). Particularly fertile was the Po valley, one of the great plains of Europe. It owed this fertility partly to nature

– a well- distributed rainfall – and partly to man. In the course of the fifteenth century several canals were dug in Lombardy, and irrigation schemes allowed formerly waste land to be brought under the plough. By the year 1500, some 85 per cent of the land between Pavia and Cremona was under cultivation, an extremely high proportion for the period when marshes and woods were much more widespread than they are today. Dairy farming was becoming important (Dowd, 1961).

South of the Po valley the picture was less rosy. In Tuscany, although the hilly terrain restricted agriculture, the interior valleys were fertile. The Valdarno was best known for grain, the Valdichiana for wine, the Mugello for fruit, and the area around Lucca for olives. However, in the fourteenth and fifteenth century land was going out of cultivation in Tuscany, and 10 per cent of the villages disappeared altogether (Klapisch-Zuber and Day, 1965). Further south, the rocky terrain and the low rainfall in the growing season have always been obstacles to cultivation and, despite pockets of prosperity around Naples and elsewhere, southern agriculture was in decline. There was a gradual shift from arable to pasture, accompanied by a fall in population. As in Thomas More's England, the sheep were eating up the men.

To maintain Italy's high urban population, it was necessary for many farmers to produce for the market. For example, the concentration in Venice of some 160,000 people who did not grow their own food led to the commercialization of agriculture not only in the Veneto but as far afield as Mantua, the Marches and even, perhaps, in Apulia. The Italian cloth industry encouraged the growing of woad in Lombardy, and the keeping of sheep in the Roman Campagna and in the south as well as in Tuscany.

This brief description of the Italian economy is intended as no more than an introduction to the question of its links with the Renaissance. Before discussing these links, however, it is necessary to tackle one major problem. Was the economy 'capitalist'? Capitalism has been defined in many different ways, but it may be useful to emphasize two features of this mode of production, the concentration of capital in the hands of a few entrepreneurs, and the institutionalization of a rational, calculating approach to economic problems. It may also be useful to draw distinctions between commercial, financial and industrial capitalism (cf. Gras, 1953).

It is not difficult to find spectacular examples of rich entrepreneurs in this period, such as Averardo di Bicci de'Medici (the grandfather of Cosimo), who left a fortune of 180,000 florins in 1428. It was possible for entrepreneurs to accumulate capital in this way because

lifestyle can itself be explained in economic terms, that the shift from entrepreneurs to rentiers was an adaptation to economic recession, a case of 'hard times and contempt for trade', a kind of sour grapes effect. It has also been suggested that the Italian economic structure was unusually favourable to the development of a luxury market, thanks not only to the accumulation of wealth but also its wide distribution among a constantly changing group of urban consumers (Goldthwaite, 1985).

In these circumstances, competition for status thrived so that building magnificently became a strategy for distinguishing some families from others.[35] It would be unhistorical to treat Renaissance art as no more than a set of status symbols, forgetting the piety that underlay the patronage of sacred images or the pleasures of a private collection. Yet it would be equally unhistorical to treat the art of this period as if it had no connections with conspicuous consumption at all. The strength of the connections was subject to change over time. To examine the links between cultural and social change is the purpose of the following chapter.

---

[35] General reflections on these strategies in Bourdieu (1979).

10

CULTURAL AND SOCIAL CHANGE

> The natural changes in worldly affairs make poverty succeed riches . . . the
> man who first acquires a fortune takes a greater care of it; having known
> how to make his money, he also knows how to keep it . . . his heirs are less
> attached to a fortune they have made no effort to acquire. They have been
> brought up to riches and have never learned the art of earning them. Is it
> any wonder that they let it slip through their fingers?
> Guicciardini, *Ricordi*, no. 33

The focus of this book has been the description and analysis of social
and cultural 'structures'; that is, factors which remain fairly constant
over a century or two. They were not static, but it makes for clarity to
analyse them as if they were. Artistic, ideological, political and
economic factors have so far been treated in relative isolation. Such a
procedure has its advantages if the aim is to analyse as well as
describe. It is obvious, however, that what contemporaries experi-
enced was the combination or conjuncture of all these factors, and
that this conjuncture was constantly changing. It may be useful,
therefore, to draw together the themes of different sections at this
point, and to concentrate on the historian's traditional business – the
study of change over time.

It is in practice useful to distinguish different kinds of change, as
Braudel (1949) did in his famous study of the Mediterranean. There is
short-term change, the time of events, of which contemporaries are
well aware, and there is long-term change, almost impossible to
notice at the time but visible to historical hindsight. There are times
when it is useful to distinguish the long term from the very long term,
as Braudel does, but not in the case of a study concerned, as this one
is, with a mere two centuries.

GENERATIONS

In the study of short-term changes, a useful and attractive concept is
that of 'generation'. The concept is attractive because it seems to grow
out of experience, that of identifying oneself with one group and
distancing oneself from others. It helps in analysing links between the

229

Donatello, or even whether Bruni's stress on liberty was a heartfelt conviction or the expression of an official attitude required by his administrative position. In any case, the argument applies only to Florence. The Florentines were the leaders in innovation, but there were other important humanists, such as Vittorino da Feltre and Guarino da Verona, and other important painters, from Pisanello to Jacopo Bellini. The two humanists did not show any distaste for princes: Vittorino was employed at the court of Mantua, Guarino at that of Ferrara.

Another political event which was supposed to have had a profound impact on culture took place in 1453: the fall of Constantinople to the Turks. Long embedded in textbooks as *the* explanation of the Renaissance, this thesis goes back to the period itself, to the Lombard humanist Pier Candido Decembrio. The fall of the city, so the argument goes, forced Greek scholars to migrate to Italy, bringing with them their knowledge of the Greek language and literature and so stimulating the revival of ancient learning. The obvious objection to this thesis is that Greek scholars were working in Italy before 1453. Gemistos Plethon and Bessarion attended the Council of Florence in 1439, and Bessarion remained in Italy. Demetrios Chalcondylas and Theodore Gaza arrived in Italy in the 1440s. As in the case of the year 1402, however, it is perhaps a mistake to focus attention too narrowly on a particular date. The crucial political event was the westward advance of the Turks, which was clear enough before 1453. Indeed, it was the Turkish threat which underlay the rapprochement between Latin and Greek Christians at the Council of Florence. The humanist Theodore Gaza went to Italy after his native city of Salonika had been taken by the Turks in 1430. After the fall of Constantinople, more Greek scholars, such as Janos Argyropoulos and Janos Lascaris, arrived in Italy

These immigrants had an important effect on the Italian world of learning, not unlike that of scholars from central Europe – including many specialists on the Renaissance – on the English-speaking world after 1933. They stimulated Greek studies. However, their importance was that they satisfied a demand which already existed. The fall of Constantinople shocked the Christian world, but it does not seem to have bound together a generation. Indeed, the artists and writers born between 1420 and 1450 (Ficino, for example, or Ghirlandaio) seem a much less politically minded group than their predecessors, whether because they reacted against them or because the age in which they were in their prime was an age of relative peace in the peninsula, the age of the balance of power within Italy.

After two essentially Florentine generations came one which was genuinely Italian. Of the 85 members of the creative elite born between 1460 and 1479, only 21 were Tuscans. In any case, political events made the generation of 1460–90 (which includes Machiavelli and Guicciardini, Ariosto and Bembo, Michelangelo, Titian and Raphael) aware of their common destiny as Italians. Their formative years were marked by the French invasion of 1494 and the long wars which followed, a struggle for mastery between the French (Charles VIII, Louis XII, Francis I) and the forces of Spain (under Ferdinand the Catholic) and the Empire (under Maximilian and Charles V). Many Italians were killed, whether fighting with or against the invaders. Many cities were captured and some were sacked. 'Crisis' is a term which is somewhat overworked by historians; it ought to be obligatory on anyone who uses the term about a particular period to show that it was preceded and followed by years of non-crisis.[4] All the same, it is clear that Italy was passing through a 'time of troubles'.

The year 1494 has been taken as a turning point in the history of Italy, indeed of Europe, from that day to this, and Francesco Guicciardini and Leopold von Ranke are only two of the distinguished historians who began their narratives with that year.[5] It cannot be assumed that 1494 marks a break in the history of Italian culture, but it is not difficult to find evidence which supports this suggestion.

The dispersal of artists and writers in this time of troubles is relatively easy to chart. In Florence, for example, the musician Heinrich Isaak left in 1494, when the Medici, his patrons, were driven out. In Naples, plans for improving the city were brought to an end by the French invasion, and the architect fra Giocondo went back to France with Charles VIII. In Milan, the black year was 1499, when Lodovico Sforza fled from the French and the artists at his court were dispersed. The architect Bramante, the sculptor Cristoforo Solari, and the musician Gasper van Weerbecke all went to Rome, while the historian Bernardino Corio retired to his country villa. In 1509, it was the turn of Venice to be attacked. Although the city was not captured, its mainland possessions were overrun. The university of Padua closed for some years, while the printer Aldo Manuzio left Venice for three years, whether for economic or political reasons (Lowry, 1979, pp. 159–61).

Two very different conscious responses to the time of troubles were given by Machiavelli and Savonarola. For Savonarola, the French invasion was the fulfilment of his prophecy of a new flood. He

---

[4] Bec (1975), who extends the notion of crisis to the whole period 1500–50, is open to this objection.

[5] So, still closer to 1494, did Bernardo Rucellai (see Gilbert, 1949).

1542, and of the Index of Prohibited Books a few years later. The increasing effectiveness of ecclesiastical censorship was a crucial factor in the development of the arts in Italy after 1550 (Rochon, 1982).

The 1520s were also the time when the style art historians now call 'Mannerism' emerged, breaking with the rules of perspective, proportion, the combination of architectural motifs and so on. A famous example of rule-breaking is to be found in the Palazzo del Te in Mantua, designed by Giulio Romano (1527–34), with its frieze in which every third triglyph is out of place and seems to be coming loose (above, p. 100). This was a kind of architectural joke, but it is worth asking whether the rejection of rules and reason, whether joking or serious, may not be a response to this time of troubles, which helped create a new generation, including the writers Aretino, Berni and Folengo and the artists Pontormo, Rosso, Giulio Romano, Cellini, Parmigianino and Vasari (all born between 1492 and 1511). The mood of this generation was an unstable one, veering between a violent rejection of the world and a cynical acceptance of it. A possible account of the movement would describe the changes in style as expressing changes in worldview and the changes in worldview as responses to changes in the world. Some writers would go so far as to talk of this as an 'alienated', generation.[9]

Such an account is too simple because it ignores the possibility of changes in style being – in part at least – reactions to art rather than to the world outside it. In any case, corroborative evidence is lacking yet again about the inner lives of most artists and their responses to the world around them. The one exception, Michelangelo, comes from an earlier generation (he was born in 1475). He was involved in the religious movements of his time, sympathetic to Savonarola in his youth and to Ignatius Loyola in his old age. His letters and poems do communicate a sense of spiritual anguish. However, the little we know about the lives and personalities of such artists as Giulio Romano and Parmigianino suggests that they were very different from Michelangelo. The most that could be safely said would be that the Mannerists responded in different ways to similar experiences, of which the sack of 1527 was the most important (Chastel, 1983, p. 169f).

STRUCTURAL CHANGES

At the same time as these dramatic events, other cultural and social changes were taking place in Italy, which were no less significant for

[9] Hauser (1965) called alienation 'the key to Mannerism'.

passing virtually unnoticed at the time. If we compare the situation in the later sixteenth century with that in 1400, certain major differences will become apparent. In 1400, for example, what we now call the Renaissance was a movement restricted to a small group of Florentines, who made important innovations in the arts and criticized some traditional assumptions and values. They were surrounded, even in Florence, by colleagues with traditional attitudes, patrons who made the usual demands, and craftsmen who went on working in the customary manner. The new ideas and the new style gradually spread from Florence to the rest of Tuscany and from Tuscany to the rest of Italy.[10]

The invention of printing helped spread the ideals of the movement more quickly than had ever been possible before. Grammars and anthologies of poems and letters familiarized literate men and women all over Italy with Tuscan usage. The illustrated architectural treatises of Vitruvius, Serlio and Palladio made the classical language of architecture equally familiar. The new art gradually created a market for itself. Patrons became aware that it was possible to commission statuettes or scenes from classical mythology, while a knowledge of the differences between the Doric, Ionic and Corinthian orders became part of a gentleman's education.

The growth of a public interested in the new ideals was itself a force for change, encouraging the development of a more allusive art and literature. Aretino and Berni were among the writers who parodied the love lyrics of Petrarch. To enjoy their poems the reader needs to have some familiarity with Petrarch and his fifteenth-century imitators, a familiarity which breeds boredom if not exactly contempt (Borsellino, 1973). In a similar way the deliberate mistakes or solecisms in Giulio Romano's frieze at Mantua imply spectators who are educated enough to know the rules, to entertain certain visual expectations, to receive a shock when those expectations are falsified, and finally to enjoy being shocked because familiarity with the rules has made them rather blasé.

Another unintended consequence of the spread of the new ideals was the ironing out of regional diversities, which had been enormously important in earlier centuries. Domenico Beccafumi, for example, was not as distinctively Sienese a painter as (say) Neroccio de'Landi had been.[11] From Milan to Naples, literature composed in dialect was

---

[10] Fifty members of the creative elite were born between 1360 and 1399; 23 in Tuscany, 14 in the Veneto, only 13 from the rest of Italy. But 176 members of the elite were born between 1480 and 1519; 50 in Tuscany, 49 in the Veneto, 77 from other parts of Italy.

[11] On the changing balance between the centre and periphery in Italian art, see Castelnuovo and Ginzburg (1979).

market in works of art, ancient and modern, originals and reproductions alike.

Yet this trend was to some degree offset by another, which historians describe as 'refeudalization' (in the wide, Marxist sense of the term 'feudal') or, as Braudel does, as the 'bankruptcy of the bourgeoisie'.[13] A number of wealthy merchants (how many in any given decade it is unfortunately impossible to say) shifted their investments from trade to land. The trend is most noticeable in the two cities that have concerned us most in this study, Florence and Venice, where the patricians, poised for a long time between bourgeoisie and nobility, opted by their changing style of life for the latter. In Florence, the movement was gradual, almost imperceptible in any one generation, though obvious enough if one compares the patriciate of 1600 with its equivalent in 1400 or the better-documented year 1427. In Venice, the movement was more sudden. It was after the year 1570 or thereabouts that the patricians began to switch their investments from trade to landed estates on the mainland, from neighbouring Padua to distant Friuli (Woolf, 1968). They changed from entrepreneurs to rentiers; from a dominant interest in profit to a dominant interest in consumption. The elegant gestures in Florentine portraits by Bronzino and others reflect the attitudes of the sitters, who were no longer prepared to get their hands dirty as their fathers and grandfathers had been (good merchants, as Giovanni Rucellai had observed in the later fifteenth century, always have inky fingers).[14] The most splendid Venetian villas, starting with Villa Maser, built by Palladio and decorated by Veronese in the early 1560s for the Barbaro family, belong to this period of the return to the land.

Why did this change take place? It looks like an example of the shirtsleeves-to-shirtsleeves cycle, the third-generation syndrome which the American economist W. W. Rostow (1960) called 'the pattern of Buddenbrooks dynamics', after the Lübeck family described in a famous novel by Thomas Mann. As in Mann's novel, so in Renaissance Italy one can point to examples (most obviously that of the Medici) of families ruined for trade by a humanist education; Lorenzo the Magnificent composed poems while the family bank went into decline. However, we are not talking about a family but about a whole social group. Families had withdrawn from trade before; what was new, in Florence, Venice and elsewhere, was the lack of new families to replace them. The fundamental explanation was probably an economic one. As a result of the discovery of America, the centre of gravity of European trade was shifting away

---

[13] On 'refeudalization', see Antal (1947) and Romano (1971); and cf. Braudel (1949).
[14] Rucellai, *Il Zibaldone*, p. 6.

from the Mediterranean and towards the Atlantic. The Italians were losing their traditional role as middlemen in international trade and it was being taken over by the Portuguese, the English and, above all, in the seventeenth century, by the Dutch. We have returned to the theme of 'hard times and contempt for trade' (above pp. 37–8). At the same time, food prices were rising, so that to wealthy urban Italians, land appeared an increasingly attractive investment.

This change in the style of life of the patriciate was good for the arts in the short term but not so beneficial in the long run. The ruling class was more inclined to patronize the arts because this was part of their new aristocratic lifestyle, but in the long term the wealth which permitted them to build palaces and buy works of art dried up. The change in values – especially the emphasis on birth and the contempt for manual labour – worked against the newly risen status of the artist. There was a kind of 'brain drain' (brains being what an artist mixed his colours with) thanks to the diffusion of Renaissance ideals abroad and the consequent demand for Italian artists in Hungary, France, Spain, England and elsewhere. In the fourteenth and fifteenth centuries, Italy, a country of merchant republics, had been as distinctive socially as she was culturally. As she came to resemble other European societies, Italy lost her cultural lead. There was also a shift of creativity from the visual arts into music which has been explained by the decline of the city-state as well as increasing ecclesiastical control of the media (Koenigsberger, 1960). All the same, Italian art remained the envy of Europe until the death of Bernini in 1680.

between the two regions. Frescos were less important in The Netherlands (where large windows left little wall space in churches), and
miniatures in manuscripts more important. The most famous contrast
between the painters of Italy and The Netherlands was made at the
time, by Michelangelo:

> They paint in Flanders only to deceive the outward eye [*vista exterior*]
> . . . Their painting is of textiles, bricks and mortar, the grass of the
> fields, the shadows of trees, and bridges and rivers, which they call
> landscapes, and little figures here and there; and all this, although it
> may appear good to some eyes, is in truth done without reason or art,
> without symmetry or proportion, without care in selecting or rejecting,
> and finally without any substance or nerve.[2]

The criticism is unfair but revealing – in its very unfairness – of the
values of Michelangelo and of Florentine visual culture, in which
idealization and the heroic were central, while the illusion of solidity
mattered more than the illusion of space.

There were economic and social as well as cultural parallels
between Italy and The Netherlands. As a fifteenth-century Spanish
traveller put it, 'two cities compete with each other for commercial
supremacy, Bruges in Flanders in the West and Venice in the East'
(Lestocquoy, 1952; Prevenier and Blockmans, 1986). These cities
were set in the most highly urbanized parts of Europe. Around the
year 1500, in the provinces of Flanders and Brabant, as much as
two-thirds of the population lived in towns. As in Italy, the commercialization of agriculture consequent on the growth of towns led to
the disappearance of serfdom earlier than elsewhere. As in Italy, the
textile industry was of great importance for export-led growth, and
within the industry there was a shift towards production for the
luxury market, as in the case of the tapestries made in Arras, Lille and
Tournai. In The Netherlands, too, the peak period for the visual arts
coincided with the peak in the development of the luxury industries.

In Flanders, as in Italy, artists were often the sons of craftsmen. Out
of 17 leading painters whose father's occupation is known, 14 were
the sons of craftsmen: a cutler, a weaver, a smith, an artist and so on.
Painting was a family business and there were well-known dynasties
of artists, such as the Bouts, Brueghel, Floris and Massys families. The
painters tended to be born in sizeable towns, and to gravitate towards
Bruges and Antwerp, the greatest commercial cities of The Netherlands. Bruges lost its economic dominance around the year 1500
owing to the silting up of the river Zwijn, and its place was taken by

---

[2] de Hollanda, *Da Pintura Antigua*, 63 (first dialogue).

Antwerp, where the population rose to about 100,000 by 1550. In painting, too, the centre shifted from Bruges to Antwerp, which is not surprising, since merchants were among the most important patrons. As in Italy, an art market developed in the sixteenth century (Floerke, 1905).

In The Netherlands, as in Italy, artists generally had the status of craftsmen, unless their patrons were rulers like Philip the Good, duke of Burgundy, who appointed Jan van Eyck his official painter and *valet de chambre*, sent him on diplomatic missions, visited his studio at Bruges and gave him six silver cups for the christening of the painter's son. However, the painters of The Netherlands seem to have lacked the self- awareness of some of their Italian colleagues. Self-portraits are more rare, and the Dutch Vasari, Karel van Mander, did not publish his collection of artists' biographies until 1604.

The relations of the music of the period to the society in which it was composed is rather more indirect and elusive. Most of this music is church music (possibly because church music had a better chance of survival). The great composers usually owed their musical training (as we have seen, on p. 56) to cathedral choir schools. Some of them held benefices. However, the increasing size of church choirs in this period was made possible only by the generosity of the laity. The money was used in part to bring laymen into the choirs; for example, the cathedral chapter at Antwerp diverted income from some benefices to pay the salaries of professional singers who did not have to be clerics. As in Italy, townspeople founded fraternities, and some, such as the Fraternity of Our Lady at Antwerp (whose members included bankers, merchants and craftsmen), financed a daily service with singers. In other words, the ecclesiastical culture of The Netherlands in the fifteenth century was founded on urban wealth.

Music was also written for the court. Duke Philip the Good made Binchois his chaplain and appointed Dufay music tutor to his son Charles the Bold, who learned to sing, play the harp and compose chansons and motets. When he became duke he employed Busnois and he took his musicians with him even on campaign. The importance of this court patronage is suggested by the fact that after Charles's death in 1477, the leading composers Isaak and Josquin left The Netherlands.

The court had, of course, to be paid for. The Feast of the Pheasant, a Burgundian banquet held in 1454 at which musicians played a prominent part, cost so much that even a courtier who took part in it, Olivier de la Marche, commented in his chronicle on what he called the 'outrageous and unreasonable expense'. It was the good fortune of Philip the Good and Charles the Bold that their dominions

reminiscent of Samuel Smiles if they did not antedate him by a century and a half.

It seems plausible to argue that the rise of the *chōnin* – not to say 'middle class' – and the cultural innovations of the period are connected. Of the major writers and artists, Moronobu was the son of an embroiderer; Saikaku, the son of an Osaka merchant; Kiseki, the best-known of Saikaku's followers, the son of Kyoto shopkeeper. The *Nō* plays had been for *samurai* only. On the other hand, *samurai* were forbidden to go to performances of *kabuki* and *jōruri*, which were for the *chōnin*, and not infrequently dealt with their lives. As for the stories of Saikaku and others, they were printed in *kana* script and so reached an audience (female as well as male) much wider than that of traditional literati. In the seventeenth century, bookselling was good business; there were 50 bookshops in Osaka in 1626. Adapting Defoe, we may say that writing was becoming 'a very considerable part of the Japanese commerce'. So were images. Woodblock prints could be massproduced cheaply, so that they were within the means of craftsmen. One of their functions was commercial; to advertise the skills and charms of the actors and courtesans they so frequently portrayed. In Japan as in Europe we see the rise of what we might call an art market and the commercialization of art and literature.

There are two qualifications to make to this picture of townsmens' culture. The first is to point out that it was associated with merchants who were no longer accumulating but indulging in conspicuous consumption. The second is to emphasize that Genroku culture was not for merchants and craftsmen alone. Edō was a capital with a court and a traditional culture associated with it. All that is being argued here is that new genres were created primarily for new social groups (or groups that were newly rich, numerous or literate). Even these new genres drew on aristocratic traditions, from *Nō* plays to the eleventh-century *Tale of Genji*, though it is not easy to say whether they are examples of imitation, parody or an ambiguous and unstable mixture of the two.

This brief comparison of Italy with The Netherlands and Japan contains obvious gaps. The available secondary literature does not permit a discussion of the merchant ethos in Flanders or the milieu of Japanese artists. In any case, these examples are not the only ones that could have been chosen. Yet they do suggest the existence of recurrent patterns of cultural and social change and they bring us back to a problem which has appeared many times in this study (sometimes in the foreground, sometimes in the background): the problem of the cultural role of the bourgeoisie.

I began work on this book, more than 20 years ago now, with the idea of juxtaposing the ideas of Jacob Burckhardt and those of Karl Marx, criticizing and rejecting where criticism and rejection were needed and attempting a synthesis. Burckhardt is not, of course, the only interesting interpreter of the Renaissance, and a good many of his successors – Baron, Baxandall, Gombrich, Lopez etc. – have contributed ideas as well as information to this study. Nor is Marx the only important social theorist, or the only one whose ideas are relevant to this period and this problem. It is a stimulating intellectual exercise (but more than just an exercise) to imagine how Max Weber might have discussed the Renaissance (emphasizing secularization, calculation, abstraction); how Emile Durkheim might have discussed it (stressing the division of labour and its effect on collective representations); how Norbert Elias might view it (as part of the civilizing process) or Erving Goffman (focusing on the presentation of self) or Pierre Bourdieu (attending to strategies for 'symbolic domi- nance') or Clifford Geertz (considering the relation between order and meaning). I have learned something from each of these thinkers, and others, and made use of them all in this book.

The central problem of this study, however, remains that of the relationship between cultural and social structures and change, and the apparent detour via The Netherlands and Japan has revealed this centrality even more clearly. The link between realism and the bourgeoisie, for example, is not as simple as some Marxists (Antal, for instance) have argued or assumed, because (as we have seen) there is more than one type of realism, more than one kind of bourgeoisie and more than one possible relationship between society and culture. Refining the concepts, however, does not dissolve the problem. There do seem to be affinities between social groups and artistic genres (if not styles). If bourgeoisies are divided into merchants and craftsmen, their contributions to the arts may be distinguished as follows. The milieu from which most artists come is urban and dominated by craftsmen, so that it can be argued (above pp. 48–51) that it is in craft-industrial towns that the abilities of potential artists are least likely to be frustrated. Merchants, on the other hand, are especially important as patrons, and often quick to take up new genres. They are, after all, professionally adaptable, and need to be able to adapt to new situations if they are to survive economically. The emphasis on novelty is important here. The argument is not that rulers, nobility (mandarins, *samurai*), or the Church (or its Hindu, Buddhist or Muslim equivalents) are unimportant patrons; this is clearly false. The focus of this study, however, has been on cultural innovation, and the Flemish and Japanese examples, no less than the Italian ones,

APPENDIX: THE CREATIVE ELITE

The 600 painters, sculptors, architects, writers, humanists, scientists and musicians whose lives form the basis of chapter 3, in particular, were selected as follows:

1 314 painters and sculptors from the article on 'Italian Art' in the *Encyclopaedia of World Art* (organized by region, this list seems to counter the Tuscan bias of Vasari).
2 88 writers from E. H. Wilkins, *A History of Italian Literature* (London, 1954).
3 74 humanists from E. Garin, *Italian Humanism* (1947: English trans., Oxford, 1965).
4 55 scientists from R. Taton (ed). *A General History of the Sciences*, 2 (London, 1965), revised with the help of Professor Marshall Clagett.
5 50 musicians selected from G. Reese, *Music in the Renaissance* (London, 1959).
6 19 writers and humanists not in Wilkins or Garin, added to round the number up to 600 and chosen because I thought them important: J. Aconcio, G. B. Adriani, Aldo Manuzio, G. Aurispa, F. Barbaro, G. Barzizza, G. Benivieni, F. Beroaldo, B. Bibbiena, A. Bonfini, V. Calmeta, J. Caviceo, B. Corio, L. Domenichi, F. Nerli, B. Rucellai, M. A. Sabellico, B. della Scala, B. Segni.

The complete list can be found in the index to this book, with asterisks against the names.

Such a list is inevitably arbitrary, at least at the edges. Contemporaries, however much in sympathy with the idea of a collection of biographies, might have found the criterion of selection, 'creativity', hard to understand, and the learned would have expected to find canon lawyers or theologians rather than artists.

The object of the exercise was to conduct something like a social survey of the dead: to look for patterns or tendencies. Hence the need to ask precise questions, as follows:

1 *Region of birth*: 9 possible answers (Lombardy; Veneto; Tuscany; States of the Church; south Italy; Liguria; Piedmont; outside Italy; not known)

251

2 *Size of birthplace*: 4 possible answers (large; medium; small; not known)

3 *Father's occupation*: 9 possible answers (cleric; noble; humanist; professional or merchant; artist; artisan or shop-keeper connected with the arts; artisan or shop-keeper unconnected with the arts; peasant; not known)

4 *Training*: 6 possible answers (University of Padua; other universities; other humanist education; apprenticeship; musical education; not known)

5 *Main discipline practised*: 7 possible answers (painting; sculpture; architecture; literature; humanism; science; music)

6 *Specialization*: 3 possible answers (1 discipline; 2; 3 or more)

7 *Relative practising these disciplines*: 5 possible answers (no known relatives; 1; 2; 3; 4 or more)

8 *Geographical mobility*: 5 possible answers (extremely sedentary: fairly sedentary; fairly mobile; extremely mobile; not known)

9 *Patronage*: 2 possible answers (Medici patronage; other)

10 *Period of birth*: 10 possible answers (dividing the years 1340–1519 into 9 periods of 20 years each, and adding a 'not known')

Punched cards were prepared and fed into a computer (1968 vintage) which printed out the results in tabular form.

BIBLIOGRAPHY

This bibliography contains all works to which reference is made in the notes, together with other studies of relevance to the field. *JWCI* = Journal of the Warburg and Courtauld Institutes.

Ackermann, J. S. (1949) 'Ars sine scientia nihil est', *Art Bulletin* 12, pp. 84–108.
— (1954) 'Architectural practice in the Italian Renaissance', *Journal of the Society for Architectural History* 13, pp. 3–10.
— (1961), *The Architecture of Michelangelo*. New York. 2nd ed., Harmondsworth, 1970.
— (1963) 'Sources of the Renaissance villa', in *The Renaissance and Mannerism*, ed. I. E. Rubin, pp. 6–18. New York.
— (1966) *Palladio*. Harmondsworth.
Ady, C. M. (1937) *The Bentivoglio of Bologna*. Oxford.
Alberigo, G. (1959) *I vescovi italiani al concilio di Trento*. Florence.
Alberti, L. B. *De re aedificatoria*, ed. P. Portoghesi, 2 vols, Milan, 1966.
— *I libri della famiglia*, ed. R. Romano and A. Tenenti, Turin, 1969; English trans., Columbia, SC. 1969.
— *On Painting*, trans. J. R. Spencer, New Haven, 1956.
— *On Painting and Sculpture*, ed. and trans. C. Grayson, London, 1972.
Albertini, R. von (1955) *Das florentinisch Staatsbewusstsein im Übergang von der Republik zum Prinzipat*. Berne.
Alpers, S. (1983) *The Art of Describing*. Chicago.
Alsop, J. (1982) *The Rare Art Traditions*. London.
Ames-Lewis, F. (1981) *Drawing in Early Renaissance Italy*. New Haven and London.
— and Wright, J. (eds) (1983) *Drawing in the Italian Renaissance Workshop*. London.
Anselmi, G. M., Pezzarassa, F. and Avellini, L. (1980) *La 'memoria' dei mercatores*. Bologna.
Antal, F. (1947) *Florentine Painting and its Social Background*. London.

Anthon, C. (1946) 'Social status of Italian musicians during the sixteenth century', *Journal of Renaissance and Baroque Music* X, pp. 111–23, 222–34.

Antoni, C. (1940) *From History to Sociology*. Florence. English trans., Detroit, 1959.

Archambault, P. (1967) 'The analogy of the body in Renaissance political literature', *Bibliothèque d'Humanisme et Renaissance* 29, pp. 21–53.

Aretino, P. *Sei Giornate* (1534–6), ed. G. Aquilecchia, Bari, 1975.

Arnaldi, G. and Pastore Stocchi, M. (eds) (1980–1) *Storia della cultura veneta dal primo '400 al concilio di Trento*, 2 vols Vicenza.

Aron, P. *Toscanello*, Venice, 1523.

Asor Rosa, A. (ed.) (1983) *Letteratura italiana 2: produzione e consumo*. Turin.

Atlas, A. W. (1985) *Music at the Aragonese court of Naples*. Cambridge.

Auerbach, E. (1939) 'Figura', in his *Scenes from the Drama of European Literature*, pp. 11–76. New York.

— (1946) *Mimesis*. English trans., Princeton, 1954.

Avery, C. (1970) *Florentine Renaissance Sculpture*. London.

Bandello, M. *Novelle* (1554), ed. G. G. Ferrero, Turin, 1974.

Barbieri, G. (1938) *Economia e politica nel ducato di Milano*. Milan.

Barolsky, P. (1978) *Infinite Jest: Wit and Humor in Renaissance Art*. London.

Baron, H. (1938) The historical background of the Florentine Renaissance', *History* 23, pp. 315–27.

— (1955) *The Crisis of the Early Italian Renaissasnce*. Princeton. Rev. ed., Princeton, 1966.

— (1960) 'Burckhardt's *Civilisation of the Renaissance* a century after its publication', *Renaissance News* 13, pp. 207–22.

Barrell, J. (1980) *The Dark Side of the Landscape*. Cambridge.

Batkin, L. M. (1978) *Die italienische Renaissance*. German trans. from Russian, Dresden, 1979.

Battara, P. (1935) *La popolazione di Firenze alla metà del '500*. Florence.

Battisti, E. (1962) *L'antirinascimento*. Milan.

Bauer, H. (1965) *Kunst und Utopie*. Berlin.

Baxandall, M. (1963) 'A dialogue on art from the court of Leonello d'Este', *JWCI* 26, pp. 304–26.

— (1964) 'B. Facius on painting', *JWCI* 27, pp. 90–107.

— (1965) 'Guarino, Pisanello and Manuel Chrysoloras', *JWCI* 28, pp. 183–201.

— (1971) *Giotto and the Orators*. Oxford.

— (1972) *Painting and Experience in Fifteenth-Century Italy*. Oxford.

— (1985) 'Art, society and the Bouguer principle', *Representations* 12, pp. 32–43.

Bec, C. (1967) *Les marchands écrivains*. Paris and The Hague.

— (ed.) (1975) *Italie 1500–50: une situation de crise?* Lyons.

— (1981) *Cultura e societá a Firenze nel tempo della Rinascenza*. Salerno and Rome.

— (1983) 'Lo statuto socio-professionale degli scrittori' in *Letteratura italiana 2: produzione e consumo*, ed. A. Asor Rosa, Turin.

— (1984) *Les livres des florentins (1413–1608)*. Florence.

Becker, H. (1963) *Outsiders*. New York.

Bellah, R. (1957) *Tokugawa Religion*. Glencoe.

Beloch, K. J. (1961) *Bevölkerungsgeschichte Italiens*, 3. Berlin.

Beltrami, D. (1954) *Storia della popolazione di Venezia*. Padua.

Bembo, P. *Prose della volgar lingua* (1525), repr, in his *Prose e rime*, ed. C. Dionisotti, Turin, 1960.

Benjamin, W. (1936) 'The work of art in the age of mechanical reproduction', English trans. in his *Illuminations*, London, 1970, pp. 219–44.

Berengo, M. (1965) *Nobili e mercanti nella Lucca del '500*. Turin.

Berlin, I. (1976) *Vico and Herder*. London.

Bertelli, S. (1976) 'L'egemonia linguistica come egemonia culturale', *Bibliothèque d'humanisme et Renaissance* 38, pp. 249–81.

Bing, G. (1965) 'A. M. Warburg', *JWCI* 28, pp. 299–313.

Binni W. and Sapegno N. (eds), (1968) *Storia letteraria delle regioni d'Italia*. Florence.

Biringuccio, V. *Pirotechnia* (1540), English trans. 1942; new ed. Cambridge, Mass., 1966.

Bloch, M. (1967) *Land and Work in Medieval Europe*. London.

Blunt, A. (1946) *Artistic Theory in Italy 1450–1600*. Oxford.

Boase, T. S. R. (1979) *Giorgio Vasari: the Man and the Book*. Princeton.

Bohannan, P. (1961) 'Artist and critic in an African society' in *The Artist in Tribal Society*, ed. M. W. Smith, pp. 85–94. London.

Bologna, F. (1977) *Napoli e le rotte mediterranee della pittura da Alfonso il Magnanimo a Ferdinando il Cattolico*. Naples.

Bombe, W. (1909) 'Die Tafelbilder des Benedetto Bonfigli', in *Repertorium für Kunstwissenschaft*.

— (ed.) (1928) *Nachlass-inventare des Angelo da Uzzano und Lodovico da Gino Capponi*. Leipzig and Berlin.

Bonomo, G. (1959) *Caccia alle streghe*. Palermo.

Borkenau, F. (1934) *Der Ubergang vom feudalen zum bürgerlichen Weltbild*. Paris.

Borsellino, N. (1973) *Gli anticlassicisti del '500*. Rome and Bari.

Bottari, G. G. (1822–5) *Raccolta di lettere*, 8 vols. Milan.

Bourdieu, P. (1972) *Outlines of a Theory of Practice*. Geneva. English trans., Cambridge, 1977.

— (1979) *Distinction*. Paris. English trans., London, 1984.

Braghirolli, W. (1877) 'Carteggio di Isabella d'Este intorno ad un quadro di Giambellino', *Archivio Veneto* 13, pp. 376–83.

Branca, V. (ed.) (1964) *Umanesimo europeo ed umanesimo veneziano*. Florence.

— (1983) *Poliziano e l'umanesimo della parola*. Turin.

Braudel, F. (1949) *The Mediterranean and the Mediterranean World in the Age of Philip II*. Paris. English trans., 2 vols, London, 1972–3.

Bridgman, N. (1964) *La vie musicale au quattrocento*. Paris.

Bronzini, G. (1966] *Tradizione di stile aedico dai cantari al Furioso*. Florence.

— (1978) 'Pubblico e predicazione popolare di Bernardino di Siena', *Lares* 44, pp. 3–31.

Brown, A. (1961) 'The humanist portrait of Cosimo de'Medici', *JWCI* 24, pp. 186–221.

— (1979) *Bartolommeo Scala*. Princeton.

Brown, H. F. (1891) *The Venetian Printing-Press*. London.

Brucker, G. (ed.) (1967) *Two memoirs of Renaissance Florence*. New York.

— (1977) *The Civic World of Early Renaissance Florence*. Princeton.

Bruni, L. *Epistolae*, ed. L. Mehus, 2 vols. Florence, 1741.

— (1978) 'Panegyric to the city of Florence' in *The Earthly Republic*, ed. B. Kohl and R. Witt, pp. 135–75. Philadelphia.

Bryson, N. (1981) *Word and Image*. Cambridge.

Burckhardt, J. (1860) *The Civilisation of the Renaissance in Italy*. Basel. English trans., 1873, repr. London, 1944.

— (1867) *The Architecture of the Renaissance in Italy*. Stuttgart. English trans. London, 1985.

— (1898) *Beiträge zur Kunstgeschichte von Italien*. Basle.

— (1906) *Reflections on World History*. Berlin/Stuttgart. English trans., London, 1943.

Burke, P. (1969) *The Renaissance Sense of the Past*. London.

— (1977) 'G. F. Pico and his *Strix*' in *The Damned Art*, ed. S. Anglo, pp. 32–52. London.

— (1978a) 'Investment and culture in three seventeenth-century cities', *Journal of European Economic History* 7, pp. 311–36.

— (1978b) *Popular Culture in Early Modern Europe*. London.

— (1982) 'A world history of what?' (a review of H. Honour and J. Fleming *A World History of Art* (1982) *Art History* 6, pp. 214–18.

— (1984a) 'How to be a counter-Reformation saint', in *Religion and Society in Early Modern Europe*, ed. K. von Greyerz. London.

— (1984b), 'Death in the Renaissance', in *Dies Illa*, ed. J. H. M. Taylor, pp. 59–70. Liverpool.

— (1986) 'Strengths and weaknesses of the history of mentalities', *History of European Ideas*, 7, pp. 439–51

Burney, C. (1776–89) *A General History of Music*, 4 vols. London.

Butters, H. (1986) *Governors and Government in Early Sixteenth-Century Florence*. Oxford.

Callmann, E. (1974) *Apollonio di Giovanni*. Oxford.

Camporesi, P. (1981) 'Cultura popolare e cultura d'élite fra Medioevo e età modernà' in *Storia d'Italia*, Annali 4, pp. 81–157. Turin.

Caplan, H. (1929) 'The four senses of scriptural interpretation', *Speculum* 4, pp. 282–94.

Caplow, H. N. (1974) 'Sculptors' partnerships', *Studies in the Renaissance* 21, pp. 145–75.

Cardano, G. *De rerum varietate*, Basel, 1557.

— *The Book of My Life* (1575) English trans., New York, 1962.

Carrithers, M., Collins S. and Lukes S. (eds) (1985) *The Category of the Person*. Cambridge.

Cartwright, J. (1903) *Isabella d'Este*, 2nd ed., 2 vols. London.

Casotti, G. B. (1714) *Memorie istoriche della miracolosa immagine di Maria Vergine dell'Impruneta*, 2 vols. Florence.

Cassirer, E., Kristeller, P. and Randall, J. H. (eds) (1948) *The Renaissance Philosophy of Man*. Chicago.

Cast, D. (1981) *The Calumny of Apelles*. New Haven and London.

Castelnuovo, E. (1973) 'Il significato del ritratto pittorico nella società', *Storia d'Italia* 5, pp. 1035–94. Turin.

— (1976) 'Per una storia sociale dell'arte', reprinted in his *Arte, industria, rivoluzioni*, Turin, 1985.

— and Ginzburg, C. (1979) 'Centro e periferia', *Storia dell'arte italiana*, 1, ed. G. Previtali, pp. 285–352. Turin.

Castiglione, B. *Il Cortegiano* (1528), ed. B. Maier, 2nd ed., Turin, 1964; English trans., New York, 1959.

Castiglione, S. di *Ricordi* (1549), Venice, 1554.

Cavalcanti, G. *Istorie fiorentine* (written in the 1420s), Milan, 1944.

Céard, J. (1977) *La nature et les prodiges*. Geneva.

Cellini, B. *Vita*, ed. E. Camesasca, Milan, 1594. English trans., Harmondsworth, 1956.

Cendali, L. (1936) *Giuliano e Benedetto da Maiano*. Florence.

Cennini, C. *Il libro dell'arte*, text and English trans., ed. D. V. Thompson, 2 vols, New Haven, 1932–3.

Chabod, F. (1958) 'Usi e abusi nell'amministrazione dello stato di Milano', *Studi storici in onore di Gioacchino Volpe*, pp. 95–194. Florence.

— (1961) *L'epoca di Carlo V*. Milan.

— (1964) 'Was there a Renaissance state?', reprinted in *The Development of the Modern State*, ed. H. Lubasz. New York.

Chambers, D. S. (1970a) *The Imperial Age of Venice, 1380–1580*. London.

— (ed.) (1970b) *Patrons and Artists in the Italian Renaissance*. London.

Chastel, A. (1961) *Art et humanisme à Florence au temps de Laurent le magnifique*. Paris.

— (1964) 'Art et humanisme au quattrocento' in *Umanesimo europeo ed umanesimo veneziano*, ed. V. Branca, pp. 395–406. Florence.

— (1965) *The Studios and Styles of the Renaissance: Italy 1460–1500*. English trans., London, 1966.

— (1983) *The Sack of Rome*. Princeton.

Cipolla, C. M. (1963–4) 'Economic depression of the Renaissance?', *Economic History Review* 16, pp. 519–24.

— (1967) *Clocks and Culture*. London.

Clark, T. (1973) *Image of the People*. London.

Clements, R. J. (ed.) (1963) *Michelangelo, a Self-Portrait*. Englewood Cliffs, NJ.

Clough, C. H. (1973) 'Federigo da Montefeltre's patronage of the arts', *JWCI* 36, pp. 129–44.

— (1976) (ed.) *Cultural Aspects of the Italian Renaissance*. Manchester and New York.

Cocchiara, G. (1966) *Le origini della poesia popolare*. Turin.

Coffin, D. R. (ed.) (1972) *The Italian Garden*. Dumbarton Oaks.

— (1979) *The Villa in the Life of Renaissance Rome*. Princeton.

Cohn, S. K. (1980) *The Laboring Classes in Renaissance Florence*. New York.

Cole, B. (1980) *Sienese Painting*. New York.

— (1983). *The Renaissance Artist at Work from Pisano to Titian*. London.

Collett, B. (1985) *Italian Benedictine Scholars and the Reformation*. Oxford.

Concina, E. (1984) *L'Arsenale della Repubblica di Venezia*. Milan.

Condivi, A. (1964) *Vita di Michelangelo Buonarrotti*, ed. E. S. Barelli. Milan.

Coniglio, G. (1951) *Il regno di Napoli al tempo di Carlo V*. Naples.

Contarini, G. *Commonwealth and Government of Venice* (1543) English trans. London, 1598.

Conti, A. (1979) 'L'evoluzione dell'artista', *Storia dell'arte italiana*, 2, pp. 117–263. Turin.

Conway, M. (1929) *Giorgione*. London.

Coor, G. (1961) *Neroccio de'Landi*. Princeton.

Corio, B. (1978) *Storia di Milano*, ed. A. Morosi Guerra, 2 vols. Milan.

Corti, G. and Hartt, F. (1962) 'New documents concerning Donatello', *Art Bulletin* 44, pp. 155–67.

Cosenza, M. (1952) *Biographical Dictionary of Italian Humanists*. New York.

Cox-Rearick, J. (1984) *Dynasty and Destiny in Medici Art*. Princeton.

Cozzi, G. (1963) 'Cultura, politica e religione nella pubblica storiografia veneziana', *Studi Veneziani* 5, pp. 215–94.

Craven, W. G. (1981) *Giovanni Pico della Mirandola, Symbol of his Age*. Geneva.

Crawcour, E. S. (1968) 'Changes in Japanese commerce in the Tokugawa period', reprinted in *Studies in the Institutional History of Early Modern Japan*, ed. J. W. Hall and M. B. Jansen, pp. 189–202. Princeton.

Crowe, J. A. and Cavalcaselle, G. B. (1881) *The Life and Times of Titian*. London.

Dacos, N. (1979) 'Arte italiana e arte antica', *Storia dell'arte italiana* 3, ed. G. Previtali, pp. 5–68. Turin.

D'Amico, J. F. (1983) *Renaissance Humanism in Papal Rome*. Baltimore.

D'Ancona, A. (ed.,) (1872) *Sacre Rappresentazioni dei secoli xiv, xv, e xvi*. Florence.

Daniello, B. *Poetica*. (1536) Venice.

D'Arco, C. (1842) *Giulio Pippi Romano*, 2nd ed. Mantua.

Davis, J. C. (1962) *The Decline of the Venetian Nobility as a Ruling Class*. Baltimore.

Caprio, V. De (1981) 'Intelletuali e mercato del lavoro nella Roma medicea', *Studi romani* 29, pp. 29–46.

— (1983) 'Aristocrazia e clero dalla crisi dell'umanesimo alla Controriforma' *Letteratura italiana 2: produzione e consumo*, ed. A. Asor Rosa, pp. 299–361. Turin.

Della Casa, G. *Galateo* (1558), ed. D. Provenzal, Milan, 1950. English trans., Harmondsworth, 1958.

Delumeau, J. (1967) 'Réinterpretation de la Renaissance', *Revue d' histoire moderne et contemporaine* 14, pp. 296–314.

— (1973) 'Mobilité sociale: riches et pauvres à l'époque de la Renaissance', in *Ordres et classes* ed. E. Labrousse, pp. 125–34. Paris and The Hague.

De Maio, R. (1978) *Michelangelo e la Controriforma*. Naples.

Dempsey, C. (1968) 'Mercurius Ver: the sources of Botticelli's Primavera', *JWCI* 31, pp. 251–69.

— (1980) 'Some observations on the education of artists at Florence and Bologna during the later sixteenth century', *Art Bulletin* 62, pp. 552–69.

Denis, A (1975) 'Charles VIII en Italie', in *Italie 1500–50: une situation de crise?*, ed. C. Bec, pp. 57–66. Lyons.

Denley, P. (1981) 'Recent studies on Italian universities of the Middle Ages and Renaissance', *History of Universities* 1, pp. 193–206.

— (1983) 'The social function of Italian Renaissance universities', *CRE Information* 62, pp. 47–58.

Dijksterhuis, E. J. (1950) *The Mechanization of the World Picture.* Amsterdam. English trans., Oxford, 1961.

Dionisotti, C. (1967) *Geografia e storia della letterature italiana.* Turin.

Dolce, L. *Aretino* (1557), text and English trans., ed. M. W. Roskill, New York, 1968.

Dominici, G. (1860) *Regola del governo di cura familiare.* Florence. English trans., Washington, DC, 1927.

Doren, A. (1901) *Die florentiner Wollentuchindustrie vom 14. bis zum 16. Jahrhundert.* Stuttgart.

— (1922) *Fortuna im Mittelalter.* Hamburg.

— (1931) 'Aby Warburg und sein Werk', *Archiv für Kulturgeschichte* 21, pp. 1–23.

Dowd, D. F. (1961) 'The economic expansion of Lombardy, 1300–1500', *Journal of Economic History* 21, pp. 143–60.

Duby, G. (1969) *The Three Orders.* Paris. English trans., Chicago, 1980.

Dundes, A. and Falassi, A. (1975) *La Terra in Piazza: an Interpretation of the Palio of Siena.* Berkeley.

Dürer, A. *Schriftlicher Nachlass,* ed. H. Rupprich, 3 vols, Berlin, 1956–69.

Eagleton, T. (1983) *Literary Theory.* Oxford.

Ebreo, Leone *Dialoghi d'Amore* (1535) Bari, 1929.

Edgerton jr, S. Y. (1975) *The Renaissance Rediscovery of Linear Perspective.* New York.

— (1985) *Pictures and Punishment: Art and Criminal Prosecution during the Florentine Renaissance.* Ithaca and London.

Edwards, J. M. B. (1968) 'Creativity: social aspects', *International Encyclopaedia of the Social Sciences,* ed. D. L. Sills, 3, pp. 442–55. New York.

Einstein, A. (1949) *The Italian Madrigal,* 3 vols. Princeton.

— (1958) *Essays on Music.* London.

Elam, C. (1978) 'Lorenzo de'Medici and the urban development of Renaissance Florence', *Art History* 1, pp. 43–56.

Elias, N. (1939) *The Civilizing Process*. Basel. English trans., 2 vols, Oxford, 1978–82.

— (1969) *The Court Society*. Neuwied. English trans., Oxford, 1983.

Errera, I. (1920) *Répertoire des peintures datées*. Brussels.

Ettlinger, L. D. (1965) *The Sistine Chapel before Michelangelo*. Oxford.

— (1977) 'The emergence of the Italian architect during the fifteenth century', in *The Architect*, ed. S. Kostof, pp. 96–121. New York.

— and Ettlinger H. S. (1976) *Botticelli*. London.

Evans-Pritchard, E. E. (1940) *The Nuer*. Oxford.

Fagiolo Dell'Arco, M. (1970) *Il Parmigianino: un saggio sull'ermetismo nel '500*. Rome.

Febvre, L. (1942) *The Problem of Unbelief in the Sixteenth Century*. Paris. English trans., Cambridge, Mass.

Fenlon, I. (1980) *Music and Patronage in 16th-Century Mantua*. Cambridge.

Ferguson, W. K. (1948) *The Renaissance in Historical Thought*. Cambridge, Mass.

ffoulkes C. J. and Maiocchi, R. (1909) *Vincenzo Foppa*. London.

Ficino, M. *De vita* (1489) Venice, n.d., c. 1525.

Filarete, A. *Treatise on Architecture*, facsimile and English trans., ed. J. R. Spencer, 2 vols, New Haven, 1965.

— *Trattato di Architettura*, ed. A. M. Finali and L. Grassi, Milan, 1972.

Finlay, R. (1978) 'The Venetian Republic as a gerontocracy', *Journal of Medieval and Renaissance Studies* 8, pp. 157–78.

— (1980) *Politics in Renaissance Venice*. London.

Firenzuola, A. *Prose*, Florence, 1548.

Fishman, J. A. (1965) 'Who speaks what language to whom and when', reprinted in *The Sociology of Language*, ed. J. B. Pride and J. Holmes, Harmondsworth, 1971, pp. 15–31.

Floerke, H. (1905) *Studien zu niederländische Kunst- und Kulturgeschichte*. Munich and Leipzig.

Folena, G. F. (1964) 'La cultura volgare e l'umanesimo cavalleresco nel Veneto' in *Umanesimo europe ed umanesimo veneziano*, ed. V. Branca, pp. 141–57. Florence.

Foscari A. and Tafuri, M. (1983) *L'armonia e i conflitti: la chiesa di San Francesco della Vigna nella Venezia del '500*. Turin.

Fossati, F. (1928) 'Lavoro e lavoratori a Milano nel 1438', *Archivio storico lombardo* 55, pp. 225–58, 496–525; and 56 (1929), pp. 71–95.

Foucault, M. (1966) *The Order of Things*. Paris. English trans., London, 1973.

Francastel, G. (1960) 'De Giorgione à Titien: l'artiste, le public et le commercialisation de l'oeuvre d'art', *Annales E. S. C.* 15, pp. 1060–75.

Francastel, P. (1950) *Peinture et société*. Paris. 2nd ed., Paris, 1965.

— (1953) 'Imagination et réalité dans l'architecture civile du quattrocento' in *Hommage à Lucien Febvre*, pp. 195–206. Paris.

— (1965) 'Valeurs socio-psychologiques de l'espace-temps figuratif de la Renaissance' in *L'Année Sociologique*, pp. 3–68.

— (1967) *La figure et le lieu: l'ordre visuel du quattrocento*. Paris.

Frey C. (ed.) (1892) *Il libro de Antonio Billi*. Berlin.

Friedländer, W. (1965) *Mannerism and Anti-Mannerism in Italian Painting*. New York.

Fumagalli, G. (1952) *Leonardo omo sanza lettere*. Florence.

Fumaroli, M. (1980) *L'age de l'éloquence*. Geneva.

Galton, F. (1869) *Hereditary Genius*. London.

Gambi. L. and Bollati, G. (eds) (1976) *Storia d'Italia 6, Atlante*. Turin.

Garin, E. (1959) 'I cancellieri umanisti della repubblica fiorentina', *Rivista storica italiana* 71, pp. 185–208.

— (1963) 'La cité idéale de la Renaissance italienne' in *Les utopies à la Renaissance*, ed. W. Lameere, pp. 13–37. Brussels and Paris.

— (1976) *Astrology in the Renaissance*. Bari. English trans., London, 1983.

Gauricus, P. *De sculptura* (1504) ed. A. Chastel and R. Klein, Geneva, 1969.

Gaye, G. (ed.) (1839–40) *Carteggio inedito d'artisti dei secoli xiv, xv, xvi*, 3 vols. Florence.

Geertz, C. (1983) *Local Knowledge*. New York.

Gelli, G. B. (1896) 'Vite d'artisti', *Archivio Storico Italiano* 17, pp. 32–62.

Ghiberti, L. *I commentari*, ed. O. Morisani, Naples, 1947.

Gilbert, C. (1952) 'On subject and not-subject in Italian Renaissance pictures', *Art Bulletin* 34, pp. 202–16.

— (1959) 'The archbishop on the painters of Florence', *Art Bulletin* 41, pp. 75–87.

Gilbert, F. (1949) 'Bernardo Rucellai and the Orti Oricellari', *JWCI* 12, pp. 101–31.

— (1951) 'On Machiavelli's idea of *virtù*', *Renaissance News* 4, pp. 53–55.

— (1957) 'Florentine political assumptions in the period of Savonarola and Soderini' *JWCI* 20, pp. 187–214.

— (1965) *Machiavelli and Guicciardini.* Princeton.

— (1970) 'Biondo, Sabellico and the beginnings of Venetian official historiography' in *Florilegium historiale,* ed. J. G. Rowe and W. H. Stockdale, pp. 276–87. Toronto.

— (1977) 'Venice in the crisis of the League of Cambrai', reprinted in his *History: Choice and Commitment,* ch. 11. Cambridge, Mass.

— (1980) *The Pope, his Banker, and Venice.* Cambridge, Mass. and London.

Gille, B. (1964) *Engineers of the Renaissance.* Paris. English trans., Cambridge, Mass., 1966.

Gilmore, M. P. (1963) 'The lawyers and the Church in the Italian Renaissance', in his *Humanists and Jurists,* pp. 61–86. Cambridge, Mass.

Ginzburg, C. (1961) 'Stregoneria e pietà popolare', *Annali Scuola Normale di Pisa* 30, pp. 269–87.

— (1966a) 'Da A. Warburg a E. H. Gombrich', *Studi medievali* 7, pp. 1015–65.

— (1966b) *The Night Battles.* Turin. English trans., London, 1983.

— (1976) *Cheese and Worms.* Turin. English trans., London, 1981.

— (1981) *The Enigma of Piero.* Turin. English trans., London, 1985.

Gnoli, D. (1938) *La Roma di Leon X.* Milan.

Goffen, R. (1986) *Piety and Patronage in Renaissance Venice.* New Haven and London.

Goffman E. (1956) *The Presentation of Self in Everyday Life.* Rev. ed., New York, 1959.

Goldthwaite, R. A. (1968) *Private Wealth in Renaissance Florence.* Princeton.

— (1972) 'Schools and teachers of commercial arithmetic in Renaissance Florence', *Journal of European Economic History* 1, pp. 418–33.

— (1980) *The Building of Renaissance Florence.* Baltimore and London.

— (1985) 'The Renaissance economy: the preconditions for luxury consumption' in *Aspetti della vita economica medievale,* pp. 659–75. Florence.

Gombrich, E. H. (1960a) *Art and Illusion.* London.

— (1960b) 'Vasari's Lives and Cicero's Brutus', *JWCI* 23, pp. 309–11.

— (1963) *Meditations on a Hobby Horse.* London.

— (1966) *Norm and Form.* London.

— (1969) *In Search of Cultural History.* Oxford.

— (1970) *Aby Warburg: an Intellectual Biography.* London.

— (1972) *Symbolic Images.* London.

— (1976) *The Heritage of Apelles*. Oxford.

Graf, A. (1888) *Attraversa il '500*. Turin.

Grafton A. and Jardine, L. (1982) 'Humanism and the School of Guarino', *Past and Present* 96, pp. 51–80.

Gras, N. S. B. (1953) 'Capitalism, concepts and history' in *Enterprise and Secular Change*, ed. F. C. Lane and J. Riemersma, pp. 66–79. London.

Greene, T. (1982) *The Light in Troy: Imitation and Discovery in Renaissance Poetry*. New Haven and London.

Greer, G. (1979) *The Obstacle Race*. London.

Grendler, P. F. (1969a) *Critics of the Italian World 1530–60*. Madison.

— (1969b) 'Francesco Sansovino and Italian popular history', *Studies in the Renaissance* 16, pp. 139–80.

— (1982) 'What Zuanne read in school', *Sixteenth-Century Journal* 13, pp. 41–53.

Grove, G. (1980) *Dictionary of Music and Musicians*, ed. S. Sadie, 20 vols. London.

Guasti, C. (ed.) (1884) *Le feste di S. Giovanni Batista in Firenze*. Florence.

Guerri, D. (1931) *La corrente popolare nel Rinascimento*. Florence.

Guglielminetti, M. (1977) *Memoria e scrittura: l'autobiografia da Dante a Cellini*. Turin.

Guicciardini, F. *Ricordi*, ed. R. Spongano, Florence, 1951; English trans., New York, 1965.

Hale, J. (1954) *England and the Italian Renaissance*. London.

— (ed.) (1973) *Renaissance Venice*. London.

Hall, J. W. and Jansen, M. B. (eds) (1968) *Studies in the Institutional History of Early Modern Japan*. Princeton.

Hansen, J. (ed.) (1901) *Quellen zur Geschichte des Hexenwahns*. Bonn.

Harff, A. von *Pilgrimage* (1496) English trans., London, 1946.

Hartt, F. (1958) *Giulio Romano*. New Haven.

— (1964) 'Art and freedom in '400 Florence' in *Essays in Memory of Karl Lehmann*, ed. L. F. Sandler, pp. 114–31. New York.

Haskell, F. (1963) *Patrons and Painters*. London.

Hatfield, R. (1970) 'The Compagnia de'magi', *JWCI* 33, pp. 107–44.

— (1973) Review of Burke. *Art Bulletin* 55, pp. 630–33.

— (1976) *Botticelli's Uffizi Adoration*. Princeton.

Hauser, A. (1951) *A Social History of Art*, 2 vols. London.

— (1965) *Mannerism*, 2 vols. London.

Hay, D. (1961) *The Italian Renaissance in its Historical Background*. Cambridge. 2nd ed., Cambridge, 1977.

— (1977) *The Church in Italy in the Fifteenth Century*. Cambridge.

Heers, J. (1961) *Gênes au 15e siècle*. Paris.

Hegel, G. W. F. (1837) *Philosophy of History*. Berlin. English trans., New York, 1956.

Heller, A. (1979) *Renaissance Man*. London.

Herder, J. G. (1784–1791) *Ideen zur Philosophie der Gerschichte der Menschheit*, 4 vols, Berlin.

Herlihy, D. (1973) 'Three patterns of social mobility in medieval history', *Journal of Interdisciplinary History* 3, pp. 633–47.

— (1974) 'The generation in medieval history', *Viator* 5, pp. 347–64.

— (1978) 'The distribution of wealth in a Renaissance community: Florence, 1427' in *Towns in Societies*, ed. P. Abrams and E. A. Wrigley, pp. 131–57. London.

— and Klapisch-Zuber C. (1978) *Les Toscans et leurs familles*. Paris. Abridged English trans., New Haven and London, 1985.

Hermes, G. (1916) 'Der Kapitalismus in der Florentiner Wollentuchindustrie' in *Zeitschrift für die gesamte Staatswissenschaft* 72, pp. 367–400.

Herrick, M. T. *Italian Comedy in the Renaissance*. Urbana.

— (1965) *Italian Tragedy in the Renaissance*. Urbana.

Hersey, G. L. (1969) *Alfonso II and the Artistic Renewal of Naples*. New Haven and London.

Hexter, J. (1973) *The Vision of Politics on the Eve of the Reformation*. London.

Heydenreich, L. H. (1967) 'Federico da Montefeltre as a building patron', in *Studies in Renaissance and Baroque Art presented to A. Blunt*, pp. 1–6. London.

— (1969) 'La villa', *Bollettino Centro Andrea Palladio* 11, pp. 11–20.

— and Lotz, W. (1974) *Architecture in Italy 1400–1600*. Harmondsworth.

Hibbett, H. (1959) *The Floating World in Japanese Fiction*. London.

Hill, G. F. (1930) *A Corpus of Italian Renaissance Medals*, 2 vols. London.

Hills, P. (1983) 'Piety and patronage in '500 Venice: Tintoretto and the Scuole del Sacramento', *Art History* 6, pp. 30–43.

Hind, A. M. (1930) *Early Italian Engraving*. London.

Hollanda, F. de *Da Pintura Antigua* (1548) Porto, 1918; English trans., London, 1928.

Holly, M. A. (1984) *Panofsky and the Foundations of Art History*. Ithaca and London.

Holub, R. C. (1984) *Reception Theory*. London.

Hook, J. (1979) *Siena: a City and its History*. London.

Hope, C. (1980) *Titian*. London.

— (1981) 'Artists, patrons and advisers in the Italian Renaissance' in *Patronage in the Renaissance*, ed. G. F. Lytle and S. Orgel, pp. 293– 343. Princeton.

Howard, D. (1975) *Jacopo Sansovino: Architecture and Patronage in Renaissance Venice*. New Haven.

Huizinga, J. (1919) *The Waning of the Middle Ages*. Leiden. English trans. London, 1924.

— (1920) 'Renaissance and realism', English trans. in his *Men and Ideas*, pp. 288–309. New York.

— (1929) 'The task of cultural history', English trans. in his *Men and Ideas*, pp. 17–76. New York 1959.

Humfrey, P. and MacKenney, R. (1986) 'The Venetian trade guilds as patrons of art in the Renaissance', *Burlington Magazine* 128, pp. 317– 30.

Hymes, D. (1964) 'Toward ethnographies of communication', reprinted in *Language and Social Context*, ed. P. P. Giglioli, pp. 21–41. Harmondsworth.

Jameson, F. (1971) *Marxism and Form*. Princeton.

Janson, H. W. (1967) 'The equestrian monument from Cangrande della Scala to Peter the Great' in *Aspects of the Renaissance*, ed. A. R. Lewis. Austin.

Jardine, L. (1983) 'Isotta Nogarola: women humanists – education for what?' in *History of Education* 12, pp. 231–44.

— (1985) 'The myth of the learned lady in the Renaissance', *Historical Journal* 28, pp. 799–820.

Jenkins, A. D. F. (1970) 'Cosimo de'Medici's patronage of architecture and the theory of magnificence', *JWCI* 33, pp. 162–70.

Jones, P. J. (1965) 'The agrarian development of medieval Italy', *Second International Conference of Economic History*, 2, pp. 69–86. Paris and The Hague.

— (1966) 'Italy' in *Cambridge Economic History of Europe* 1, ed. M. M. Postan, pp. 340–431. Cambridge.

— (1978) 'Economia e società nell'Italia medievale: la leggenda della borghesia', *Storia d'Italia, Annali* 1, pp. 185–372. Turin.

Jones, R. and Penny, N. (1983) *Raphael*. New Haven and London.

Kaegi, W. (1933) 'Das Werk Aby Warburgs', *Neue Schweize Rundschau*.

— (1947–82) *Jacob Burckhardt: eine Biographie*, 7 vols. Basle.

Kearney, H. F. (1970) *Scholars and Gentlemen*. London.

Keene, D. (1976) *World within Walls: Japanese Literature of the Premodern Era, 1600–1867*. London.

Kelley, D. (1970) *Foundations of Modern Historical Scholarship.* New York.

Kelly, J. (1977) 'Did women have a Renaissance?', in *Becoming Visible*, ed. R. Bridenthal and C. Koonz, pp. 137–61. Boston.

Kemp, M. (1981) *Leonardo da Vinci: the Marvellous Works of Nature and of Man.* London.

Kent, D. V. (1975) 'The Florentine Reggimento in the fifteenth century', *Renaissance Quarterly* 28, pp. 575–620.

— (1978) *The Rise of the Medici: Faction in Florence, 1426–1434.* Oxford.

— and Kent, F. W. (1982) *Neighbours and Neighbourhood in Renaissance Florence.* Locust Valley.

Kent, F. W. (1977) *Household and Lineage in Renaissance Florence.* Princeton.

Kernodle, G. F., (1944) *From Art to Theatre: Form and Convention in the Renaissance.*

King, M. L. (1976) 'Thwarted ambitions: six learned women of the Italian Renaissance', *Soundings* 59, pp. 280–300.

— (1986) *Venetian Humanism in an Age of Patrician Dominance.* Princeton.

Kirshner J. and Molho, A. (1978) 'The dowry fund and the marriage market in early fifteenth-century Florence', *Journal of Modern History* 50, pp. 403–38.

Klapisch-Zuber, C. (1985) *Les maîtres du marbre.* Paris.

— (1985) *Women, Family and Ritual in Renaissance Italy.* Chicago and London.

— and Day, J. (1965) 'Villages désertés en Italie' in *Villages désertés,* ed. F. Braudel, pp. 420–59. Paris.

Klein, R. (1979) *Form and Meaning.* New York.

— and Zerner, R. (1966) *Italian Art 1500–1600.* Englewood Cliffs, NJ.

Klibansky, R., Panofsky E. and Saxl, F. (1964) *Saturn and Melancholy.* London.

Koch, D. (1967) *Die Kunstaustellung.* Berlin.

Koenigsberger, H. G. (1960) 'Decadence or shift? Changes in the civilization of Italy and Europe', *Transactions of the Royal Historical Society* 10, pp. 1–18.

Kraus, A. (1960) 'Secretarius und Sekretariat', *Römische Quartalschrift* 55, pp. 43–84.

Krautheimer R. and Krautheimer-Hess, T. (1956) *Lorenzo Ghiberti.* Princeton.

Kris, E. and Kurz, O. (1934) *Legend, Myth and Magic in the Image of the Artist.* Vienna. English trans., New Haven, 1979.

Kristeller, P. O. (1955) *Renaissance Thought*. New ed., New York, 1961.

— (1956) 'Lay religious traditions and Florentine Platonism', in his *Studies in Renaissance Thought and Letters*, pp. 99–123. Rome.

Kroeber, A. L. (1944) *Configurations of Culture Growth*. Berkeley and Los Angeles.

Kurczewski, J. (1983) 'Spoleczny Mechanizm Odrodzenia', *Znak* 35, pp. 1333–40.

Kurz, O. (1948) *Fakes*, Rev. ed., New York, 1967.

Landes, D. (1983) *Revolution in Time*. Cambridge, Mass.

Landino, C. *Commento sopra la Comedia di Dante* (1481) Venice, 1507.

Landucci, L. *A Florentine Diary*, ed. J. del Badia, Florence 1883; English trans., London, 1927.

Lane, F. C. (1934) *Venetian Ships and Shipbuilders of the Renaissance*. Baltimore.

— (1973) *Venice: a Maritime Republic*. Baltimore.

Lane, R. (1962) *Masters of the Japanese Print*. London.

Larivaille, P. (1980) *Pietro Aretino fra Rinascimento e Manierismo*. Rome.

Larner, J. (1971) *Culture and Society in Italy 1290–1420*. London.

— (1980) *Italy in the Age of Dante and Petrarch*. London.

Leach, E. (1976) *Culture and Communication*. Cambridge.

Lee, R. W. (1940) 'Ut pictura poesis: the humanistic theory of painting', *Art Bulletin* 3. Reprinted New York, 1967.

Lenzi, M. L. (ed.) (1982) *Donne e madonne: l'educazione femminile nel primo rinascimento italiano*. Turin.

Leonardo da Vinci, *Literary Works*, ed. J. P. Richter. Oxford, 1939.

Lerner-Lehmkuhl, H. (1936) *Zur Struktur und Geschichte des florentinischen Kunstmarktes im 15. Jht*. Wattenscheid.

Le Roy Ladurie, E. (1975) *Montaillou*. Paris. English trans., New York, 1978.

Lestocquoy, J. (1952) *Les villes de Flandre et d'Italie*. Paris.

Levey, M. (1971) *Painting at Court*. London.

Lewis, C. S. (1964) *The Discarded Image*. Oxford.

Lipset S. M. and Bendix, R. (1959) *Social Mobility in Industrial Society*. Berkeley.

Lockwood, L. (1984) *Music in Renaissance Ferrara*. Oxford.

Logan, O. (1972) *Culture and Society in Venice 1470–1790*. London.

Lopez, R. S. (1953) 'Hard times and investment in culture' in W. K. Ferguson et al., *The Renaissance*. New York.

— (1963) 'Quattrocento genovese', *Rivista Storica Italiana* 75, pp. 709– 27.

— (1970) *The Three Ages of the Italian Renaissance*. Charlottesville.

Lord, A. B. (1960) *The Singer of Tales*. Cambridge, Mass.

Lorenzo, G. (1868) *Monumenti per servire alla storia de Palazzo Ducale*. Venice.

Lovejoy, A. O. (1936) *The Great Chain of Being*. Cambridge, Mass.

Lowinsky, E. E. (1954) 'Music in the culture of the Renaissance'. *Journal of the History of Ideas* 15, pp. 509–53.

— (1966)'Music of the Renaissance as viewed by Renaissance musicians' in *The Renaissance Image of Man and the World*, ed. B. O'Kelly, pp. 129–64.

Lowry, M. (1979) *The World of Aldus Manutius*. Oxford.

Ludwig, G. (1905) 'Archivalische Beiträge zur Geschichte der Venezianische Malerei', *Jahrbuch der Königlich Preussischen Kunstsammlungen*. Beiheft.

Machiavelli, N. *Istorie fiorentine*, English trans., New York, 1960.

MacKenney, R. (1981) 'Arti e stato a Venezia tra tardo medioevo e '600', *Studi veneziani* 5, pp. 127–43.

— (1984) 'Guilds and guildsmen in 16th-century Venice', *Bulletin of the Society for Renaissance Studies* 2, no. 2, pp. 7–18.

Maffei, D. (1973) *Il giovane Machiavelli banchiere con Berto Berti a Roma*. Florence.

Maikuma, Y. (1985) *Der Begriff der Kultur bei Warburg, Nietzsche und Burckhardt*. Königstei.

Malaguzzi-Valeri, F. (1902) *Pittori Lombardi del '400*. Milan.

Mâle, E. (1925) *L'art religieux du 13e siècle en France*. Paris.

— (1951) *L'art religieux après le concile de Trente*. Paris.

Manetti, A. (1970) *Vita di Brunelleschi*, text and English trans., ed. H. Saalman. University Park.

Mannheim, K. (1952) *Essays on the Sociology of Knowledge*. London.

Marabottini, A. (1968) 'I collaboratori' in *Raffaello*, ed. M. Salmi, 2 vols, 1, pp. 199–203. Novara.

Mare, A. de la (1965) *Vespasiano da Bisticci*, unpublished PhD thesis, University of London.

Martin, A. von (1932) *The Sociology of the Renaissance*. Stuttgart. English trans., London, 1944; new ed., New York, 1963.

Martines, L. (1963) *The Social World of the Florentine Humanists, 1390–1460*. London.

— (1974) 'A way of looking at women in Renaissance Florence', *Journal of Medieval and Renaissance Studies* 4, pp. 15–28.

— (1979) *Power and Imagination: City-States in Renaissance Italy*. New York.

Martini, G. S. (1956) *La bottega di un cartolaio fiorentino*. Florence.

Maruyama, M. (1974) *Studies in the Intellectual History of Tokugawa Japan*. Princeton and Tokyo.

Marx, K. and Engels, F. (1846) *The German Ideology*. English trans., Moscow, 1964.

Mather, R. (1948) 'Documents relating to Florentine painters and sculptors', *Art Bulletin* 30, pp. 20–65.

Mattingly, G. (1955) *Renaissance Diplomacy*. London.

Medcalf, S. (1981) 'On reading books from a half-alien culture', in *The Later Middle Ages*, ed. S. Medcalf, pp. 1–55. London.

Medin, A. and Frati, L. (eds.) (1890) *Lamenti storici* 3. Bologna.

Meiss, M. (1948) Review of Antal, *Florentine Painting and its Social Background'*, *Art Bulletin* 30, pp. 143–50.

— (1951) *Painting in Florence and Siena after the Black Death.* Princeton.

— (1963) 'Masaccio and the Early Renaissance' in *Renaissance and Mannerism*, ed. I. E. Rubin, pp. 123–43. Princeton.

Merton, R. K. (1957) *Social Theory and Social Structure*, rev. ed. Glencoe.

Michelangelo, *Carteggio*, ed. G. Poggi, 5 vols. Florence, 1965–83. Trans. E. H. Ramsden, London, 1963.

Mills, C. Wright (1959) *The Sociological Imagination*. London.

Mitchell, C. (1960) 'Archaeology and romance in Renaissance Italy', in *Italian Renaissance Studies*, ed. E. F. Jacob, pp. 455–83. London.

Molho, A. (1968) 'Politics and the ruling class in Early Renaissance Florence', *Nuova Rivista Storica* 52, pp. 401–20.

— (1977) 'The Brancacci Chapel: studies in its iconography and history', *JWCI* 40, pp. 50–85.

Molmenti P. and Ludwig, G. (1903) *Vittore Carpaccio et la confrérie de St Ursule*. Florence.

Mondolfo, R. (1954) 'The Greek attitude to manual labour', *Past and Present* 6, pp. 1–5.

Montaigne, M. de *Journal de voyage en Italie*, ed. M. Rat, Paris, 1955.

Monti, G. M. (ed.) (1920) *Un laudario umbra quattrocentista dei Bianchi*. Città di Castello.

— (1927) *Le confraternite medievali dell'alta e media Italia*, 2 vols. Venice.

Morisani, O. (1953) 'C. Landino', *Burlington Magazine* 95, pp. 267–70.

Mortier, A. (1930) *Etudes italiennes*. Paris.

Mosher, F. J. (1978) 'The fourth catalogue of the Aldine Press', *La Bibliofilia* 80, pp. 229–35.

Motta, E. (1887) 'Musici alla corte degli Sforza', *Archivio Storico Lombardo* 14, pp. 29–64, 278–340, 514–57.

— (1895) 'L'università dei pittori milanesi nel 1481', *Archivio Storico Lombardo* 22, pp. 408–33.

Muir, E. (1981) *Civic Ritual in Renaissance Venice*. Princeton.

Müntz, E. (1888) *Les collections des Médicis au xve siècle*. Paris.

Muraro, M. A. (1961) 'The statutes of the Venetian Arti and the mosaics of the Mascoli Chapel', *Art Bulletin* 43, pp. 263–74.

Murray, A. (1978) *Reason and Society in the Middle Ages*. Oxford.

Murray, P. (1978) *The Architecture of the Italian Renaissance*. London.

— (1966) 'The Italian Renaissance architect', *Journal of the Royal Society of Arts* 144, pp. 589–607.

Nardi, B. (1964) 'La scuola di Rialto' in *Umanesimo europeo ed umanesimo veneziano*, ed. V. Branca, pp. 93–140. Florence.

Nelson, N. (1933) 'Individualism as a criterion of the Renaissance', *Journal of English and Germanic Philology* 32, pp. 316–34.

Niccoli, O. (1979) *I sacerdoti, i guerrieri, i contadini*. Turin.

Nigro, S. (1985) *Le brache di San Griffone. Novellistica e predicazione tra '400 e '500*. Bari.

Novelli, L. and Massaccesi, M. (1961) *Ex voto del santuario della Madonna del Monte di Cesena*. Forli.

O'Kelly, B. (ed.) (1966) *The Renaissance Image of Man and the World*. Kent, Ohio.

O'Malley, J. (1979) *Praise and Blame in Renaissance Rome*. Durham, NC.

Onians, J. (1971) 'Alberti and Filarete', *JWCI* 34, pp. 96–114.

Origo, I. (1957) *The Merchant of Prato*. London. 2nd ed., Harmondsworth.

Ortalli, G. (1979) *La pittura infamante nei secoli xiii–xvi*. Rome.

Ossola, C. (ed.) (1980) *La corte e il cortegiano*, vol. 1. Rome.

Palisca, C. (1985) *Humanism in Renaissance Italian Musical Thought*. New Haven.

Palladio, A. *I Quattro Libri dell'Architettura*. Venice, 1570. English trans., 1738, reprinted New York, 1965.

Palmieri, M. (1982) *La vita civile*, ed. G. Belloni. Florence.

Panofsky, E. (1924) *Idea*. Leipzig and Berlin. English trans., New York, 1968.

— (1924–5) *Perspective as Symbolic Form*. Undated unauthorized English trans., c. 1975.

— (1939) *Studies in Iconology*. New York.

— (1953a) 'Artist, scientist, genius' in W. K. Ferguson et al. *The Renaissance*. New York. New ed., New York, 1962.

— (1953b) *Early Netherlandish Painting.* Cambridge, Mass.

— (1955) *Meaning in the Visual Arts.* New York.

Partner, P. (1958) *The Papal State under Martin V.* London.

— (1976) *Renaissance Rome 1500–59.* Berkeley.

— (1980) 'Papal financial policy in the Renaissance and the Counter-Reformation', *Past and Present* 88, pp. 17–62.

Partridge, L. and Starn, R. (1980) *A Renaissance Likeness: Art and Culture in Raphael's Julius II.* Berkeley.

Petrucci, A. (ed.) (1978) 'Per la storia dell'alfabetismo e della cultura scritta', *Quaderni Storici* 38, pp. 437–50.

— (1983a) 'Il libro manoscritto', in *Letteratura italiana 2: produzione e consumo,* ed. A. Asor Rosa, pp. 499–524. Turin.

— (1983b) 'Le biblioteche antiche', in *Letteratura italiana 2: produzione e consumo,* ed. A. Asor Rosa, pp. 527–54. Turin.

Pevsner, N. (1940) *Academies of Art.* Cambridge.

— (1942) 'The term "architect" in the Middle Ages', *Speculum* 17, pp. 549–62.

Peyre, H. (1948) *Les générations littéraires.* Paris.

Pignatti, T. (ed.) (1981) *Le scuole di Venezia.* Milan.

Pinder, W. (1926) *Das Problem der Generation in der Kunstgeschichte Europas.* Berlin.

Pino, P. *Dialoghi di pittura* (1548) ed. E. Camesasca, Milan, 1954.

Pius II, *De curialium miseriis epistola,* ed. W. P. Mustard, Baltimore, 1928.

Pius II, *Commentarii,* Frankfurt, 1614. English trans., 1959.

Plaisance, M. (1973) 'Une première affirmation de la politique culturelle de Côme ler', in *Les Ecrivains et le pouvoir en Italie à l'époque de la Renaissance,* ed. A. Rochon, pp. 361–433.

— (1974) 'Culture et Politique à Florence de 1542 à 1551' in *Les Ecrivains et le pouvoir en Italie à l'époque de la Renaissance,* ed. A. Rochon, pp. 149–228. Paris.

— (1975) 'La politique culturelle de Côme ler et les fêtes annuelles à Florence de 1541 à 1550' in *Les fêtes de la Renaissance,* 3, ed. J. Jacquot, pp. 133–48. Paris.

Plekhanov, G. (1898) *The Role of the Individual in History.* Moscow English trans., New York, 1940.

Pocock, J. G. A. (1975) *The Machiavellian Moment.* Princeton.

Podro, M. (1982) *The Critical Historians of Art.* New Haven.

Poggi, G. (ed.) (1909) *Il duomo di Firenze.* Berlin.

Poliziano, A. *Panepistemon,* Venice, 1495.

Pomponazzi, P. *De incantationibus,* written c. 1520; posthumously published, 1556; reprinted Hildesheim and New York, 1970.

Pope-Hennessy, J. (1958) *Italian Renaissance Sculpture.* London.

— (1966) *The Portrait in the Renaissance.* London.

Pottinger,G. (1978) *The Court of the Medici*. London.

Prager F. D. and Scaglia, G. (1970) *Brunelleschi*. Cambridge.

Prevenier W. and Blockmans, W. (1986) *The Burgundian Nether-lands*. English trans., Cambridge.

Procacci, U. (1960) 'Compagnie di pittori', *Rivista d'Arte* X, pp. 3–37.

Prodi, P. (1982) *Il sovrano pontefice*. Bologna.

— and Johanek, P. (eds.) (1984) *Strutture ecclesiastiche in Italia e in Germania prima della Riforma*. Bologna.

Prosperi, A. (ed.) (1980) *La corte e il cortegiano*, vol. 2. Rome.

Pullan, B. (1971) *Rich and Poor in Renaissance Venice*. London.

— (1981) 'Natura e carattere delle scuole' in *Le scuole di Venezia*, ed. T. Pignatti pp. 9–26. Berlin.

Puppi, L. (1973) *Andrea Palladio*. Venice. English trans., London, 1975.

Putelli, R. (1935) *Vita, storia ed arte mantovana nel '500*, 2. Mantua.

Quondam, A. (1977) 'Mercanzia d'honore, mercanzia d'utile: prod-uzione libraria e lavoro intelletuale a Venezia nel '500', in *Libri editori e pubblico nell'Europa moderna*, ed. A. Petrucci, pp. 53–104. Bari.

— (ed.) (1978) *Le corti farnesiane*. Rome.

— (1983) 'La letteratura in tipografia' in *Letteratura italiana 2: produzione e consumo*, ed. A. Asor Rosa, pp. 555–686. Turin.

Ramsden, H. (1974) *The 1898 Movement in Spain*. Manchester.

Rashdall, H. (1936) *The Universities of Europe in the Middle Ages*. Oxford.

Renouard, Y. (1950) 'L'artiste ou le client?' *Annales ESC* 5, pp. 361–5.

Reti, L. (1968) 'The two unpublished Mss of Leonardo', *Burlington Magazine* 110, pp. 10–22.

Ricci, C. (1924) *Il tempio malatestiano*. Milan and Rome.

Rice, E. (1985) *St Jerome in the Renaissance*. Baltimore and London.

Ringbom, S. (1965) *From Icon to Narrative*. Abo.

Robertson, C. (1982) 'Annibal Caro as iconographer', *JWCI* 45, pp. 160–75.

Rochon, A. (1963) *La jeunesse de Laurent de Médicis*. Clermont-Ferrand.

— (ed.) (1972) *Formes et significations de la beffa dans la littérature italienne de la Renaissance*. Paris.

— (ed.) (1973) *Les Ecrivains et le pouvoir en Italie à l'époque de la Renaissance*, 1. Paris.

— (ed.) (1982) *Le pouvoir et la plume: incitation, contrôle et repression dans l'Italie du 16e siècle*. Paris.

Romano, R. (1971) *Tra due crisi: l'Italia del Rinascimento*. Turin.

Roover, R. de (1941) 'A Florentine firm of cloth manufacturers', *Speculum* 16, pp. 3–30.

— (1963) *The Rise and Decline of the Medici Bank*, rev. ed. Cambridge, Mass.

Rosand, D. (1982) *Painting in Cinquecento Venice: Titian, Veronese, Tintoretto*. New Haven and London.

Roscoe, W. (1795) *The Life of Lorenzo de'Medici*. London.

Rose, P. L. (1975) *The Italian Renaissance of Mathematics*. Geneva.

Rostow, W. W. (1960) *The Stages of Economic Growth*. Cambridge.

Rotunda, D. P. (1942) *Motif-Index of the Italian Novella in Prose*. Bloomington.

Rowe, J. G. and Stockdale, W. H. (eds.) (1971) *Florilegium historiale*. Toronto.

Rubin, I. E. (1963) *The Renaissance and Mannerism*. Princeton.

Rubinstein, N. (1966) *The Government of Florence under the Medici*. London.

— (ed.) (1968) *Florentine Studies*. London.

— (1971) 'Notes on the word stato in Florence before Machiavelli' in *Florilegium historiale*, ed. J. G. Rowe and W. H. Stockdale, pp. 314–21. Toronto.

Rucellai, B. *Il Zibaldone*, ed. A. Perosa, London, 1960.

Rupprecht, B. (1966) 'Villa: Geschichte eines Ideals' in *Probleme der Kunstwissenschaft* 2, pp. 210–50. Berlin.

Rusconi, R. (1981) 'Predicatori e predicazione (secoli ix-xviii)' *Storia d'Italia, Annali* 4, pp. 951–1053.

— (1984) 'Dal pulpito alla confessione. Modelli di comportamento religioso' in *Strutture ecclesiastiche in Italia e in Germania prima della Riforma*, ed. P. Prodi and P. Johanek, pp. 259–315. Bologna.

Ryder, A. F. (1976a) *The Kingdom of Naples under Alfonso the Magnanimous*. Oxford.

— (1976b) 'Antonio Beccadelli' in *Cultural Aspects of the Italian Renaissance*, ed. C. H. Clough, ch. 7. Manchester and New York.

Saalman, H. (1958) 'Filippo Brunelleschi', *Art Bulletin* 40, pp. 113–37.

— (1959) 'Antonio Filarete', *Art Bulletin* 41, pp. 89–106.

Sabbadini, R. (1916) 'Come il Panormita diventò poeta aulico', *Archivio Storico Lombardo* 43, pp. 5–28.

Sannazzaro, J. *L'Arcadia* (1504).

Santangelo, G. (ed.) (1954) *Le epistole de imitatione di G. F. Pico e di P. Bembo*. Florence.

Santillana, G. de (1966) 'Paolo Toscanelli and his friends', in *The*

Renaissance Image of Man and the World, ed. B. O'Kelly, pp. 105–28. Kent, Ohio.

Santoro, C. (1948) *Gli uffici del dominio sforzesco, 1450–1500*. Milan.

Sardella, P. (1948) *Nouvelles et spéculations à Venise*. Paris.

Savonarola, G. *Prediche e scritti*, ed M. Ferrara, Florence, 1952.

Saxl, F. (1934) *La fede astrologica di Agostino Chigi*. Rome.

— (1957) *Lectures*. London.

Schaffran, E. 'Der Inquisitionsprozesse gegen Paolo Veronese', *Archiv für Kulturgeschichte* 42, pp. 178–93.

Schmitt, C. (1975) 'Philosophy and science in sixteenth-century universities' in *The Cultural Context of Medieval Learning*, ed. J. E. Murdoch and E. D. Sylla. Dordrecht.

Scholderer, V. (1949) *Printers and Readers in Italy in the Fifteenth Century*. London.

Schutte, A. J. (1980) 'Printing, piety and the people in Italy: the first thirty years', *Archiv für Reformationsgeschichte* 71, pp. 5–20.

Schutz, A. M. (1977) *The Sculpture of Bernardo Rossellino and his Workshop*. Princeton.

Segarizzi, A. (ed.) (1916) *Relazioni degli ambasciatori veneti*, 3. Bari.

Seigel, J. (1966) 'Civic humanism or Ciceronian rhetoric?' *Past and Present* 34, pp. 3–48.

Serafino dell'Aquila, *Opere*. Venice, 1505.

Sereni, E. (1961) *Storia del paesaggio agrario italiano*. Bari.

— (1973) 'Agricoltura e mondo rurale', *Storia d'Italia* 1, pp. 136–252. Turin.

Settis, S. (1978) *La Tempestà interpretata*. Turin.

— (1981) Artisti e committenti fra Quattro e Conquecento', *Storia d'Italia, Annali* 4, pp. 791–64. Turin.

Seymour, C. (1966) *Sculpture in Italy, 1400 to 1500*. Harmondsworth.

— (1967) *Michelangelo's David: a Search for Identity*. Pittsburgh. 2nd ed., New York, 1974.

Seznec, J. (1940) *The Survival of the Ancient Gods*. London. English trans., New York, 1953.

Shaftesbury, Lord, *Second Characters*, written c. 1712; ed. B. Rand, Cambridge, 1914.

Shearman, J. (1965) *Andrea del Sarto*, 2 vols. New Haven.

— (1967) *Mannerism*. Harmondsworth.

— (1971) 'The Vatican Stanze: functions and decoration', *Proceedings of the British Academy* 57, pp. 369–424.

— (1975) 'The Florentine Entrata of Leo X, 1515', *JWCI* 38, pp. 136–44.

Sheldon, C. D. (1958) *The Rise of the Merchant Class in Tokugawa Japan*. New York.

Simeoni, L. (1903) 'Una vendetta signorile nel '400', *Nuovo Archivio Veneto* 5, pp. 252–8.

Singleton, C. (ed.) (1936) *Canti carnascialeschi*. Bari.

Skinner, Q. (1978) *Foundations of Modern Political Thought*, 2 vols. Cambridge.

Smyth, C. H. (1962) *Mannerism and Maniera*. Locust Valley.

Soria, A. (1956) *Los humanistas de la corte de Alfonso el Magnanimo*. Granada.

Sorrentino, A. (1935) *La letteratura italiana e il Sant'Ufficio*. Naples.

Spencer, J. R. (1957) 'Ut rhetorica pictura', *JWCI* 20, pp. 26–44.

Steinberg, R. M. (1977) *Fra Girolamo Savonarola, Florentine Art and Renaissance Historiography*. Athens, Ohio.

Steinmann, E. (1905) *Die Sixtinische Kapelle*, 2 vols. Munich.

Stephens, J. N. (1983) *The Fall of the Florentine Republic, 1512–1530*. Oxford.

Sterling, C. (1959) *Still Life Painting*. Paris.

Stone, L. (1971) 'Prosopography', *Daedalus*, Winter, pp. 46–73.

Straeten, E. van der (ed.) (1882) *La musique aux pays bas, 6: Les musiciens néerlandais en Italie*. Brussels. Reprinted New York, 1969.

Strozzi, A. Macinghi negli *Lettere*, ed. C. Guasti, Florence, 1877.

Summers, D. (1981) *Michelangelo and the Language of Art*. Princeton.

Tacchi-Venturi, P. (1910) *Storia della compagnia di Gesù in Italia*, 1. Rome.

Tafuri, M. (1985) *Venezia e il Rinascimento*. Turin.

Tenenti, A. (1957) 'Luc'Antonio Giunti il giovane, stampatore e mercante', *Studi in onore di Armando Sapori*, pp. 1023–60. Milan.

— (1959) *Naufrages, corsaires et assurances maritimes à Venise, 1592–1609*. Paris.

Thieme U. and Becker, F. (1907–50) *Allgemeines Lexikon der bildenden Künstler*, 37 vols. Leipzig.

Thomas, K. V. (1971) *Religion and the Decline of Magic*. London.

Thompson, J. B. (1984) *Studies in the Theory of Ideology*. Cambridge.

Thorndike, L. (1934–58) *History of Magic and Experimental Science*, 8 vols. New York.

Tietze, H. (1939) 'Master and workshop in the Venetian Renaissance', *Parnassus* 11, pp. 34–45.

Tietze-Conrat, E. (1934) 'Marietta, fille du Tintoret', *Gazette des BeauxArts* 76, pp. 258–62.

Tillyard, E. M. W. (1943) *The Elizabethan World Picture.* Cambridge.

Tinctoris, J. *De arte contrapuncti* (1477), English trans., *Musicological Studies and Documents* 5, Rome, 1961.

Tolnay, C. (1943–60) *Michelangelo,* 5 vols, Princeton.

Trexler, R. (1972a) 'Florentine religious experience: the sacred image', *Studies in the Renaissance,* 19, pp. 7–41.

— (1972b) 'Les religieuses de Florence', *Annales ESC* 27, pp. 1329–50.

— (1973) 'Charity and the defence of urban elites in the Italian communes' in *The Rich, the Well-born and the Powerful,* ed. F. C. Jaher, pp. 64–105. Urbana.

— (1980) *Public Life in Renaissance Florence.* New York.

Trinkaus, C. (1970) *In Our Image and Likeness,* 2 vols. London.

Turner, A. R. (1966) *The Vision of Landscape in Renaissance Italy.* Princeton.

Ugolini, P. (ed.) (1971) *Un altra'Firenze: l'epoca di Cosimo il Vecchio.* Florence.

Usmiani, M. A. (1957) 'Marko Marulic', *Harvard Slavic Studies* 3, pp. 1– 48.

Valeriano, G. P. *De litteratorum infelicitate,* c. 1527, Venice, 1620.

Varchi, B. *Due lezioni,* Florence, 1549.

Vasari, G. *Literarische Nachlass,* ed. K. Frey, 2 vols, Munich, 1923.

— *Vite,* ed. G. Milanesi, Florence, 1878–81. A new edition, ed. P. Barocchi and R. Bettarini, is in progress. English trans., London, 1850, London, 1897, London, 1912.

Venezian, S. (1921) *Olimpo da Sassoferrato.* Bologna.

Ventura, A. (1964) *Nobiltà e popolo nella società veneta del '400 e '500.* Bari.

Verde, A. (1973) *Lo studio fiorentino,* 3 vols. Florence. Pistoia, 1977.

Vespasiano da Bisticci, *Vite di uomini illustri,* ed. P. d'Ancona and E. Aeschlimann, Milan, 1951. English trans., London, 1926.

Vicentino, N. *L'antica musica,* Venice, 1555.

Vida, M. G. *De arte poetica* (1527) English trans., London, 1725.

Voltaire, *Essai sur les moeurs* (1756) ed. R. Pomeau, 2 vols, Paris, 1963.

Wackernagel, M. (1938) *The World of the Florentine Renaissance Artist.* Leipzig. English trans., Princeton, 1981.

Waley, D. (1969) *The Italian City-Republics.* London. Rev. ed., London, 1978.

Walker, D. P. (1958) *Spiritual and Demonic Magic from Ficino to Campanella.* London.

Walser, E. (1932) *Gesammelte Schriften.* Basel.

Warburg, A. (1932) *Gesammelte Schriften*. Leipzig–Berlin. Reprinted 1969; selection in Italian trans., *La rinascita del paganesimo antico*, Florence, 1966.

Weber, M. (1968) *Economy and Society*. English trans., New York.

Weinberg, B. (1961) *A History of Literary Criticism in the Italian Renaissance*, 2 vols. Chicago.

Weinstein, D. 'The myth of Florence', in *Florentine Studies*, ed. N. Rubinstein, pp. 15–44. London.

— (1970) *Savonarola and Florence*. Princeton.

Weise, G. (1950) 'Maniera und Pellegrino', *Romanistisches Jahrbuch* 3, pp. 321–403.

— (1961–5) *L'ideale eroico del Rinascimento*, 2 vols. Naples.

Weisinger, H. (1950) 'The English origins of the sociological interpretation of the Renaissance', *Journal of the History of Ideas* 11, pp. 321–38.

Weiss, R. (1969) *The Renaissance Discovery of Classical Antiquity*. Oxford.

Weissmann, R. (1982) *Ritual Brotherhood in Renaissance Florence*. New York.

Wellek, R. 'Auerbach's special realism', *Kenyon Review*, pp. 299–307.

— (1963) 'The concept of realism in literary scholarship' in his *Concepts of Criticism*, pp. 222–55. New Haven and London.

Wendorff, R. (1980) *Zeit und Kultur*, 2nd ed. Opladen.

Westfall, C. W. (1974) *In this Most Perfect Paradise: Alberti, Nicholas V and the Invention of Conscious Urban Planning in Rome, 1447–55*. University Park.

Wilde, J. (1944) 'The Hall of the Great Council of Florence', reprinted in *Renaissance Art*, ed. C. Gilbert, New York, 1970, pp. 92–132.

Williams, R. (1958) *Culture and Society*. London.

— (1974) *Television: Technology and Cultural Form*. London.

— (1977) *Marxism and Literature*. Oxford.

Williamson G. C. (ed., trans.) (1903) *The anonimo: Notes on Pictures and Works of Art in Italy*. London.

Winckelmann, J. J. (1764) *Geschichte der Kunst des Altertums*. English trans., London, 1881.

Wind, E. (1948) *Bellini's Feast of the Gods*. Cambridge, Mass.

— (1958) *Pagan Mysteries in the Renaissance*. London. Rev. ed., Oxford, 1980.

— (1969) *Giorgione's Tempestà*. Oxford.

Witt, R. G. (1983) *Hercules at the Cross-Roads: the Life, Work and Thought of Coluccio Salutati*. Durham, NC.

Wittkower, R. (1949) *Architectural Principles in the Age of Humanism*. London. 3rd ed., London, 1962.

— (1961) 'Individualism in art and artists', *Journal of the History of Ideas* 22, pp. 291–302.

— and Wittkower, M. (1963) *Born under Saturn*. London.

Wölfflin, H. (1888) *Renaissance and Baroque*. Munich. English trans., London, 1964.

— (1898) *Classic Art*. Munich. English trans., London, 1952.

— (1915) *Principles of Art History*. Munich. English trans., New York, 1950.

Woolf, S. (1962) 'Venice and the terraferma', reprinted in *Crisis and Change in the Venetian Economy*, ed. B. Pullan, London, 1968, pp. 175–203.

Wyrobisz, A. (1965) 'L'attivitá edilizia a Venezia', *Studi Veneziani* 7, pp. 307–43.

Yates, F. (1964) *Giordano Bruno and the Hermetic Tradition*. London.

Zanetti, D. (1964) *Problemi alimentari di una economia preindustriale: cereali a Pavia dal 1338 al 1700*. Turin.

Zarlino, G. *Institutioni harmoniche*, Venice, 1558.

Zarri, G. (1984) 'Aspetti dello sviluppo degli Ordini religiosi' in *Strutture ecclesiastiche in Italia e in Germania prima della Riforma*, ed. P. Prodi and P. Johanek, pp. 207–57. Bologna.

Zilsel, E. (1926) *Die Entstehung des Geniebegriffs*. Tübingen.

Zimmermann, T. C. P. (1976) 'Paolo Giovio and the evolution of Renaissance art criticism', in *Cultural Aspects of the Italian Renaissance*, ed. C. H. Clough, pp. 406–24. Manchester and New York.

INDEX